W9-CZN-807

Dangerous But Not Omnipotent

Exploring the Reach and Limitations of Iranian Power in the Middle East

Frederic Wehrey · David E. Thaler · Nora Bensahel · Kim Cragin
Jerrold D. Green · Dalia Dassa Kaye · Nadia Oweidat · Jennifer Li

Prepared for the United States Air Force
Approved for public release; distribution unlimited

PROJECT AIR FORCE

The research described in this report was sponsored by the United States Air Force under Contract FA7014-06-C-0001. Further information may be obtained from the Strategic Planning Division, Directorate of Plans, Hq USAF.

Library of Congress Cataloging-in-Publication Data

Dangerous but not omnipotent : exploring the reach and limitations of Iranian power in the Middle East / Frederic Wehrey ... [et al.].
    p. cm.
    Includes bibliographical references.
    ISBN 978-0-8330-4554-6 (pbk. : alk. paper)
    1. United States—Foreign relations—Iran. 2. Iran—Foreign relations—United States. 3. Iran—Politics and government—1997– 4. Iran—Military policy.
5. Political culture—Iran. 6. State-sponsored terrorism—Iran. 7. Terrorism—Middle East. 8. Weapons of mass destruction—Iran. 9. Iran—Foreign relations—Middle East. 10. Middle East—Foreign relations—Iran. I. Wehrey, Frederic M.

E183.8.I55D355 2009
327.73055—dc22

                                                                2009009797

The RAND Corporation is a nonprofit research organization providing objective analysis and effective solutions that address the challenges facing the public and private sectors around the world. RAND's publications do not necessarily reflect the opinions of its research clients and sponsors.

RAND® is a registered trademark.

Published 2009 by the RAND Corporation
1776 Main Street, P.O. Box 2138, Santa Monica, CA 90407-2138
1200 South Hayes Street, Arlington, VA 22202-5050
4570 Fifth Avenue, Suite 600, Pittsburgh, PA 15213-2665
RAND URL: http://www.rand.org/
To order RAND documents or to obtain additional information, contact
Distribution Services: Telephone: (310) 451-7002;
Fax: (310) 451-6915; Email: order@rand.org

Preface

Canvassing a range of global threats, the 2006 U.S. *National Security Strategy* warns:

> We may face no greater challenge from a single country than from Iran.[1]

Indeed, following the U.S. invasions of Iraq and Afghanistan, the Iranian threat to U.S. interests has taken on seemingly unprecedented qualities of aggressiveness and urgency. Defying international condemnation, the Islamic Republic appears inexorably committed to the pursuit of nuclear energy that will, at the very least, allow for a breakout weapon capability. Its longstanding support to Levantine terrorist groups earned it newfound acclaim in the Arab world following Hezbollah's 2006 war with Israel. Within its conventional arsenal, Iran is developing new and worrisome naval capabilities for impeding maritime access to the Strait of Hormuz, as well as longer-range ballistic missiles that would put U.S. military assets and American allies in the region at risk. In Iraq and Afghanistan, Tehran's clandestine paramilitary wing, the Qods Force, has been implicated in supplying lethal technology to insurgents and paramilitaries.

Added to these immediate provocations is the sense that Iran is trying to effect far-reaching changes on the regional and even global stage. Iran has long exercised broad-ranging influence inside Iraq,

---

[1] National Security Council, *The National Security Strategy of the United States of America*, Washington, D.C.: The White House, March 2006, p. 1 of opening statement.

spreading alarm among Sunni Arab states and raising the specter of Iran filling the power vacuum following the departure of U.S. forces. Similarly, the cascading sense of regional insecurity arising from its nuclear ambitions has spurred warnings of proliferation among Arab states. Further afield, Tehran has worked assiduously to leapfrog U.S. encirclement by courting partners as diverse as Latin American demagogues, the post-apartheid government of South Africa, and the Shanghai Cooperation Organization.

Yet the U.S. ability to gauge the extent and totality of these challenges is ultimately handicapped by the lack of official relations between the two states since the Islamic Revolution and, more subtly, by a lingering sense of national trauma from the hostage crisis of 1979–1981.

Working within this context, this study aims to provide U.S. Air Force (USAF) and Department of Defense (DoD) planners a new framework for anticipating and preparing for the strategic challenges Iran will present over the next ten to fifteen years. We adopted as an analytical point of departure the observation that although Iranian power projection is marked by strengths, it also has serious *liabilities* and *limitations*. We survey the nature of both by assessing four critical areas—the Iranian regime's underlying perception of itself in the world as a regional and even global power, Iran's conventional military capabilities and aspirations for asymmetric warfare, its support to Islamist militant groups, and its appeal to Arab public opinion. Based on this assessment, we offer a new U.S. policy paradigm that seeks to manage the challenges Iran presents through the exploitation of regional barriers to its power; we also identify the sources of caution in the regime's strategic calculus.

The bulk of the research for this monograph was completed in late 2007. To the extent practicable, the authors have updated descriptions of major events and conditions described throughout the monograph through early 2009.

The research reported here was sponsored by the U.S. Air Force Director of Operational Plans and Joint Matters (A5X), Headquarters USAF, and conducted within the Strategy and Doctrine Program of RAND Project AIR FORCE for a fiscal year 2007 study "Persia Rising: Meeting Future Security Challenges Presented by Iran." This monograph should be of interest to U.S. security policymakers, military planners, and analysts and observers of regional affairs in the Middle East and Central and South Asia.

RAND Project AIR FORCE

RAND Project AIR FORCE (PAF), a division of the RAND Corporation, is the U.S. Air Force's federally funded research and development center for studies and analyses. PAF provides the Air Force with independent analyses of policy alternatives affecting the development, employment, combat readiness, and support of current and future aerospace forces. Research is conducted in four programs: Force Modernization and Employment; Manpower, Personnel, and Training; Resource Management; and Strategy and Doctrine.

Additional information about PAF is available on our Web site at http://www.rand.org/paf

Contents

Figures

Table

Summary

Iranian power projection and regional ambitions are among the most pressing foreign policy challenges facing the United States. U.S. observers of the Islamic Republic, regardless of their political persuasion, have noted with alarm the country's new assertiveness on the Middle Eastern stage, its buildup of conventional military capability, and its apparently inexorable drive for nuclear energy in defiance of international criticism. The challenges posed by the Islamic Republic are especially acute from the perspective of the USAF: Airpower will likely be the military instrument of "first resort" to project U.S. power into Iran's unstable neighborhood, reassure allies, and dissuade Iran from aggression or adventurism. In the minds of Iranian policymakers, U.S. airpower has assumed a similar prominence. Tehran's fear of encirclement and strangulation by the United States stems in large measure from the proximity of the USAF's presence in neighboring states. And as evidenced by the 1996 Khobar Towers bombing,[1] this proximity places USAF lives and assets at risk from asymmetric terrorist attacks and, increasingly, Iran's ballistic missiles.

To accurately gauge the strategic challenges from Iran over a ten- to fifteen-year horizon, this study sought to assess the *motivations* of the Islamic Republic, not just its *capabilities*. This approach, although difficult given the complexities of the Iranian system, is critical in identifying potential sources of caution and pragmatism in Iran's policy formulation. Our exploration of Iranian strategic thinking revealed

---

[1] See *The 9/11 Commission Report: Final Report of the National Commission on Terrorist Attacks upon the United States*, U.S. Government Printing Office, July 26, 2004, p. 60.

that ideology and bravado frequently mask a preference for opportunism and realpolitik—the qualities that define "normal" state behavior. Similarly, when we canvassed Iran's power projection options, we identified not only the extent of the threats posed by each but also their limitations and liabilities. In each case, we found significant barriers and buffers to Iran's strategic reach rooted in both the regional geopolitics it is trying to influence and in its limited conventional military capacity, diplomatic isolation, and past strategic missteps. Similarly, tensions between the regime and Iranian society—segments of which have grown disenchanted with the Republic's revolutionary ideals—can also act as a constraint on Iranian external behavior.

This leads to our conclusion that analogies to the Cold War are mistaken: The Islamic Republic does not seek territorial aggrandizement or even, despite its rhetoric, the forcible imposition of its revolutionary ideology onto neighboring states. Instead, it feeds off existing grievances with the status quo, particularly in the Arab world. Traditional containment options may actually create further opportunities for Tehran to exploit, thereby amplifying the very influence the United States is trying to mitigate. A more useful strategy, therefore, is one that exploits existing checks on Iran's power and influence. These include the gap between its aspiration for asymmetric warfare capabilities and the reality of its rather limited conventional forces, disagreements between Iran and its militant "proxies," and the potential for sharp criticism from Arab public opinion, which it has long sought to exploit. In addition, we recommend a new U.S. approach to Iran that integrates elements of engagement and containment while de-escalating unilateral U.S. pressure on Tehran and applying increased *multilateral* pressure against its nuclear ambitions. The analyses that informed these conclusions also yielded the following insights for U.S. planners and strategists concerning Iran's strategic culture, conventional military, ties to Islamist groups, and ability to influence Arab public opinion.

Assertiveness and Caution Define Iran's Strategic Culture

Our assessment of Iranian leadership dynamics, threat perception, and regional strategy reveals competing tendencies toward adventurism and pragmatism. This stems from a number of factors.

Many within the current regime appear to view Iran as an indispensable regional power, but not necessarily a revolutionary hegemon. There is the further belief that the Islamic Republic is a model for Islamic enlightenment everywhere and the preeminent Islamic state in the region, providing a geopolitical bridge between Asia and the Middle East. As a result of these perceived attributes, the Iranian leadership has shown a marked tendency not only to push for a greater role in regional affairs but also to exaggerate Iran's strategic profile on the world stage.

Yet it does not follow that Iran is currently an expansionist, revolutionary state. Its revolutionary ideology has certainly featured prominently in the rhetoric of its officials. However, the record of Iranian actions suggests that these views should be more accurately regarded as the *vocabulary* of Iranian foreign policy rather than its *determinant*. Nationalism, sovereignty, and regime survival are the more fundamental drivers of Iran's external behavior. For example, even in Shi'ite-dominated Iraq, Iran is not seeking to export its revolutionary goals, despite the fact that it would ultimately prefer clerical rule as a final outcome. Today, many officials in Tehran see the United States as an anti–status quo, revolutionary power seeking to reshape the Middle East by exporting secularism, democracy, and, more recently, sectarianism. (See pp. 8–14.)

The Iranian threat perception blurs internal and external concerns. The regime has a marked tendency to conflate domestic instability with external meddling. Although the U.S. invasions of Afghanistan and Iraq eliminated Iran's most serious regional adversaries, it still faces serious threats with the potential to wreak internal havoc. The spread of crime, weapons, and sectarian tensions from Iraq has animated ethnic activists in the provinces of Kordestan and Khuzestan (which border Iraq) and even in the eastern province of Baluchestan. These concerns have informed Iran's trilateral cooperation with Syria and Turkey over the Kurds, its involvement in Iraq, and its decision to repatriate Afghan refugees. Leading clerics in Iran are also concerned about the theological challenge stemming from Shi'ite seminaries in Iraq. The learning centers of Najaf and Karbala long dominated Shi'ite discourse before being suppressed by Ba'athist regimes in Iraq; they are now reemerging with the potential to overshadow their Iranian counterparts in Qom. Finally, the Iranian leadership continues to perceive an existential threat posed to the Islamic Republic by the United States. This has made it highly sensitive to internal "interference" by the United States, particularly U.S. promotion of civil society and support for ethnic activists. One result of these fears has been an intensified crackdown on academic exchanges, social liberalism, and freedom of expression. In some cases, however, the regime is cynically exploiting this threat to bolster sagging popular support for the revolution. (See pp. 15–22.)

Regime factionalism affects external behavior. The Iranian system is beset with factionalism. Decisionmaking requires consensus; therefore, the number and complexity of these factions, combined with the individual reluctance and inability to make decisions, make it very difficult for the system to change course or to make significant decisions. Moreover, competing factions frequently use foreign policy issues to subvert or outmaneuver their rivals. This is particularly the case given the Revolutionary Guard's efforts to consolidate its control over key domestic institutions. Also, the country's worsening economic situation and increasing isolation over the nuclear issue has been a boon to factional opponents of President Ahmadinejad. Finally, the ongoing nuclear crisis may be at least partially fueled by internal maneuvering and bureaucratic competition. The net effect of these internal dynamics is an erratic, unpredictable, and frequently escalatory foreign policy. (See pp. 22–31.)

Iran Pursues a Multifaceted Regional Strategy Marked by Strengths and Limitations

As noted above, Iran views itself as a status quo power, preferring to assert a greater role for itself within the existing regional system rather than refashion that system according to its revolutionary vision. This has resulted in an ambitious, activist policy that hinges on three themes: deterrence and homeland defense, support for Islamist militant groups (both for symbolic reasons and as a retaliatory capability), and the currying of favor with publics in the Arab world to circumvent official hostility from other regimes in the region. Within each of these vectors are factors that both aid Iranian power and circumscribe it. (See pp. 31–37.)

Despite asymmetric doctrinal ambitions, Iran fields a weak conventional force. Iranian leaders have long trumpeted their shift to an asymmetric strategy of homeland defense that would exact intolerable costs from an invader. Much of this rests on notions of "mosaic defense," partisan warfare, and popular mobilization of Basiji auxiliaries. On the whole, however, Iran's military remains mired in conventional doctrine because of bureaucratic inertia in procurement and frequent infighting between the Revolutionary Guard and conventional forces. Most of Iran's military equipment is out of date and poorly maintained, and its ground forces suffer from both personnel and equipment shortages. With its outdated aircraft, the Iranian Air Force, in particular, is no match for its neighbors and certainly not for U.S. airpower. (See pp. 58–64.)

Tehran's layered and overlapping security structures, while useful for regime survivability, inhibit battlefield performance and reduce its capability to defend against external threats. This is reflected in the shortcomings evident in Iran's nationwide exercises between the air, ground, and sea components of the Revolutionary Guard and regular forces. Although touted as "joint," they usually devolve into organizational or service-specific training that appears highly scripted and choreographed. (See pp. 42–49.)

Some of Iran's asymmetric capabilities are threatening. Because of its inferior conventional military forces, Iran's defense doctrine, particularly its ability to deter aggressors, relies heavily on asymmetric warfare. Iranian strategists favor guerilla efforts that offer superior mobility, fighting morale, and popular support (e.g., the Hezbollah model in Lebanon) to counter a technologically superior conventional power—namely, the United States. At the high end of the spectrum, Iran has strong motives and means to develop advanced ballistic missile and nuclear weapon capabilities. This reliance on asymmetric capabilities can threaten Western interests in a variety of ways, particularly on the naval front. Iran's mining capability, antiship cruise missiles, and innovative "swarming" tactics could impede maritime access in the Strait of Hormuz. (See pp. 64–70.)

The Revolutionary Guard also possesses a significant arsenal of short- and medium-range ballistic missiles that can reach the small Persian Gulf states, Afghanistan, Israel, eastern Turkey, and most of Saudi Arabia. Although these missiles are currently inaccurate and thus have limited military utility, improvements in their range, ability to carry unconventional warheads, and accuracy would significantly enhance Iran's ability to threaten large population centers, economic infrastructure, and military bases. (See pp. 65–66.)

Iran has limited leverage over so-called proxy groups. To compensate for its conventional inferiority, Iran has long provided financial and military support to a variety of non-state Islamist groups. According to Revolutionary Guard doctrine, this "peripheral strategy" is intended to give strategic depth to Iran's homeland defense, taking the fight deep into the enemy's camp. In the cases of Hamas and Hezbollah, this strategy also buys Iran legitimacy among Arab publics who are frustrated with their regimes' seemingly status quo approach. In effect, Tehran is being "more Arab than the Arabs" on issues such as Palestine. (See pp. 34–35 and pp. 84–86.)

In supporting major Shi'ite militant groups in Iraq and Lebanon, Tehran may expect a degree of reciprocity. This is particularly the case in the event of a U.S. strike, in which Iran might expect these groups to act unflinchingly as retaliatory agents. Yet this expectation may be misplaced. In Iraq, for instance, Iranian funds and military assistance are not essential to the survival of major Shi'ite political factions. Furthermore, some of these groups depend extensively on promoting an image of Iraqi nationalism for domestic support and thus prefer to maintain a degree of separation from Tehran. In Lebanon, Hezbollah's behavior is also informed by questions of domestic legitimacy; it has recently taken great pains to publicly distance itself from Iranian patronage. (pp. 86–123.)

Thus, in the event of conflict between the United States and Iran, the willingness of these groups to retaliate purely in the service of Tehran should not be assumed as automatic. Instead, they will carefully weigh the benefits of such actions against the risks to their own local agendas. Fractionalization and dissent may occur between pro-Iranian, anti-Iranian, and neutral factions. In some cases, Tehran may actively cultivate these splits, or the groups' leadership may secretly subcontract attacks to a spin-off or "rogue element." (See pp. 102–103 and p. 123.)

In short, it is best to conceive of Iran as exerting *influence* over its Shi'ite allies, but not control.

Iran has long sought to exploit Arab opinion, with mixed success. Aside from its support to non-state actors, Tehran also views Arab public opinion as an important vector for power projection. Tehran uses this strategy to exert pressure on unfriendly regimes and their Western allies. Employing both local media and its own transnational outlets (such as its Arabic-language satellite channel al-Alam), Iran has portrayed itself as a populist challenger of the status quo, a champion of the Palestinian cause, the patron of Hezbollah, and a beleaguered victim of Western double standards on the nuclear issue. Tehran's belief that it can count on Arab public support and its attempts to be "more Arab than the Arabs" have resulted in frequently bellicose behavior. Indeed, Ahmadinejad's antagonism toward Israel, defiance of U.S. pressure on the nuclear program, and populist charisma have earned him accolades from Arab publics. Iran's appeal in the region skyrocketed following Hezbollah's summer 2006 war with Israel. (See pp. 36–37 and pp. 129–130.)

However, our analysis of key media outlets and external polling reveals that popular Arab support for Iran remains a fickle strategic resource. In many cases, Arab opinion can rapidly swing from praise to condemnation based on events that are beyond Iran's control or because of its own strategic missteps. Growing sectarian tensions in Iraq and the perception of Shi'ite political ascendancy in the region have spurred trepidation about Iran throughout the Arab world, particularly after the execution of Saddam Hussein. Arab governments in particular are concerned about Tehran's ability to circumvent official diplomatic channels and appeal directly to ordinary Arabs, thereby threatening their own legitimacy. Among the Persian Gulf states, the Saudi and Bahraini governments fear Iran's attempts to mobilize Shi'ite populations within their borders, particularly in the event of a

U.S. strike. Yet our own field research on this issue reveals these worries are overblown: Most Shi'ite groups have worked peacefully within the system for political change and reject Iran as a political patron. (See pp. 131–144.)

Arab opinion on Iran is often split between publics and their regimes. Arab regimes fear Iran's nuclear aspirations but are cognizant that its nuclear program is largely endorsed by their Arab publics as a critique of Western double standards and interference. Consequently, they are reticent about appearing too hostile to the prospect of an Iranian bomb lest their publics perceive this as tacit support for a U.S. strike. As a result, some Arab officials are exploiting Sunni Arab fears of Shi'ite ascendancy and sectarian strife in their media outlets to curry favor for what is essentially a classic balance-of-power strategy against Iran. Regarding a U.S. attack against Iran, both official and popular opinion is largely opposed, voicing deep concern about Iran's retaliatory options and insufficient U.S. protection. These divergent and ambivalent views suggest caution for U.S. policymakers who would take Arab hostility toward Iran as de facto support for a U.S. attack or U.S. efforts to contain Iran through a Cold War–style bloc of Sunni states. (See pp. 144–151.)

Recommendations: Toward a New U.S. Policy Paradigm

Over the years, the United States has attempted a variety of approaches to address the Iranian challenge. To date, none has succeeded in making Iran less menacing to U.S. interests or more compliant with United Nations Security Council resolutions. The existing policy of creating a Cold War–like containment regime against Iran does not take into account features of the regional geopolitics and Iranian strategic culture discussed in this report. Although more appealing, policies relying only on bilateral engagement and/or hopes for some sort of grand bargain are equally unrealistic. And efforts to foment internal unrest and to play one faction off another within Iran are also likely to backfire because of limited U.S. understanding of Iran's complex political landscape and the regime's ability to manipulate such interference to its advantage. (See pp. 163–174.)

Given these shortcomings, we propose a different approach that involves a series of unilateral de-escalation measures by Washington and continued muscular multilateral efforts targeted at Iranian behaviors that are at odds with international norms (e.g., the nuclear issue and links to terrorism). Rather than a broad U.S.-based containment strategy, we suggest leveraging international pressure while unilaterally de-escalating U.S. rhetoric and policy toward Iran (essentially, reversing the traditional good cop/bad cop roles).[2] Keeping the pressure components of this approach multilateral (including support from Russia and China) is critical because it helps deprive the Iranian leadership of the ability to deflect domestic critique by focusing discontent solely on the United States and the United Kingdom or other European Union powers. At the same time, the United States should avoid unilateral actions that would escalate conflict with Iran, as these are unlikely to work and are likely to exacerbate tensions significantly. Although no panacea, multilateral pressure—when combined with less-hostile U.S. rhetoric and policy—may prove more effective than past policies, at least in terms of the more limited aims regarding Iran's nuclear ambitions. That said, the likelihood of sustained support for this approach by Russia and China remains questionable. The specific components of this approach are as follows (see pp. 175–179):

- **Continue strengthening international sanctions and other financial pressures targeted on the nuclear issue, but avoid unilateral punitive measures that are not likely to generate broad support.** Secondary sanctions are particularly counterproductive in maintaining European and international support for nuclear-related sanctions in the United Nations.
- **Pursue bilateral dialogues related to areas of common interest, such as instability in Iraq and Afghanistan, narcotics trafficking,**

---

2 For more on this idea of role reversals in the context of transatlantic diplomacy toward the Iranian nuclear challenge, see Robert J. Einhorn, "Transatlantic Strategy on Iran's Nuclear Program," *Washington Quarterly*, Autumn 2004.

natural disaster relief, refugees, and other humanitarian crises.
The United States should identify and exploit areas where genuine
collaboration can be productive and profitable, without harboring
expectations for broader diplomatic breakthroughs. These more-
limited efforts should not be trivialized by over-hyping them.
News of good works will spread on its own. That said, the United
States should temper any expectation that engagement will produce dramatic results. However, even limited engagement efforts
may improve the prospects for a broader dialogue and normalization process should political conditions improve.

- **Issue unambiguous statements about U.S. interests and intentions in the region, particularly regarding Iraq.** These must be
simple and easily understood, and the United States must stick
to them long enough for them to be taken seriously. The United
States should reinforce the Status of Forces Agreement with Iraq
by clearly stating that it has no long-term interest in occupying
Iraq or establishing a permanent military presence there. At the
same time, the United States has a right to maintain a military
presence in the region and to use force to protect its interests and
those of its allies against threats from both state and non-state
actors. These statements would underscore that U.S. military postures are for defensive purposes and to ensure stability, not to
develop U.S. bases for launching attacks on regional neighbors
(i.e., Iran).

- **Engage in efforts to build a multilateral regional security framework that is simultaneously inclusive of Iran and sensitive to
the needs of the United States' Arab friends and allies.** The
Arab states remember the exceedingly close U.S.-Iranian relations during the Pahlavi era and thus would be ambivalent at best
about closer ties between Tehran and Washington. Yet despite
these difficulties, the United States needs to aggressively pursue a
broad-based multilateral regional security framework that would
include Iran alongside Washington's traditional Arab allies, as well
as key international players like the European Union, Russia, and
China. Such a structure would not be based on a specific threat
(such as a collective security organization like NATO), but would

provide an open-ended security forum where regional states could discuss and address a range of regional challenges (starting with more-consensual issues such as narcotics trafficking, responses to natural disasters, maritime security, and economic and energy development) and engage in military confidence-building measures. The model for such a forum could be a cooperative security organization like the Organisation for Security and Co-operation in Europe, where mutual threat perceptions are aired and conflict resolution measures pursued.

Although an inclusive multilateral security structure in the Persian Gulf region would take time to build, it would contribute more to regional stability over the long run than would continuing to rely solely on competitive, balance-of-power strategies designed to isolate Iran. Such narrow strategies are more likely to encourage, even reify, Iranian hegemonic aspirations than remove them. Furthermore, a U.S.-led "containment" of Iran is also unlikely to be sustainable among Persian Gulf states that desire to maintain cordial relations with Iran, if not active political and economic engagement.

Acknowledgments

The authors wish to thank a number of individuals for their support of our research. Major General Frank Gorenc, then–Director of Operational Planning, Policy and Strategy, Headquarters USAF, was the sponsor of this study. Colonel William "Shoes" DelGrego, then–Chief, AF/A5XS, Concepts, Strategy and Wargaming (Skunk Works), and Lieutenant Colonel Greg "Elroy" Hillebrand were instrumental in guiding this project throughout its various stages. Also with Skunk Works, Renee Maisch was critical in ensuring the smooth coordination of meetings and flow of information. We would also like to thank Andrew Hoehn, Vice President and Director, RAND Project AIR FORCE, and David Ochmanek, Director of PAF's Strategy and Doctrine Program, who conceived of the study and offered valuable guidance, advice, and encouragement. David Ochmanek also offered a useful and thorough critique of draft versions of this monograph.

RAND colleagues Bruce Nardulli and Theodore Karasik sent illuminating dispatches from the Persian Gulf region that supplemented and updated previous fieldwork on Arab perceptions of Iran. Natasha Hall provided helpful research on the concluding sections. On Iranian military issues, we benefited tremendously from the insights and previous research of Lieutenant Commander Anthony Butera (U.S. Navy) and RAND colleagues Derek Eaton, David Frelinger, and Bruce Pirnie. Pardee RAND Graduate School Fellow Second Lieutenant Dave Shulker, USAF, added valuable suggestions for the concluding section. Outside RAND, we benefited from the insights and comments of Karim Sadjadpour, Michael Eisenstadt, and Barbara Slavin.

Several people at RAND deserve kudos for preparing the manuscript. Jane Siegel, Joanna Nelsen, Pamela Severson, Terri Perkins, and Isabel Sardou assembled the report, formatted the draft version, and developed the bibliography. We also thank Mary Wrazen and Sandi Petitjean for their proficiency in producing high-quality graphics. In the RAND Library, Roberta Shanman was helpful in locating hard-to-find source material.

We extend our appreciation to the numerous analysts from DoD and other government organizations who took the time to share their insights with us. Added to this are the numerous officials and scholars from the Middle East who, for both this project and previous RAND endeavors, gave us new and important perspectives on Iran and regional geopolitics. We also benefited tremendously from the views of Iranian scholars and policy analysts during telephone conversations and at meetings in the Persian Gulf region conducted from 2005 to 2006. The current political climate in Iran, explored in Chapter Two, prevented us from continuing this dialogue and from traveling to Iran; it is our hope that these fruitful exchanges will soon resume.

Finally, we wish to express great appreciation to RAND colleagues Bruce Nardulli and James Dobbins and to Shahram Chubin for their insightful technical reviews of the document, and to RAND colleague Alireza Nader for carefully perusing the document more than once for factual errors, strength of argument, and coherence. Their comments significantly strengthened the substance of the report and its recommendations.

Of course, the content of this report is the sole responsibility of the authors.

Abbreviations

AMAL	*Afwaj al-Muqawama al-Lubnaniya*
CIA	U.S. Central Intelligence Agency
CONOP	concept of operations
DoD	Department of Defense
EFP	explosively formed projectile
GCC	Gulf Cooperation Council
GDP	gross domestic product
HQ	headquarters
IDF	Israel Defense Forces
IED	improvised explosive device
IFLB	Islamic Front for the Liberation of Bahrain
IRGC	Islamic Revolutionary Guard Corps
IRGCAF	Islamic Revolutionary Guard Corps Air Force
IRGC-QF	Islamic Revolutionary Guards Corps-Qods (Jerusalem) Force
IRIAF	Islamic Republic of Iran Air Force
IRIB	Islamic Republic of Iran Broadcasting

ISCI	Islamic Supreme Council of Iraq
ISR	intelligence, surveillance, and reconnaissance
LEF	Law Enforcement Forces
MANPADS	man-portable air defense system
MFA	Ministry of Foreign Affairs
MOIS	Ministry of Intelligence and Security
NATO	North Atlantic Treaty Organization
NAVCENT	U.S. Naval Forces Central Command
OIC	Organization of the Islamic Conference
OIR	Organization for the Islamic Revolution
PAF	Project AIR FORCE
PIJ	Palestinian Islamic Jihad
PKK	Kurdistan Workers Party
PLO	Palestinian Liberation Organization
SAM	surface-to-air missile
SCIRI	Supreme Council for the Islamic Revolution in Iraq
SCNS	Supreme Council for National Security
SCO	Shanghai Cooperation Organization
SOFA	Status of Forces Agreement
TEL	Transporter Erector Launches
UAE	United Arab Emirates
UAV	unmanned aerial vehicle
UN	United Nations
USAF	U.S. Air Force

CHAPTER ONE

Introduction: Understanding the Iranian Challenge

Since the 1979 revolution, Iran's regional ambitions and power-projection efforts have been among the most critical foreign policy challenges facing the United States in the Middle East. U.S. policymakers from that time have grappled with variations on a question that continues to challenge their successors today: Is Iran an unequivocal threat to U.S. interests in the region, undermining the evolution of, as then–Secretary of State Condoleezza Rice put it, "the kind of Middle East that we want to see"?[1] In recent years, Tehran has pursued an increasingly aggressive foreign policy, leading President G. W. Bush to declare before a group of U.S. veterans in August 2007 that "Iran's actions threaten the security of nations everywhere."[2]

Although such pronouncements may appear excessively strident to some, all observers of Iran, regardless of their political orientation, recognize the significance of Iran's nuclear ambitions and the country's new assertiveness in the Middle East. For the Department of Defense (DoD) and the U.S. Air Force (USAF), this activism is most visible in Iran's supply of lethal improvised explosive device (IED) technology to Iraqi insurgents and its conventional military buildup, including the development of short- and medium-range ballistic missiles and the

---

[1] See Robin Wright, "Iran Is Critical as U.S. Unveils Arms Sales in the Middle East," *Washington Post*, July 31, 2007, p. 15.

[2] The White House, "President Bush Addresses the 89th Annual National Convention of the American Legion," August 28, 2007.

capability to threaten shipping in the Strait of Hormuz. Elsewhere in the region, Tehran continues to sponsor terrorist groups such as Hamas and the Lebanese Hezbollah—an organization that has been termed the "A-team" of terrorism and that arguably destroyed the image of Israeli military invincibility during the Lebanon conflict in the summer of 2006.[3] Added to these threats, Tehran has strong motives and the means to acquire nuclear weapons. Although questions remain about the extent and nature of the Iranian nuclear program, there is little doubt that the Islamic Republic is actively seeking an indigenous uranium enrichment capability that would, at the very least, allow for a nuclear breakout capacity.[4]

Tehran has other less lethal but possibly more effective means to challenge U.S. interests and pressure U.S. allies. For example, Arab audiences widely applauded Hezbollah's battlefield performance in 2006 and Iranian President Mahmoud Ahmadinejad's nuclear posturing, topics that have opened up fissures between Arab publics and their regimes. Indeed, the resulting trepidation from America's Arab allies may pose a greater long-term challenge to U.S. interests than Iran itself. The states of the Gulf Cooperation Council (GCC), presumably at the urging of Saudi Arabia, have announced an interest in developing a nuclear capability of their own, as have Egypt and Jordan.[5] In Iraq and Afghanistan, Iran exerts significant influence through "soft-power" projection in the forms of reconstruction aid, infrastructure development, media, and financial investments. These levers only serve to strengthen Iran's self-perception of geo-strategic centrality. Taken in sum, these factors suggest an Iranian bid for regional dominance that could significantly challenge U.S. interests over the ten- to fifteen-year time horizon.

---

[3] In a September 2002 speech, then–Deputy Secretary of State Richard Armitage noted, "Hezbollah may be the A-team of terrorists and maybe al-Qaeda's actually the B-team" ("US Official Calls Hezbollah 'A-Team of Terrorists'," Reuters, September 5, 2002). For a concise overview, see Laura Deeb, "Hizballah: A Primer," *Middle East Report*, July 31, 2006.

[4] See, for example, Tim Guldimann, "The Iranian Nuclear Impasse," *Survival*, Vol. 49, No. 3, Autumn 2007, pp. 169–178.

[5] Although nuclear *weapons* are never explicitly mentioned, the timing and meaning of such developments in a part of the world with few energy challenges are unmistakable.

Iranian Motives Are Ambiguous

Yet Tehran's true motives may belie their outward appearance. What seems like a drive for hegemony may in fact be a form of deterrence or the manifestation of an ambition for increased stature and "indispensability" in the midst of isolation and encirclement. Although its major regional adversaries, the Taliban regime in Afghanistan and the government of Saddam Hussein in Iraq, are gone and its principal enemy (the United States) has been entangled in Iraq, Iran remains fundamentally bereft of any real allies. Adding to this diplomatic loneliness are transnational threats that affect Iran's internal stability: refugee crises, ethnic irredentism, narcotics smuggling, and Sunni radicalism.[6] Thus, Tehran has strong *defensive* incentives to break out of what Iranian leaders perceive as U.S.-imposed isolation by asserting a critical role for itself in the region's affairs—often in ways that are inimical to U.S. objectives. An article in the Islamic Revolutionary Guard Corps (IRGC) weekly magazine captures this dynamic from an Iranian viewpoint:

> The U.S. considers Iran as a challenge to its hegemony in the region. At the same time, the U.S. has realized that its victory in Iraq, Lebanon and Palestine is dependent on its relations with Iran.[7]

Airpower Is a Critical Element of U.S. Power Against Iran

Among the instruments of U.S. national power arrayed against Iran, airpower will likely assume increasing prominence—both for U.S. decisionmakers and in the minds of the Iranian leadership. Along with maritime power—to include carrier-based airpower—the USAF is the force of "first resort" to project power into Iran's unstable environs; to reassure and protect U.S. allies and partners; and to dissuade, coerce,

---

[6] Anoushiravan Ehteshami, "Iran's International Posture After the Fall of Baghdad," *Middle East Journal*, Vol. 58, No. 2, Spring 2004, p. 187.

[7] Farsan Shahidi, "Unsuccessful U.S. Policies in the Middle East," *Sobhe Sadegh* (weekly magazine of the Islamic Revolutionary Guard Corps), in Persian, n.d.

and deter Iranian aggression. This role is all the more critical in times when the regional security environment is in flux and local states are rethinking old paradigms of confrontation and cooperation. In addition, USAF assets deployed around Iran continue to cast a long shadow over the regime's strategic worldview, reinforcing the aforementioned sense of encirclement. Witness Tehran's preoccupation with Shindand Airfield in western Afghanistan, located less than 100 km from the Iranian border, and Tehran's repeated calls that the Iraqi government exercise control over "foreign air bases."[8]

Yet, as we discuss at length below, it is not clear whether Tehran's siege mentality spurs Iran toward greater caution or activism in its regional strategy. Certainly, U.S. airpower acts as a visible deterrent against conventional belligerence by Iran. But Tehran has other nontraditional and asymmetric means for challenging U.S. interests, means that are not easily contained by military action. The 1996 Khobar Towers bombing is a potent reminder of this strategy's potential lethality, as well as its ability to target USAF personnel and assets.[9]

Our Study Addresses Four Key Aspects of the Iranian Challenge

Guided by these observations, this study aims to prepare the USAF leadership and the U.S. defense community to anticipate and confront future challenges from Iran. To do so, we examine the motivations behind Iranian strategy; Iran's military doctrine and capabilities; Iran's interactions with non-state Islamist groups; and the Arab public's per-

---

[8] "Iranian Radio Criticizes Reported US Plans for Military Base in West Afghanistan," Mashhad Voice of the Islamic Republic of Iran External Service in Dari, FBIS IAP20041220000065, 1330 GMT December 19, 2004. See also Ron Synovitz, "Afghanistan: How Would Permanent U.S. Bases Impact Regional Interests?" Radio Free Europe/Radio Liberty, February 23, 2005. On Iraq, see "Iranian Defense Minister Urges Iraq to 'Exercise Its Authority' over Foreign 'Bases'," Tehran Fars News Agency, Web page, in Persian, FBIS IAP20050706011012, 0421 GMT July 6, 2005.

[9] See *The 9/11 Commission Report: Final Report of the National Commission on Terrorist Attacks upon the United States*, U.S. Government Printing Office, July 26, 2004, p. 60. The commission implicates Iran, Saudi Hezbollah, and al-Qaeda in the attacks.

ception of Iran. More broadly, we present a framework for assessing future trends in Iranian strategy. Because Tehran often acts in ways that are intentionally ambiguous, U.S. leaders must avoid making presumptions about Iranian *intentions* that are derived simply from Iranian *capabilities*. Thus, any analysis of future threats from the Islamic Republic must be grounded in an understanding of the domestic roots of Tehran's behavior. Similarly, the United States must identify the buffers and barriers to Iran's power-projection efforts. Some of these limitations are present in the regional system Iran is trying to influence, but they are also found inside Iran's unique strategic culture.

In Chapter Two, therefore, we begin by addressing the domestic drivers for assertiveness and caution in Iranian behavior, focusing on the regime's perception of Iran's place in the world and weighing the role of ideology, pragmatism, and factionalism in its policy calculations. To set the stage for subsequent analysis, we identify three principal themes that inform Iran's regional strategy: deterrence, support for Islamists and non-state actors, and an appeal to Arab public opinion.

In Chapter Three, we cover Iran's developing conventional military buildup, discussing the significant gap between its doctrinal aspirations for asymmetric warfare and the reality of its rather limited conventional capability.

In Chapter Four, we explore Tehran's interactions with non-state Islamists in Lebanon and Iraq, assessing the extent of Iranian control over these groups and the resulting threat to U.S. interests.

In Chapter Five, we cover Tehran's appeal to Arab public opinion, revealing how Arab sentiment frequently swings between acclaim for and criticism of the Islamic Republic, making it an unstable strategic resource.

Finally, our concluding chapter surveys previous U.S. policies toward the Islamic Republic and formulates a new U.S. strategy paradigm by acknowledging the aforementioned limitations on Iranian power and adopting a more multilateral approach.

Our Methodology Is Grounded in Primary Sources

Although discerning Tehran's motivations and future strategy is challenging, it is possible to derive insights from a number of sources. We analyzed Iranian media, the statements of key Iranian leaders, and Persian-language publications of Iranian think tanks and policy journals. We also drew from phone and email discussions with Iranian scholars and interactions with former Iranian diplomats at meetings in the Middle East.[10]

In assessing Arab opinions of Iran, we benefited from extensive discussions with Arab officials, military commanders, diplomats, scholars, and religious clerics, principally in the Persian Gulf region but also in Egypt and Jordan. Moreover, we made use of Arabic-language print and broadcast resources. Finally, our research drew from consultations with government analysts and USAF personnel, as well as previous RAND work on Iran's security policy, the behavior of nuclear-armed states, and U.S. strategies for dealing with a post-nuclear Iran.[11] Based on a thorough examination of these sources, we present an empirically rooted analysis to inform U.S. decisionmakers who need to anticipate patterns and variations in Iranian behavior.

---

[10] However, some of this material is dated because the regime's current ban on academic exchanges with the West, reflected most poignantly in the arrest of the Iranian-American scholar Haleh Esfandiari, has affected our access. Indeed, one of our researchers was scheduled to participate in a panel discussion with the former Iranian defense minister at a seminar in Tehran hosted by a prominent Iranian think tank. In the midst of the recent crackdown, however, this invitation was quietly withdrawn.

[11] Daniel Byman, Shahram Chubin, Anoushiravan Ehteshami, and Jerrold D. Green, *Iran's Security Policy in the Post-Revolutionary Era*, Santa Monica, Calif.: RAND Corporation, MR-1320-OSD, 2001.

CHAPTER TWO

Assertiveness and Caution in Iranian Strategic Culture

Each of Iran's vectors for power projection presents both assets and liabilities for Iranian leaders. As we discuss below, some of these limitations are inherent in Iranian capabilities, particularly in its conventional military, as well as structural features in the Middle East political environment. Yet the *motives* and *intentions* of the regime's leadership will ultimately determine whether and how these instruments are used: with assertiveness and risk or caution and prudence. Shaping long-term DoD and USAF options and posture requires an understanding of the interplay of these contending poles of Iranian behavior. This understanding is also important for constructing a new U.S. policy paradigm toward the Islamic Republic that exploits existing buffers and checks on Iranian power and that does not inadvertently amplify the threats the United States is trying to mitigate.

Therefore, in this chapter, we explore the domestic context for Iran's power projection to identify the sources of assertiveness and caution in Iran's future strategy. First, we offer an overview of trends in Iranian worldview and threat perception, focusing on the impact of pragmatism and ideology. Of critical importance is discerning how Iranian leaders see an overlap between external and internal threats. Like all revolutionary regimes, the leaders of the Islamic Republic have perceived a web of conspiracies and plots against the regime with origins outside their country—and in many cases have cynically cultivated public paranoia to bolster their sagging legitimacy. We then explore the role of factionalism within the regime as a driver for Iranian external behavior. Finally, we highlight some prominent themes in Iranian regional strategy—deterrence, pan-Islamism and support to proxy groups, and an appeal to Arab public opinion—that, while seemingly hegemonic, are for Tehran more likely a multilayered homeland defense strategy.

Iran's Strategic Worldview Appears Revolutionary But Leans Toward Realpolitik

The strategic motives of the Islamic Republic and its place in the international system have been the subject of a long-running policy and academic debate. Some observers have pointed to Tehran's inflammatory rhetoric on the Palestinian issue, denial of the Holocaust, recent territorial claims in the Persian Gulf region, and support for international terrorism to characterize the regime as expansionist and ideologically driven.[1] Adherents of this argument often posit that the revolutionary origins of the regime predispose it toward the acquisition of nuclear weapons and other weapons of mass destruction. Along these lines, some have argued that clerical factionalism and the seemingly messianic aspects of the Islamic Republic's Shi'ite ideology make certain leadership factions immune to the normal rules of international behavior.[2] Others see Iran as a less-exceptional case in the international system, a country whose behavior has been characterized by realpolitik

---

[1] Patrick Clawson and Michael Rubin, *Eternal Iran: Continuity and Chaos*, New York: Palgrave-MacMillan Press, 2005; Ilan Berman, *Tehran Rising: The Iranian Threat to the United States*, New York: Rowman and Littlefield, 2005; Kenneth Timmerman, *Countdown to Crisis: The Coming Nuclear Showdown With Iran*, New York: Three Rivers Press, 2005; Michael Rubin, "Dealing with Iran," interview with Kathryn Jean Lopez, *National Review Online*, April 25, 2006.

[2] For the resonance of apocalyptic thinking among certain segments of the elite, see Mehdi Khalaji, "Apocalyptic Politics: On the Rationality of Iranian Policy," Policy Focus 79, Washington, D.C.: The Washington Institute for Near East Policy, January 2008. Khalaji writes that, "in the military forces, especially in the Islamic Revolutionary Guard Corps (IRGC) and the Basij militia, apocalypticism has a very strong following." For regime factionalism and its effect on deterrence, see Michael Eisenstadt, "Living with a Nuclear Iran," *Survival*, Vol. 41, No. 3, Autumn 1999, p. 36.

since the death of Khomeini.[3] These analysts interpret Iran's nuclear ambitions and even its support for terrorism as serving more-pragmatic goals related to regime survival and deterrence.

The immediate post-revolutionary period was certainly marked by a calculated effort by Tehran to export the revolution, most notably to Lebanon but also to neighboring Persian Gulf states and Iraq. Even in faraway Egypt, the Sunni Muslim Brotherhood was animated by Khomeinist themes of anti-imperialism, prompting the government of Egyptian President Anwar Sadat to emphasize the revolution's sectarian motives—a tactic that has re-emerged today among jittery Arab leaders.[4] In the Persian Gulf states, the very names of Tehran's principal Shi'ite allies following the revolution indeed suggest a real threat to the old political order: the Islamic Front for the Liberation of Bahrain (IFLB), the Organization for the Islamic Revolution on the Arabian Peninsula (OIR–Saudi Arabia), and the Supreme Council for the Islamic Revolution in Iraq (SCIRI).[5]

---

[3] For Iran as a more pragmatic, conservative power pursuing what is fundamentally a defensive, albeit assertive, foreign policy in a hostile strategic neighborhood, see R. K. Ramazani, "Ideology and Pragmatism in Iranian Foreign Policy," *Middle East Journal*, Vol. 58, No. 4, Autumn 2004; Nader Entessar, "Iran's Security Challenges," *The Muslim World*, Vol. 94, October 2004; Mark Gasiorowski, "The New Aggressiveness in Iran's Foreign Policy," *Middle East Policy*, Vol. 14, No. 2, Summer 2007, pp. 125–132; Shahram Chubin, "Iran's Strategic Environment and Nuclear Weapons," in *Iran's Nuclear Weapons Options: Issues and Analysis*, Washington, D.C.: The Nixon Center, January 2001, pp. 22–30; Ray Takeyh and Nikolas K. Gvosdev, "Pragmatism in the Midst of Iranian Turmoil," *The Washington Quarterly*, Vol. 27, No. 4, Autumn 2004, pp. 33–56; Ray Takeyh, "Time for Détente with Iran," *Foreign Affairs*, March/April 2007. For Iranian views of pragmatism, see Kaveh Afrasiabi and Abbas Maleki, "Iran's Foreign Policy After 11 September," *Brown Journal of World Affairs*, Vol. 9, No. 2, Winter/Spring 2003, pp. 263–264; Abbas Maleki "Iran's Foreign Policy: From Idealism to Realism," *Majalleh Siasat Khareji* [*The Journal of Foreign Policy*], in Persian, Vol. 10, 1999; Kamran Taremi, "Beyond the Axis of Evil: Ballistic Missiles in Iran's Military Thinking," *Security Dialogue*, Vol. 36, No. 1, March 2005a; Byman et al., 2001.

[4] Rudee Mathee, "The Egyptian Opposition on the Iranian Revolution," in Juan R. I. Cole and Nikki R. Keddie, *Shi'ism and Social Protest*, New Haven: Yale University Press, 1986, pp. 247–274.

[5] For more on these organizations, see Yitzhak Nakash, *Reaching for Power: The Shi'a in the Modern Arab World*, Princeton, N.J.: Princeton University Press, 2006, pp. 42–71.

Yet Tehran's ambition to graft its ideology onto the region ultimately foundered, reflected most visibly by the fact that all three of the Persian Gulf–based Shi'ite organizations have changed their names, effectively shedding their affiliation with Tehran.[6] The dynamics of this distancing is addressed more thoroughly in Chapter Four, but it is sufficient to mention here that differing political milieus, the termination of the Iran-Iraq and Lebanese civil wars, Arab-Persian cultural distinctions, and competing Shi'ite clerical networks all played a role in the failure.

The most prominent reason for Iran's failure to spread its ideology throughout the region was the death of Ayatollah Khomeini. As conveyed to RAND by a senior Shi'ite cleric in Saudi Arabia, "When Ayatollah Khomeini died, his idea of *velayat-e faqih* (literally, "rule of the jurisconsult"—the political theory that legitimizes clerical rule in Iran) died."[7] Inside Iran, his system of government has endured, but former President and current Chairman of the Assembly of Experts 'Ali Akbar Hashemi Rafsanjani's more pragmatic administration sought to cultivate better bilateral ties throughout the Arab world and to emphasize the peaceful political integration of Arab Shi'ites.[8] As a result, Tehran's strategy since the passing of Khomeini has been shaped by conservatism, caution, and a general preference for realpolitik. The Iraqi Shi'ite uprising after the 1991 Persian Gulf War, when Tehran did little to aid its co-religionists, is a vivid illustration of this shift away from ideological absolutism.[9] Iran's lack of action during this watershed event reflects

---

[6]   The IFLB in Bahrain became the Islamic Action Society and has participated in Bahraini parliamentary elections, and the OIR became the Shi'ite Reform movement and has also worked peaceably for reform. Most recently, in May 2007, the SCIRI changed its name to the Islamic Supreme Council of Iraq (ISCI).

[7]   RAND interview with a leading Saudi Shi'ite cleric, Qatif, Saudi Arabia, March 10, 2007.

[8]   For the implications of Rafsanjani's shift on Hezbollah's orientation, to be discussed more thoroughly in Chapter Three, see Nizar A. Hamzeh, "Lebanon's Hizbullah: From Islamic Revolution to Parliamentary Accommodation," *Third World Quarterly*, Vol. 14, No. 2, 1993, p. 324.

[9]   Faleh Abd al-Jabbar, "Why the Uprisings Failed," *Middle East Report*, No. 176, May–June 1992, pp. 2–14.

a decisionmaking process that ultimately favored pragmatism and real-politik over revolutionary fervor. Today, Iran's support for militant groups, particularly in the Levant, serves more-state-centric geopoliti-cal aims, such as providing a form of "forward defense" and deterrence against a U.S. invasion and driving a wedge between the United States and its "client" Arab regimes by exploiting the Arab-Israeli dispute.

Today, many Iranian leaders argue that the United States is an anti–status quo, predatory power that cannot reconcile itself to the Islamic Republic's natural role in the region. Those who hold this view see Washington as seeking to secularize and democratize the Middle East while sowing internal discord inside Iran, with the ultimate goal of demolishing the revolution and the institutions it spawned. As noted by Iranian scholar and former diplomat Mahmoud Vaezi, the strat-egy of the United States has placed the entire region at risk by caus-ing the "disintegration of specific Islamic countries through organized riots and ethnic diversity."[10] Since 2006, Iranian officials have routinely blamed sectarian tensions in the Middle East on a U.S.-engineered plot designed to weaken pan-Islamic solidarity and isolate Iran.

Iran Aims for Regional and Global Preeminence

The Islamic Republic today is perhaps best described as a highly nation-alistic country that sees itself as a symbolic beacon for global Islamic enlightenment, but whose more immediate aims are rooted in a drive for regional preeminence. Many in the Iranian leadership, regardless of their political orientation or factional affiliation, appear to conceive of the Islamic Republic as an "exceptional" case in the international system—but not because of its revolutionary foundations. Iranian leaders no longer seek to radically reshape the regional order as they did after the revolution, but rather to raise the stature of their country within it. They see Iran as being entitled to a higher position in global affairs and a more active role on the regional stage.

---

[10] "'Experts' Warn U.S. Plan Uses Arab States to Cause Sunni-Shiite Split," *Hezbollah* [Tehran], in Persian, OSC IAP20070119011004, January 14, 2007, p. 2.

This newfound confidence is probably more reflective of changes in the regional environment that have enhanced Iran's existing leverage rather than any new changes in Iranian power. The "new assertiveness" in Iranian external behavior can therefore be characterized as an attempt to *consolidate* and *preserve* the strategic gains that were in some sense handed to the Islamic Republic by the U.S. invasions of Iraq and Afghanistan. Other enabling factors include the following:

- The perception among Iran's leadership and other regional governments that U.S. credibility, moral standing, and maneuverability in the region are at an all-time low—due principally to the U.S. entanglement in Iraq. This is perhaps best illustrated by President Ahmadinejad's public invitation to Saudi Arabia that the two states cooperate in filling the regional "power vacuum" created by the impending departure of U.S. forces from Iraq.[11]

- The disappearance of Iraq as an Arab buffer state, the so-called eastern flank of the Arab world, has amplified Iran's influence in the Arab world, both in the minds of Arab leaders and the imaginations of their publics. Thus, Arab leaders in the Levant speak of Iran having "reached the shores of the Mediterranean" through its militant allies Hamas, the Palestinian Islamic Jihad, and Hezbollah.[12] As we will discuss in subsequent chapters, however, these relationships—although real and lethal—do not constitute any sort of unified geopolitical "bloc."

- Until recently, rapid increases in the price of oil had given Iran more financial leeway, empowering the regime to spend more on external policy, to include support for militant groups abroad and for building influence in Iraq, Lebanon, and Palestine.

- The Ahmadinejad government perceives the utility of an "Eastern option," i.e., soliciting diplomatic and economic support from

---

[11] "Article Views Iranian President's 'Dangerous' Proposal to Fill Vacuum in Iraq," *Al-Sharq al-Awsat* [London], Web page referencing an article by Bilal al-Hasan entitled "Ahmadinejad's Grave Mistake: The Theory of Vacuum Filling," in Arabic, OSC GMP20070902913006, September 2, 2007.

[12] RAND discussion with Egyptian analyst, Cairo, March 14, 2008.

Asian countries to counterbalance the West. This has manifested itself in Iran's increased push for membership in the Shanghai Cooperation Organization (SCO). Ultimately, however, the leadership perceives this as a "card" to play with the West rather than a radical diplomatic reorientation.

Aside from these regional and global variables, the leadership in Tehran also believes that Iran's *intrinsic* attributes entitle it to a greater role. These qualities are rooted in the country's unique geography, economic resources, cultural heritage, intellectual capacity, and military might and are perhaps best described in a 2006 article by an Iranian scholar attached to a think tank run by former President Rafsanjani:

- Iran's long history of democracy, unique in the Middle East, stemming from the 1906 Constitutional Revolution
- Iran's independence from the West, which contrasts with the servitude of other regional powers, such as Turkey and Israel
- its ancient culture, which connects Central Asia, Afghanistan, and South Asia, and strong and influential immigrant presence throughout the world
- the recognition the Islamic Republic receives as the most important Shi'ite country in the world, which plays an important role in counterbalancing radical Sunni culture
- Iran's location between Afghanistan and Iraq, which makes it important in the U.S. war on terrorism to block the transfer of terrorism in the region[13]
- its access to various energy resources in the Persian Gulf and the Caspian Sea.[14]

---

[13] The article asserts that one reason that the U.S. effort to stabilize both countries has not succeeded is because Iran was not allowed to play a constructive role in either.

[14] Kayhan Barzegar, "Tazad-e Naghshha: Baresiye rishehaye monazeeye Iran va Amrica bad az havadese 11 September [Conflicting Role: A Study on the Roots of Iran and U.S. Disputes After September 11]," International Relations Research Division, Center for Strategic Research, Expediency Council, 2006.

In recent years, these attributes have informed a policy outlook that attaches inflated geopolitical weight to Iran's presence on the global stage. In the past several years, IRGC think tanks and policy journals have embraced a strategy that tries to push the world toward greater multipolarity in an effort to preserve Iranian sovereignty, reduce U.S. influence, and thus ensure the survival of the Republic.[15] According to one interpretation, Iran is trying, albeit unsuccessfully, to use the U.S. occupation of Iraq as "bait" to woo China and Russia closer to Iran's orbit.[16] Illustrating this ambitious reading of the global balance of power, the head of the IRGC noted in September 2006 that

> The U.S. claim to make the world unipolar in economic, political and security aspects has failed and the world is rather moving toward multipolarism . . . [A] big power will possibly appear in the Asian continent centering in China, Russia and India.[17]

This attraction to Asia as a means of leapfrogging encirclement by the West and, most recently, the Arab world, illustrates a shift in Tehran's diplomatic orientation since the election of President Ahmadinejad. Its most visible manifestation has been a concerted push by Iran for full-member status in the SCO and the evolution of this body toward a more security-oriented mandate that can counterbalance NATO.[18]

---

[15] RAND phone interview with a Tehran-based political scientist, November 12, 2005.

[16] RAND phone interview with a Tehran-based political scientist, November 15, 2005.

[17] "Iranian Military Chief Says Evidence Shows Global Power Balance Changing," IRNA, Web page, in English, OSC IAP20060902950063, 1410 GMT September 2, 2006.

[18] For more on the "Eastern shift," see Sanam Vakil, "Iran: Balancing East Against West," *The Washington Quarterly*, Vol. 29, No. 4, Autumn 2006, pp. 51–65; Hamid Reza Anvari, "A Look at the Shanghai Cooperation Organization," *Central Asia and the Caucasus Review*, No. 34, Summer 2001, p. 80.

Iran's Threat Perception Blurs Internal and External Concerns

Aside from the role of pragmatism and the drive for regional preeminence, it is important to understand the dynamics of Iranian threat perception. Iranians have a strong tendency, which is deeply rooted in their political culture and history, to view external events as having internal reverberations. Highlighting this, political scientist Marvin Zonis identified four characteristics of the prerevolutionary leadership: political cynicism, personal mistrust, interpersonal exploitation, and manifest insecurity.[19] While a fear of outside plots is inherent in most revolutionary regimes, Zonis has argued that this suspicion is especially pronounced in Iran. This is partly due to the very real conspiracy by the U.S. Central Intelligence Agency (CIA) and Britain's Secret Intelligence Service in 1953 to overthrow Iran's first elected prime minister, Mohammad Mossadegh, and reinstall the Shah. Today, the Iranian leadership appears hypersensitive to U.S. associations with oppositionists, attaching conspiratorial significance to the continued presence of the *Mujahidin-e Khalq* (MeK) at the U.S.-monitored Camp Ashraf in Iraq and the appearance on the U.S.-sponsored Voice of America of Abdulmalik Riga, the head of a Baluchi militant group active in Iran's underdeveloped province of Sistan-va Baluchestan.[20]

The most-recent salient examples of this blurring of internal and external threats include ethnic activism against the regime, threats to Iran's claim to Shi'ite theological supremacy, and the degradation of the citizenry's revolutionary ardor due to U.S. "psychological warfare" or attempts to inspire a velvet revolution.[21]

---

[19] Marvin Zonis, *The Political Elite of Iran*, Princeton, N.J.: Princeton University Press, 1971, p. 11.

[20] On April 2, 2007, Iran's *Press TV* noted that the Voice of America "interviews Iranian terrorist culprit in a sign of backing."

[21] The term *velvet revolution* has been used in Iran to draw analogies with nonviolent dissent by Iranian reformists and activists and the peaceful overthrow of the Stalinist-backed Czech government in 1989.

Internal Ethnic Dissent Influences Iran's External Strategy

Although ethnic and religious dissent inside Iran is not sufficient to mount a potent challenge to the leadership's survival, the issue has recently risen to the top of Tehran's domestic agenda and continues to inform its external calculations.[22] Only 51 percent of Iran's 65 million people are ethnic Persians, with ethnic Kurds, Azeris, Arabs, Baluch, and other groups forming a complex demographic mosaic throughout the country's provinces (see Figure 2.1).

The presence of anti-regime Kurdish insurgents in the northwest Kordestan province has figured prominently as a driver for both aggressive and pragmatic behavior by Tehran. Examples include the notorious Mykonos Affair in 1992, in which Ministry of Intelligence and Security (MOIS) agents assassinated Kurdish dissidents in Germany, and Tehran's burgeoning trilateral cooperation with Syria and Turkey, which face similar threats from Kurdish nationalism.[23] In the latter case, the Iranian regime appears to have adroitly used its campaign against Kurdish insurgents, particularly the anti-Turkish KADEK/Kongra Gel (formerly the Kurdistan Workers Party, or PKK) sheltering inside Iran, as part of a quid pro quo to secure Ankara's cooperation on investment and natural gas transfer. Iranian counterinsurgency operations in Kordestan are usually conducted in advance of critical bilateral meetings, such as the July 2004 visit to Tehran by Turkish Prime Minister Recep Tayyip Erdogan.[24]

---

[22] Among the significant ethnic groups, Azeris constitute 24 percent of the population, the Kurds 7 percent, Arabs 3 percent, and Baluch 2 percent (for more details, see U.S. Central Intelligence Agency, *The 2007 World Factbook*, 2007). Much has been made of Iran's ethnic fissures, yet the regime has proven surprisingly adept at co-opting ethnic minorities from the periphery into the center. Former Defense Minister 'Ali Shamkhani is an ethnic Arab (on several occasions, he was dispatched by the Khatami administration to Khuzestan to allay Arab fears of marginalization), and the Supreme Leader himself is an Azeri. For more on ethnic dissent, see John R. Bradley, "Iran's Ethnic Tinderbox," *The Washington Quarterly*, Vol. 30, No. 1, Winter 2006–2007, pp. 181–190.

[23] For background on the principal anti-regime Kurdish insurgent group in Iran, the Kurdistan Free Life Party (PJAK), see Graeme Wood, "The Militant Kurds of Iran," *Jane's Intelligence Review*, August 1, 2006.

[24] "Turkish PM in Iran to Ease Business Spats," Agence France Presse, July 29, 2004; Entessar, 2004, p. 547.

Figure 2.1
Geographic Breakdown of Iran's Ethno-Religious Diversity

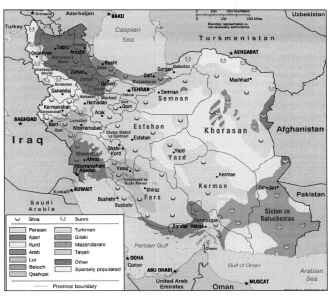

SOURCE: University of Texas, Perry-Castañeda Library Map
Collection, 2004.
RAND *MG781-2.1*

A similar dynamic is at work in the southeast province of Sistan-va Baluchestan. As German scholar Wilfried Buchta notes, much of Tehran's opposition to the Taliban regime was spurred by a domestic concern that its dominance in Afghanistan "had brought to light the existence of a minority (the ethnic Baluch and other Sunnis) in Iran that had been severely discriminated against since 1979."[25] Indeed, when Iran was preparing to attack Afghanistan over the murder of seven Iranian diplomats in 1998, the Taliban threatened to incite Iranian Sunnis against the regime.[26] Tehran's more recent policies toward

---

[25] Wilfried Buchta, *Who Rules Iran? The Structure of Power in the Islamic Republic,* Washington, D.C.: The Washington Institute for Near East Policy and the Konrad Adenauer Stiftung, 2000, p. 103.

[26] Buchta, 2000, p. 220.

Afghanistan have also been driven by concern over ethnic dissent in this drought-plagued province; much of its irrigation depends on the Helmand River, which originates in Afghanistan. Blockage of this waterway in 2004 by the Karzai government damaged Tehran's legitimacy in the eyes of the Iranian Baluch and thus became a major source of bilateral tension between Tehran and Kabul.[27] Similarly, Iran has reacted with alarm to the destabilizing effects of the massive opium influx across its borders since the fall of the Taliban and the presence on its soil of more than 1 million Afghan refugees.[28]

Elsewhere, in the southwest province of Khuzestan, Iranian officials have noted an increase in crime and weapon trafficking and a rise in Sunni Salafi ideology—all due to the effects of the Iraq war.[29] This spillover of instability is especially worrisome to Tehran because Khuzestan provides Iran with 80 percent of its crude oil revenue yet is populated by 2 million ethnic Arabs who suffer from political marginalization and economic underdevelopment. The area has been wracked by a wave of pipeline bombings and assassinations by dissident Iranian Arabs, attacks that Iranian officials allege are covertly backed by U.S. and British forces.[30]

Concern over internal instability and ethnic dissent has informed Tehran's external posturing, particularly on the nuclear issue. Speaking to Khuzestan Arabs, President Ahmadinejad has repeatedly emphasized the province's centrality in the Iranian nationalist narrative and,

---

[27] The stoppage of the river by the Karzai government in 2004 fueled widespread speculation in the Iranian press that the United States was using the Helmand River to pressure Tehran. As of December 2005, Tehran and Kabul had failed to agree on any sort of water-sharing protocol ("Iranian Official Calls for Implementation of 1972 Agreement on Helmand River," IRNA, Web page, in English, FBIS IAP20050201000031, 1255 GMT February 1, 2005; "Southeastern Iran Seeks Its Share from Hirmand River in Afghanistan," Tehran Mehr News Agency, Web page, in English, FBIS IAP20041110000084, 1756 GMT November 10, 2004).

[28] RAND phone interview with a Tehran-based political scientist, November 12, 2005.

[29] "Iranian Daily: Theologians Concerned by Reported Sunni Preaching in Khuzestan," *Aftab-e Yazd*, in Persian, FBIS IAP20051221011046, December 20, 2005.

[30] "Iran: Intelligence Minister Says 'Terrorist Act' Foiled in Khuzestan Province," Tehran Fars News Agency, Web page, in English, OSC IAP20070808950147, 1025 GMT August 8, 2007.

more importantly, promised them economic improvement via nuclear energy. This, he argues, is "their unalienable right," which has been repeatedly blocked by the "arrogant powers" (i.e., the United States and the West).[31] This accusation is a common refrain in the president's speeches to other rural audiences, illustrating the combined utility of a siege-like mentality and the issue of nuclear power in consolidating internal support for the regime and mitigating dissent.

The Regime Perceives a Threat from Najaf to Its Religious Legitimacy
Tehran's threat perception of Iraq and its resulting policies toward that country are inextricably linked with concerns of regime survival and legitimacy.[32] One important illustration of this is the regime's concern about the rise of the Iraqi Shi'ite city of Najaf as a center for Shi'ite learning and potential anti-Iranian activism.[33] Prior to its repression by successive Ba'athist regimes, Najaf's seminaries had overshadowed those in the Iranian city of Qom through the sophistication of their scholarship and their larger influence on regional Shi'ites.[34] With a significant following in these schools, Grand Ayatollah 'Ali al-Sistani has long been seen as the most serious challenger to the Supreme Leader's claim of moral leadership in the Shi'ite world. It was only the stifling restrictions placed on Najaf by Saddam Hussein that prevented

---

[31] "Khuzestan, Beating Heart of Great Iran: Ahmadinejad," Tehran Mehr News Agency, Web page, in English, OSC IAP20070102950116, 2010 GMT January 2, 2007.

[32] This concern appears especially acute among clerical communities in Qom, who forced their rivals in Mashhad, another prominent center of Shi'ite learning, to flee to Najaf following the ascendancy of Khomeini and the 1979 revolution (comments by a scholar of Iran at a Washington, D.C., conference on Shi'ism and the impact of the Iraq war, September 30, 2004).

[33] Kamran Taremi, "Iranian Foreign Policy Towards Occupied Iraq, 2003–2005," *Middle East Policy*, Vol. 12, No. 4, Winter 2005b, p. 29.

[34] For more on Qom-Najaf dynamics, see, Jawdat al-Qazwini, "The School of Qum" and "The School of Najaf," in Faleh Abd al-Jabar, ed., *Ayatollahs, Sufis and Ideologues: State, Religion and Social Movements in Iraq*, London: Saqi Books, 2002, pp. 245–281.

al-Sistani from exercising the spiritual, and possibly political, influence commensurate with his stature.[35]

Al-Sistani's philosophy of political rule is obliquely critical of Khomeini's principle of *velayat-e faqih* that legitimates clerical primacy in the Islamic Republic. Al-Sistani also enjoys widespread popularity as a *marja' al-taqlid* (a clerical "source of emulation" or spiritual guide for Shi'ites) inside Iran, particularly among those citizens dissatisfied with the current political system. For instance, prior to the February 2004 Iranian parliamentary elections, more than 400 reform activists in Iran petitioned al-Sistani to publicly condemn the elections as fraudulent.[36] The regime in turn issued statements that al-Sistani was to be regarded as a *marja'* only for citizens of the country where he resided— an attempt to circumscribe his transnational appeal.[37] This imperative to limit al-Sistani's influence (and that of Najaf in general) is made all the more urgent by the fact that every major anti-regime movement in Iran's modern history, from the 1906 Constitutional Revolution to the 1979 revolution, has found sanctuary in Najaf.[38]

The Regime Fears a U.S.-Incited Velvet Revolution

Tehran's perception of external threats has spurred or helped legitimate increasingly repressive internal policies. The first half of 2007 saw an intensified crackdown on liberal social mores, the arrest of visiting Western academics, and widespread accusations that the United States is attempting to foment a velvet revolution inside Iran using Western think tanks, nongovernmental organizations, and international aca-

---

[35] For instance, in his study of Iranian leadership dynamics, Wilfried Buchta noted, "Sistani is the main challenger to Khamenei" (Buchta, 2000, p. 89).

[36] "Reformists Ask Sistani to Intervene in the Electoral Crisis," *Al-Sharq al-Awsat*, in Arabic, February 5, 2004.

[37] Comments by a scholar of Iran at a Washington, D.C., conference on regional Shi'ite dynamics, September 30, 2004.

[38] For example, al-Sistani's powerful Qom-based representative, Jawad Shahristani, may be pursuing a "Sistani" policy independent of the Grand Ayatollah, and possibly with the encouragement or support of Iran (Reidar Visser, *Sistani, the United States and Iraqi Politics: From Quietism to Machiavellianism? Politics in Iraq*, Oslo: Norsk Utenrikspolitisk Institut, 2006).

demic conferences as covers.[39] According to one observer, most Iranians expected that the election of President Ahmadinejad in 2005 would curtail the relative openness of the Khatami era with a crackdown on the "usual suspects"—clerical dissidents, intellectuals, students, and journalists.[40] What has reportedly taken many by surprise is the pervasive and widening circle of repression since early 2007, extending to virtually every quarter of Iranian society. Accompanying this campaign was an outbreak of rioting and sporadic, country-wide violence over the government's announcement of gas rationing in June 2007, along with a 25-percent price increase.[41]

One interpretation of this siuation that the regime's intensified accusations of foreign meddling in early 2007 were a preemptive tactic designed to rally public support in the name of national security while stifling dissent over planned gas rationing. This argument is buttressed by the very public nature of the repression: Aside from the normal instruments, such as the hard-line vigilante or "pressure" groups, the state-run media have been harnessed to publicize the misdeeds of offenders, ranging from espionage by a senior member of the nuclear negotiating team under Khatami to women accused of improper wear of the *hijab*.[42]

It is important to note that bureaucratic politics may also be driving this juxtaposition of internal dissent and external interference. The MOIS has been at the forefront of this campaign: MOIS chief Mohseni-Ezhe'i has been the most vocal in sounding the warning of

---

[39] For the arrest of Western think-tank scholars, most notably Iranian-American Haleh Esfandiari, see "Iranian TV Describes Detained Iranian-American Esfandiari as 'Mosad Spy'," Islamic Republic of Iran Network Television (IRINN) (Tehran), in Persian, OSC IAP20070512011017, 1640 GMT May 12, 2007. For the broader cultural and political crackdown, see "Iran: Ahmadinezhad Government Reverses Civil Society Gains," OSC Analysis IAF20070620564001, June 20, 2007.

[40] Farideh Farhi, "Iran's Security Outlook," *Middle East Report Online*, July 9, 2007.

[41] "Rationing Leads to Clashes at Gas Stations in Tehran," OSC Feature—SHANA FEA20070627205751, 0810 GMT June 27, 2007.

[42] For the media's role in this repression, see "Iranian Media Under Pressure Tilts in Favor of Government," BBC, OSC Feature—Iran FEA20070711226066, July 11, 2007.

"soft subversion" from foreign intelligence agencies.[43] Since the purge of hardliners within its leadership and the reduction of its domestic profile during the Khatami era, the MOIS has been jockeying with other security institutions to "redeem" and assert itself.[44] The extent to which the United States increases its pressure on Iran may actually be empowering this repressive organ of the regime—a dilemma that is more thoroughly explored in our concluding chapter.

This dynamic also raises the primacy of factional and bureaucratic competition as an impetus for assertiveness in Iranian foreign policy, to which we now turn.

Factionalism Affects Iranian Foreign Policy

As in any country, the Iranian foreign policy apparatus is characterized by competing bureaucratic interests and informal networks jockeying for privilege and power. Yet what distinguishes the Islamic Republic from other cases is that the ponderous nature of decisionmaking, its multiple veto points, and the built-in demand for consensus have the effect of *encouraging* and *formalizing* factional rivalry. As noted by one observer, "Rather than serve as an autonomous regulator and arbiter of (elite) rivalry, the state is the principal arena in which the competition (over power and influence) takes place."[45] Thus, leadership factions frequently wield foreign policy issues as tools to outmaneuver their rivals and form tactical alliances that will aid their domestic standing. One scholar has gone so far as to state that in this factional contest, the actual issues debated are secondary to the larger prizes of patronage, power, and privilege.[46] The net effect of this dynamic is a state that

---

[43] "Iran: Ahmadinezhad Government Reverses Civil Society Gains," 2007.

[44] Farhi, 2007. For more on factionalism in the security services, see Abbas William Samii, "Factionalism in Iran's Domestic Security Forces," *Middle East Intelligence Bulletin*, Vol. 4, No. 2, February 2002.

[45] International Crisis Group, "Iran: Ahmadinejad's Tumultuous Presidency," Middle East Briefing No. 21, Brussels, 2007, p. 2 (as quoted in Kamrava, 2007, p. 86).

[46] RAND phone interview with an Iranian-born scholar, March 10, 2008.

seems unable to articulate a coherent strategic vision and whose frequently erratic and escalatory behavior may be serving the parochial goals of key elites rather than the state's larger interests. On the positive side, this system lends Iranian foreign policy a certain fluidity and flexibility that is lacking in more-authoritarian, single-party states.

To illustrate these dynamics, we have adopted the following broad typology for Iran's political factions.[47] These rough fissures began to surface soon after the success of the revolution but arguably reached their apogee at the end of the Iran-Iraq War and, especially, during the administration of President Muhammad Khatami (1997–2005), whose efforts to promote a more open political culture had the unintended effect of encouraging elite factionalism. It is important to highlight that these are *ideological* clusterings that in many cases transcend and overlap political institutions and other forms of association based on region or family. The most important example is the Islamic Revolutionary Guard Corps, which although sometimes treated as monolithic in outlook, is actually marked by subtle splits between pragmatists and conservatives (discussed in greater detail below). Broadly speaking, Iran's ideological factions divide as follows:

Traditional Conservatives. This current can be best described as the main and largest faction, advocating a patriarchal Islamic government, consolidation of the revolution's gains, the preservation of a traditional lifestyle, self-sufficiency with no dependence on the outside world, and cultural purity. This trend counts among its constituents the lower-middle classes, lower-ranking clerics, and *bazaari* merchants. Its reach extends into nearly all the major institutions of the state, from the Office of the Supreme Leader on down. Key formal groupings include the Association of Qom Seminary Teachers and the *Jameeh Rowhaniyyat-e Mobarez* [Association of Militant Clergy].

---

[47] This framework draws from RAND discussions with a number of scholars of Iran at a RAND-sponsored workshop in Rome, Italy. For an analysis of the implications of this dynamic on Iranian foreign policy, see Mehran Kamrava, "Iranian National-Security Debates: Factionalism and Lost Opportunities," *Middle East Policy*, Vol. 14, No. 2, Summer 2007. See also "Iran's Domestic Political Battles Exacerbate International Crisis," *Gulf States Newsletter*, Vol. 30, No. 781, May 12, 2006.

Reformist Cluster. From the mid- to late 1980s onward, the conservative trend was subjected to fissures over questions of pragmatism, doctrinal purity, and Iran's relationship with the world. A group of more-moderate clerics emerged from these debates in 1988, splitting from the Association of Militant Clergy to form the *Majma-e Rowhani-youn-e Mobarez* [Society for Militant Clerics]. Clustered around Mehdi Karrubi and Muhammad Khatami, this group argues for the promotion of civil society, a relaxation of political and social controls, economic openness, a cultural renaissance, and more interaction with the outside world. In this sense, they draw inspiration from a tradition of Iranian thinkers such as Ali Shariati and, later, Abdul Karim Saroush, who synthesized Islamic moral concepts with modern Enlightenment political philosophy to argue that there is no inherent tension between democracy and Islamic society. This broad clustering became ascendant in the mid-1990s, first inserting supporters into the *Majlis*[48] and then having its candidate, Muhammad Khatami, elected to the presidency in 1997. The popularity of this current has been strongest among the intelligentsia, writers, and students, though it never succeeded in marshaling any institutional resources behind its popular support—a fatal flaw and one that was to eventually spur the de facto political involvement of the IRGC acting in support of the conservatives to oust the reformists from power.

Pragmatic Conservatives. Situated somewhere between the first and the second factions is a cluster of what can be termed "pragmatic conservatives." This trend is organized within two parties: the *Hezbe Kargozaran Sazandegi* [Executives of Construction Party], which supports the reformists' approach to culture, and the *Hezbe E'tedal va Tose'eh* [Justice and Development Party], which leans toward the traditional conservatives on cultural issues. As a whole, this camp is inspired by the intellectual work of a number of economic theorists who believed in economic modernization from above (the so-called China model) and argues for increased technical and financial cooperation with the West (including the United States); but, unlike the reformists, this faction shows little interest in the democratization of

---

[48] The *Majlis* is the Iranian Parliament.

politics. This current has often reversed its position on critical domestic issues, spurring charges of opportunism from its rivals among the conservative traditionalist and the new conservative clusters, who depict themselves quite literally and self-righteously as "principlists" who have remained steadfast to the revolution's ideals. The pragmatists have traditionally derived support from the *bazaari* merchant class, students, the urban middle classes, and technocrats.

New Conservatives or Radicals. This is the grouping that has been most closely identified with the rise of the IRGC as a political force, beginning with its assumption of provincial administration posts in 2003 and leading up to the election of President Ahmadinejad in 2005. The political group encapsulating this current is the *Abadgaran-e Iran-e Eslami* [Developers of Islamic Iran], which was originally comprised of IRGC and Basiji war veterans. Many of them rose to mid- and senior-level positions but were subsequently marginalized during the Rafsanjani era. During the 2005 elections, the new conservatives appealed principally to the urban poor and provincial classes.

Although the Office of the Supreme Leader and other key institutions have generally remained squarely the purview of the traditional conservatives, each of the other currents has also had its heyday, enjoying a period of formal political power through control of the *Majlis* and the presidency:

- From 1989 to 1997, President Rafsanjani and the pragmatists presided over Iran's postwar reconstruction. During this period, the IRGC and ex-IRGC personnel were largely marginalized from political power.
- From 1997 to 2005, President Khatami and the reformist cluster emphasized the growth of civil society and the so-called dialogue of civilizations. The IRGC's ascendancy began during this period as it allied with conservatives to challenge Khatami's reforms.
- From 2005 to the present, President Ahmadinejad, the new conservatives, and the Revolutionary Guard came to power. Some have labeled this Iran's "Third Revolution."

It is important to highlight where the different factions diverge and converge in their views of Iran's foreign policy priorities and strategic outlook. All the factions agree on the need for the Islamic Republic to maintain its sovereignty, regional status, economic power, and access to technology. The splits emerge over the means and path to accomplish these goals. Specifically, the key differences revolve around whether Iran should continue to re-intensify its role as a confrontational and revolutionary state or whether it should adopt a more conciliatory posture that embraces globalization and moves toward normalization with the United States.

Much of this debate is embodied in deliberations over the purpose and scope of Iran's nuclear program; more-hardline factions see nuclear energy as an "equalizer" with which Iran can confront the United States on terms of greater parity, while more-pragmatic currents perceive it as giving Iran a more favorable bargaining position in the normalization of relations with the United States. The nuclear program has thus emerged as an intensely factional issue: President Ahmadinejad has appropriated it as a populist and nationalist theme to outmaneuver his rivals, while his more pragmatic opponents have highlighted the economic opportunity costs that the program—and Iran's handling of negotiations with the European Union (EU) and the United Nations (UN)—have inflicted on the country.

Factionalism Complicates the Iran-U.S. Relationship

Although there is near unanimous distrust of the United States across the factional spectrum, there are disagreements about the utility of engagement. The more radical conservative elements see any steps toward dialogue as a potentially slippery slope that will delegitimize the Islamic Republic and whittle away its sovereignty. More-pragmatic elements see the opening of relations with the United States as a way to advance the nation's economic interests and, perhaps more importantly, secure an imprimatur for the Islamic Republic from other states in the region and continued political dominance by the faction that negotiated the deal. There is more than a hint of factional self-interest in the statement of the former Secretary General of the Supreme Council for National Security (SCNS), Hassan Rohani, on this issue. "We have to be realistic. One day ties will have to be re-established," he remarked to the French newspaper *Le Figaro* in an interview. "Our skill—I would say our artistry—will be to choose the right moment."[49]

It should be emphasized that with the election of President Ahmadinejad and the domestic rise of the IRGC, several observers predicted a decrease in factional infighting over security and foreign policy issues. This argument stems from the apparent homogeneity in outlook of the so-called war generation of Iranian leaders, whose ranks are dominated by former IRGC commanders and who broadly define themselves as populist, technocratic, nationalistic, and faithful to the revolution's founding ideals.[50] After the election, one Iranian analyst forecasted continued policy "skirmishing," but at a far softer volume than the contentious maneuvering that defined the Khatami era.[51]

Yet the faltering presidency of Mahmoud Ahmadinejad has opened up significant splits within his own radical camp and within the IRGC and its veterans—between a more conservative "old guard" that seeks to confront the United States in the Levant, the Persian Gulf, and Iraq and a more pragmatic current that appears more focused on economic concerns.[52] The former head of the IRGC-Air Force (IRGCAF), former presidential contender and current mayor of Tehran General Muhammad Baqer Qalibaf, is a key figure in the latter current—one of his campaign slogans was "Iranians have the right to the a good life," and he has obliquely attacked President Ahmadinejad for the excessive deprivation his policies have inflicted on the populace.

---

[49] Hassan Rohani, interview in *Le Figaro* (Paris), January 17, 2004.

[50] According to one observer, the former IRGC leadership has embraced the motto "authoritarianism at home, engagement abroad from a position of strength" (RAND phone interview with a Tehran-based political scientist, November 10, 2005). More-recent scholarship has indicated splits within this cadre among pragmatists and ideologues (see Takeyh, 2007). Alone among other presidential candidates, President Ahmadinejad did not raise the possibility of normalizing ties with the United States. After the election, he stated, "Iran is on a path of progress and elevation and does not really need the United States on this path" (Pepe Escobar, "Twelve More Years," *Asia Times*, June 28, 2005).

[51] RAND phone interview with a Tehran-based political scientist, November 15, 2005.

[52] RAND phone interview with an Iranian-born scholar of Iran, March 13, 2008.

Several historical and current examples illustrate how factionalism can produce provocative and unpredictable foreign policy behavior —a pattern that is likely to remain an enduring feature of Iran's strategic culture.

The Salman Rushdie Fatwa Stemmed from Domestic Infighting

The *fatwa* issued in February 1989 by Ayatollah Khomeini against Anglo-Indian author Salman Rushdie for his alleged defamation of the Prophet Muhammad was a classic case of a provocative foreign policy initiative whose motivations were ultimately rooted in domestic infighting. The decree was effectively a power play against a growing pragmatic trend led by then–Parliamentary Speaker and future President Rafsanjani, a trend that had been pushing for rapprochement with Europe.[53] Aside from sabotaging this initiative, the *fatwa* was, in the words of Gilles Keppel, a "coup" that "restored Khomeini's position at home" by offering the citizenry a new moral crusade to distract them from the country's worsening economic situation.[54] Decades after its issuance, the document continues to cause factional dissonance inside Iran: The regime has refrained from sending assassination teams, but quasi-official economic foundations, or *bonyads,* close to the Supreme Leader routinely call for its implementation and for the murder of those who ignore it.[55]

Parochial IRGC Concerns Led to the Closure of the Imam Khomeini Airport

Factional economic interests played a role in the IRGC's abrupt closure on May 9, 2004, of the new Imam Khomeini International Airport on its first day of operations. The IRGC claimed that a Turkish-led consortium, which had been selected to operate the airport, presented a security risk to the state by placing foreign workers at a sensitive trans-

---

[53] Shaul Bakhash, *The Reign of the Ayatollahs*, New York: Basic Books, 1989, pp. 279–280.

[54] Gilles Keppel, *Jihad: The Trail of Political Islam*, Cambridge, Mass.: The Belknap Press of Harvard University Press, 2002, p. 190.

[55] Wilfried Buchta, *Iran's Security Sector: An Overview*, Geneva: Geneva Center for the Democratic Control of Armed Forces (DCAF), Working Paper No. 146, August 2004, pp. 8–9.

portation node. The outcome of this episode was to cause significant embarrassment to Iran internationally, damage bilateral relations with Turkey, and hasten the growing impotence of the Khatami administration by forcing the impeachment of his transportation minister. One of the IRGC's motives for closing the airport was that its own engineering firm had failed to win the contract.[56] In addition, the IRGC may have sought total oversight over the airport's operations to further its use as a key transportation hub in the IRGC's illicit smuggling activities.[57]

Security Agency Competition Has Made Iranian Foreign Policy More Confrontational

Under the Khatami administration, the main axis of foreign policy rivalry was between the Ministry of Foreign Affairs (MFA) and the combined efforts of the MOIS and the IRGC-Qods (Jerusalem) Force (IRGC-QF). This competition manifested itself most visibly in Afghanistan, where the MFA engaged the central Kabul government while the MOIS/IRGC-QF backed militant tribal factions in the rural periphery. With the sidelining of the MFA, competition has reportedly intensified between the MOIS and IRGC-QF, both of which aggressively vie for agents and influence over paramilitary and terrorist groups, often with little coordination. This has been especially true in Iraq, where the two institutions' traditional "niche capabilities" have frequently clashed and overlapped. One result of this escalatory competition has been a drift toward brinksmanship in Tehran's "proxy strategy," particularly in Iraq.[58]

---

[56] "Iranian Paper Says Airport Controversy Takes Iran's Internal Divisions 'Sky-High'," *Iran Daily* (Tehran), Web page, in English, OSC IAP20040510000022, May 10, 2004; "Iranian Paper Says Iran's Prestige Damaged by 'Embarrassing' Airport Closure," *Iran News* (Tehran), Web page, in English, OSC IAP20040510000031, 0001 GMT May 10, 2004; "Iranian Transportation Ministry Denies Blaming IRGC for Closure of New Airport," IRNA, Web page, in English, OSC IAP20040831000004, 0420 GMT August 31, 2004.

[57] Kim Murphy, "Iran's Guard Builds a Fiscal Empire," *Los Angeles Times*, August 26, 2007.

[58] Samii, 2002. See also Anthony Cordesman, *Iran's Revolutionary Guards, the Al Quds Force, and Other Intelligence and Paramilitary Forces*, working draft, Washington, D.C.: Center for Strategic and International Studies, 2007; Doron Zimmerman, "Calibrating Disorder: Iran's Role in Iraq and the Coalition Response, 2003–2006," *Civil Wars*, Vol. 9, No.

The Nuclear Crisis Is Partly a Symptom of Factionalism

The nuclear issue deserves special attention as an example of how factional and bureaucratic competition can result in belligerent external actions. Several scholars, including theorists of nuclear proliferation, have argued for the salience of the "bureaucratic model" as a driver for Iran's nuclear program, pointing to key constituencies within the Iranian power structure that derive enormous economic and political benefits from nuclear research.[59] Thus, Tehran's nuclear ambitions may have acquired a domestic momentum that is independent of any larger strategic calculations about the utility of this capability for Iran's interests. Contradictory and frequently conflicting statements from the Atomic Energy Organization of Iran, the MFA, and the SCNS portray a nuclear bureaucracy that is uncoordinated, if not openly competitive.[60]

Inside this bureaucratic web, the IRGC has certainly bolstered its domestic power and prestige by controlling nearly every aspect of nuclear research and operations. Nuclear energy as a national right for the Iranian citizenry has enormous symbolic value for the aforementioned "war generation" of former IRGC officers who have dominated key domestic institutions since the election of President Ahmadinejad. Members of this leadership cadre have presented themselves to the public as a technically savvy alternative to the elitism, corruption, and esoterism of the clerical class, particularly the oil oligarchy clustered around former President Rafsanjani.[61] The Iranian nuclear program

---

1, March 2007, pp. 8–31; Joseph Felter and Brian Fishman, "Iranian Strategy in Iraq: Politics and 'Other Means'," Occasional Paper Series, Combating Terrorism Center at West Point, U.S. Military Academy, West Point, N.Y., October 13, 2008.

[59] Scott D. Sagan, "Why Do States Build Nuclear Weapons? Three Models in Search of a Bomb," *International Security*, Vol. 21, No. 3, Winter 1996/1997, pp. 54–86. For the regime debate on nuclear weapons, see Shahram Chubin, "Whither Iran? Reform, Domestic Politics and National Security," International Institute for Strategic Studies, Adelphi Paper No. 342, 2002, pp. 80–85.

[60] For more on bureaucratic nuclear competition, see Shahram Chubin, *Iran's Nuclear Ambitions*, Washington, D.C.: The Carnegie Endowment for International Peace, 2006. Also, Abbas William Samii, "The Iranian Nuclear Issue and Informal Networks," *Naval War College Review*, Vol. 59, No. 1, Winter 2006.

[61] As noted by Frédéric Tellier, "To the *Pasdaran* (IRGC), the people ignored by the shah are the same people now groaning beneath the feet of the mullahs" (Frédéric Tellier, "The

and its attendant foreign policy challenges are important tactics in this strategy because they demand a certain policy expertise that the clerics lack. As noted by Alireza Nourizadeh, a researcher at the Center for Arab-Iranian Studies in London,

> The clerics are facing a serious identity crisis. They want to be part of this critical debate on the nuclear program and maintain their prestige. They just don't have what's needed for the moment.[62]

President Ahmadinejad appears especially well suited to play the role of what one scholar called a "nuclear Mossadegh," wielding indigenous enrichment capability for much the same set of aims that drove then–Prime Minister Muhammad Mossadegh to nationalize Iranian oil production in 1951: as leverage over his domestic rivals, to consolidate his nationalist appeal, and to carve out space for Iranian sovereignty abroad.[63]

Iranian Regional Strategy Incorporates Three Key Themes

Despite the aforementioned effects of factionalism on Iranian foreign policy, there appear to be a number of enduring principles that inform Tehran's current strategy in the region. To conclude this chapter, we examine those that present the most-significant challenges to U.S. interests: deterrence, support to non-state Islamist groups, and an appeal to Arab opinion. Each of these informs the key vectors of Iranian power projection that are discussed at length in the following chapters; understanding them is also critical for formulating a new U.S. policy paradigm that can successfully address the Iranian challenge over the next ten to fifteen years.

Iranian Moment" Washington Institute for Near East Policy, Policy Focus No. 52, February 2006).

[62] Brian Murphy, "Standoff Leaves Iran Clerics on Sidelines," *Washington Post*, May 26, 2006.

[63] Tellier, 2006, p. vii.

Deterrence Is Central to Iran's Political and Military Strategy

Writing in the December 1998 issue of Iran's *Journal of Defense Policy*, an Iranian scholar defined "to deter" using the Persian verb *bazdashtan*, meaning to "prevent, to arrest, or to imprison." For the author, its strategic meaning is unequivocal:

> Deterrence has a psychological impact on the enemy and prevents him from planning an assault or starting a war. This kind of threat should have a clear message and convey the menace of suffering or inflicting damage.[64]

For Iran's strategists, deterrence not only constitutes the centerpiece of the country's military doctrine, which is discussed more thoroughly in the following chapter, but also informs the country's larger political-military strategy, to include pan-Islamism, support to "proxies," and an appeal to Arab opinion. The actual military components of this deterrence strategy include, most obviously, the drive for an indigenous enrichment capability and a potential nuclear weapon; short- and medium-range ballistic missiles; asymmetric warfare and terrorism; and popular mobilization to defend the homeland, should an invasion occur.[65] While this may appear to Western observers as a push for hegemony, Tehran likely sees it as a multilayered form of strategic defense that extends deep into the enemy's camp and encompasses a variety of political, military, and economic levers.

Underlying these elements is the important precept of *strategic ambiguity*, which Iranian military officials frequently refer to when unveiling a new weapon system. "We should not hastily reveal our military capabilities," the prominent conservative Amir Mohebbian asserted during a February 2005 interview. "In fact, this lack of clarity regarding the consequences of a military attack is one of the factors

---

[64] Abu Mohammad Ashgar Khan, "A Look at Theories of Deterrence, Disarmament and Arms Control," *Journal of Defense Policy* (Tehran), in Persian, FBIS IAP 20021126000059, December 20, 1998, pp. 9–48.

[65] For an overview, see Steven R. Ward, "The Continuing Evolution of Iran's Military Doctrine," *Middle East Journal*, Vol. 59, No. 4, Autumn 2005.

that can deter Washington."[66] Tehran also appears to trumpet the virtues of *strategic patience* as part of its deterrence doctrine—the belief that superior indoctrination and morale will be essential to outlasting a better-equipped adversary. As proof, IRGC commanders routinely cite Hezbollah's campaign against Israel in 2006 as Iran's laboratory for homeland defense.

Given this reliance on popular mobilization and partisan warfare as a deterrence strategy, there is considerable fixation on blocking any adversary's attempts at "psychological warfare" and on the importance of sustaining revolutionary fervor.[67] As argued by the author of an IRGC-sponsored history of Iranian military thought, the center of gravity in any conflict will be the willpower of the Iranian people. Deterrence thus has an additional *internal* meaning in cultivating this fighting spirit and mitigating dissent:

> Regarding internal threats . . . "deterrent strategy" through reduction of dissatisfaction, establishment of equality and equity, establishing precautionary defensive measures, preventive measures, transfer of tribes and clans from one location to the other . . . will prove meritorious.[68]

In keeping with the paranoid tradition of Iranian political culture, the regime cannot be certain of the public's sustained support for a strategy of popular mobilization against an invading aggressor, and this uncertainty shapes its external behavior. Much of President Ahmadinejad's confrontational foreign policy may be calculated to revive this flagging "martyrdom culture" among the citizenry.

---

[66] "Interview with Amir Mohebbian in *Der Spiegel*," *E'tedal va Towse'eh*, Mohammad Nasiri, trans., FBIS IAP20050715339003, February 20, 2005.

[67] "Iranian Army Personnel Undergo Irregular Warfare Training," IRNA, FBIS IAP2005041000040, April 15, 2005. Also, "Iranian Military Practices Asymmetrical War Tactics in Final Phase of Exercises," Iranian Student News Agency, in Persian, FBIS IAP20041208000037, December 8, 2004.

[68] "Iran: Author Describes Islamic Republic's Military Doctrine," *Basis and History of Military Thought in Iran* (Tehran), in Persian, OSC IAG20021113000150, January 1, 2001, pp. 600–604.

Another critical question is whether Iran's actual and projected military capabilities are sufficient to meet its doctrinal ambitions for deterrence; we explore these deficiencies more thoroughly in the next chapter.

Support to Non-State Islamists Has Both Symbolic and Political Value

Political, financial, and, in some cases, lethal support to Sunni and Shi'ite Islamists has long been an important feature of Iran's power projection. It has enormous symbolic currency in bolstering the legitimacy of the regime and, as will be discussed at length in Chapter Four, serves an important retaliatory and deterrence function in the calculus of Iranian leaders.

It is important to note, however, that this religious dimension of Iranian strategy is not a principal driver; it will always be subject to more-realpolitik calculations. The most pertinent example is Iran's support for Christian Armenia against Muslim Azerbaijan during the Nagorno-Karabakh conflict. Another indication is the regime's support to both Sunni and Shi'ite groups abroad, which is at least partially calculated to help it win legitimacy at home among Iranian Sunnis. For example, in a speech in the Sunni-dominated province of Baluchestan, then–*Majlis* speaker Gholam-Ali Haddad-Adel attempted to downplay the Shi'ite character of Iranian foreign policy, noting that Iran has supported Palestinian Sunni groups, such as Hamas, as well as the Shi'ite Hezbollah.[69]

Tehran is beset by a host of challenges in its support for various Islamist "proxy groups." First, there is the danger that these local clients will place their own domestic agendas ahead of Iran's, thus reducing their responsiveness to Iranian control.[70] In addition, clandestine military aid to these groups carries the risk of disclosure; the January 2002 seizure by Israeli commandos of the *Karine A,* a freighter carry-

[69] "US, Israel Fomenting Shiite-Sunni Discord," *Iran-Daily*, November 28, 2006.

[70] For a general discussion of the dynamics behind state patronage to terrorism, see Daniel L. Byman, *Deadly Connections: States That Sponsor Terrorism*, New York: Cambridge University Press, 2005.

ing Iranian arms to the Palestinian Authority, and 2006 disclosures by the United States that the Qods Force was supplying explosively formed projectiles (EFPs) to Iraqi insurgents are notable examples. Inside Iran, public and factional support for the "proxy strategy" often varies tremendously. While there is reportedly near-universal acclaim for Hamas, there is anecdotal evidence that Iran's financial support for Hezbollah during the summer 2006 Israel-Lebanon conflict provoked criticism among the lower and middle classes, who questioned Tehran's lavish expenditure on a foreign entity when their own economy was in shambles.[71] Adopting a somewhat different argument, conservative clerics from Qom called for an Iranian boycott of Muqtada al-Sadr during the mid-2004 Najaf fighting, arguing that the young cleric's political immaturity had endangered Najaf's holy shrines.[72] Therefore, the various risks of the "proxy strategy" may rein in Iranian assertiveness. The risks are perhaps best summarized in an editorial written during the 2004 Sadr uprising:

> The senseless support given to Muqtada al-Sadr, who has twice shown his anti-Iranian proclivities, is an example of the policies of the past that began with our support for certain personalities or groups and ended with their indifference to us, if not their open insults against us.[73]

---

[71] Mehran Kamrava has written that Iranian support for Hezbollah enjoys support across the political spectrum—President Ahmadinejad's radicals, former President Rafsanjani's conservative-traditionalists, and the reformists (Kamrava, 2007, p. 92). Nevertheless, Azadeh Moaveni of *Time* reported popular dissent against Iranian support to Hezbollah in 2006 (see Azadeh Moaveni, "Why Iran Isn't Cheering," *Time*, July 23, 2006). On Hamas, see "Growing Support for HAMAS Observed in Iran," BBC Monitoring, OSC Feature FEA20070622199586, June 22, 2007.

[72] "Iran: Conservative Cleric Criticizes al-Sadr for Making Karbala, Najaf U.S. Targets," *Vaghaye'-ye Ettefaghiyeh* (Tehran), Web page, in Persian, OSC IAP20040520000056, May 18, 2004; "Iran: Commentator Says Shi'i Scholars Should 'Boycott' Al-Sadr," *Baztab* (Tehran), Web page, in Persian, OSC IAP20040515000085, 1122 GMT, May 15, 2004.

[73] "Commentary Criticizes Iran's Fruitless Political Alliances," *Aftab-e Yazd* (Tehran), Web page, in Persian, OSC IAP20040605000057, June 5, 2004.

An Appeal to Arab Publics Helps Tehran Circumvent Official Hostility
Tehran has traditionally been adept at speaking over the heads of Arab regimes to their publics through the use of transnational media and building support among such publics by portraying itself as more faithful to pan-Arab causes, such as Palestine, and at times deriding Arab rulers as U.S. lackeys. Should an open conflict between the United States and Iran arise, this strategy will likely form the core of Tehran's retaliatory propaganda effort—prolonging the war and stoking public opposition to Arab regimes hosting or supporting U.S. forces. Within the Middle East, this approach is not new; for example, Egyptian President Gamal 'Abd al-Nasser's pan-Arab broadcasts via *Sawt al-Arab* [Voice of the Arabs] radio were tremendously unsettling to conservative Arab monarchies allied with the West during the 1950s and 1960s. What is novel is that Iran—a Persian, Shi'ite power—has effectively co-opted the same themes of anti-imperialism and pan-Arabism deployed by President Nasser.[74]

While the traditional centerpiece of this strategy is the exploitation of the Palestine conflict,[75] Tehran has also been able to garner acclaim through Hezbollah's campaign against Israel and the Iranian drive for nuclear energy. One important example of Iran's ability to outmaneuver Arab rulers by being "more Arab than the Arabs" occurred during President Ahmadinejad's speech at the 2005 Organization of the Islamic Conference (OIC) summit in Mecca. Here, in the presence of King 'Abdallah, he made an unequivocal denial of the Holocaust and called on Europeans to open their land to Jewish settlement. For

---

[74] Graham Fuller, "The Hezbollah-Iran Connection: Model for Sunni Resistance," *The Washington Quarterly*, Winter 2006–2007, pp. 139–150. Morten Valbjørn and André Bank have argued that post-Lebanon regional alignments approximate the strategic environment in the 1980s and, more distantly, the 1950s, when the region was split between monarchists and pan-Arab nationalists, as embodied in the charismatic figure of Egyptian President Gamal 'Abd al-Nasser. See Morten Valbjørn and André Bank, "Signs of a New Arab Cold War: The 2006 Lebanon War and the Sunni-Shi'i Divide," *Middle East Report,* Spring 2007, pp. 6–11.

[75] For a discussion of the strategic, as opposed to moral or ideological, benefits of Iran's endorsement of the Palestinian cause, see Chubin, 2002. Chubin writes, "The Palestine cause serves as a card for entering regional politics and upstaging the Arab states in the process" (p. 102).

the al-Saud, who have long endeavored to be the premiere champions of the Palestinian cause, this speech was an appropriation of a key pan-Arab issue and a brazen act of one-upsmanship about which they were mortified and to which they were unable to respond.[76]

Yet this "Arab street" strategy has its limits. Tehran's frequent missteps, such as the recent insinuation by a newspaper editor close to Supreme Leader Khamenei that Bahrain was rightfully a province of Iran, often detract from whatever previous acclaim it has garnered.[77] In other instances, regional events beyond Iran's control, such as the execution of Saddam Hussein, result in a rapid reversal of Arab popular support when they are "read" through a sectarian or Arab-Persian prism. Finally, many Arab regimes in the region, particularly the al-Saud, have deliberately exploited sectarian tensions stemming from Iraq to garner public support for what is essentially a classic balance-of-power strategy against Iran.[78] Since the fall of Saddam Hussein, for example, the Saudi clerical establishment has issued a stream of anti-Iranian, anti-Shi'ite statements, recalling the 1980s, when Riyadh mobilized radical Salafi-jihadism to offset the ideological challenge from Khomeini's Iran.[79]

---

[76] For more on this tactic, see Renaud Girard, "The Calculated Provocations of the Islamist Iranian President," *Le Figaro* (Paris), in French, December 19, 2005.

[77] The incident also sparked debate inside Iran ("Analysis: Iran's Claim to Bahrain Sparks Media Debate," OSC Feature FEA20070723241746, July 23, 2007).

[78] For an example from Cairo, see "Egyptian Officials, Media Escalate Anti-Iranian Rhetoric, Prompting Restrained Iranian Response," OSC Analysis GMF20070208282001, February 8, 2007.

[79] For examples of anti-Shi'ite, anti-Iranian writings by Saudi and Gulf Salafi clerics, see Nasr al-Umar, "The Situation of the *Rafida* (Shiites) in the Land of Tawhed," Web page, in Arabic, date not available; Nasr al-Umar, "If Iran Occupies Iraq," Web page, in Arabic, date not available. It should be recalled that one indirect outcome of this strategy was al-Qaeda. See Gregory Gause, "Saudi Arabia: Iraq, Iran, the Regional Power Balance, and the Sectarian Question," *Strategic Insights*, Vol. 6, No. 2, March 2007.

Conclusions

This chapter surveys key features of Iran's strategic culture to set the stage for subsequent analysis. In meeting the future challenge from Iran, it is important to understand how the regime's worldview and threat perception can shape its foreign policy actions, impelling it toward both assertiveness and pragmatism. Similarly, the blurring of internal and external threats has shaped Iran's behavior, as has internal factional maneuvering. These domestic features help inform Iran's larger strategy, which is characterized by deterrence, support for non-state Islamists, and the exploitation of popular Arab grievances.

Our exploration of Tehran's strategic motivations reveals that its behavior, while frequently masked by ideology and bravado, is more deeply informed by a realpolitik strategy that defines "normal" state behavior. Certainly, Iran is prone to miscalculation, brinksmanship, and belligerence. But its new activism is also vulnerable to certain liabilities and buffers inherent in Iran's unique political culture and also present in the regional system it is trying to influence. Understanding this interplay, we argue, is critical for shaping both DoD and USAF responses, as well as larger U.S. policy options. In particular, it is important that U.S. strategy should exploit existing checks on Iranian power and avoid inadvertently creating conditions that bolster Tehran's influence. The following chapters examine the reach of Iranian power projection along various dimensions, but also its limitations.

CHAPTER THREE

Asymmetric Ambition and Conventional Reality: Iran's Evolving Defense Strategy, Doctrine, and Capabilities

This chapter analyzes Iran's national defense requirements and considers the challenges and opportunities Iranian strategists and planners face in meeting those requirements. First, it describes the foundations and elements of Tehran's defense strategy based on the discussion of its worldview and threat perceptions in Chapter Two, provides an overview of Iran's security establishment, and explores major themes in Iranian doctrine. It then characterizes and assesses the current and potential capabilities of Iran's armed forces and evaluates the extent to which Iran's doctrine is reflected in these capabilities. Next, the chapter examines the potential roles of nuclear weapons in Iranian strategy and how Tehran's defense priorities might evolve if it possessed these weapons and the means to deliver them. Some concluding remarks are offered in the final section.

The analysis in this chapter indicates that Iran's military is beset with structural, organizational, and capacity problems that prevent it from completely operationalizing Tehran's doctrinal ambitions for asymmetric warfare, and these problems are likely to persist over the next five to ten years. The bifurcated nature of the Islamic Republic's security structures continues to create institutional friction that stunts development of a truly integrated force. Bureaucratic inertia and other features of Iran's defense establishment will likely keep Iran's military capability mired in industrial-age conventional warfare, even as Tehran aspires toward an asymmetric warfighting doctrine. Iran's efforts to attain self-sufficiency in military equipment are limited by a wasteful and inefficient defense industry that is unable to produce the quality and quantity of systems the Iranian military requires. However, Tehran is likely to continue enhancing its military posture in ways that could present real challenges to U.S. and USAF operations in the region.

Foundations of Iran's "Diverse" Defense Strategy and Doctrine

As with any nation, Iran seeks to attain its national security objectives by fashioning a strategy informed by perceived threats and opportunities that affect Iranian interests.[1] In August 2004, Iranian Deputy Defense Minister Mohammad Shafii-Rudsari declared that Iran has a "diverse" defense strategy to meet threats from foreign powers "such as America," and that its "defense capacity and power are entirely adequate for regional . . . threats." Shafii-Rudsari did not specify the manner in which Iran's strategy was diverse. But he did claim that it compensated for any inferiority in "classical" military power and therefore deemed it unlikely that even nuclear powers would strike Iran. Iran's strategy is primarily a defensive one, in which deterrence is of central importance; yet the strategy also serves ideological tendencies that may be perceived as offensive in nature. Regime survival and consolidation of the revolution are primary aims of the strategy, but positioning Iran as a "first power" in the region and on the global stage is also a key objective.

Iran follows a four-pronged defense strategy. First, it assigns military, law enforcement, intelligence, and paramilitary forces to maintain internal stability and unity and to "guard the Islamic reign and supremacy over Iran," which includes safeguarding the "political power and sovereignty of the regime."[2] The security arms of the state are used

---

[1] Our understanding of Iranian strategy, military doctrine, and concepts of operations (CONOPs) is derived from official statements, exercises, a limited number of doctrinal publications by Iranian think tanks, and Iranian military journals such as *Saff* and *Sobhe Sadegh*, a weekly online magazine published by the Supreme Leader's representative to the IRGC.

[2] Muhammad Husayn Jamshidi, "Basis and History of Military Thought in Iran," published by the IRGC College of Command, found in "Iran: Author Describes Islamic Repub-

to quell threats emanating from political opponents, from minority ethnic groups, and from cross-border and internal criminal activity.

Second, Iran seeks to deter aggression against it by using exaggeration, ambiguity, and obfuscation about its ability to exact a prohibitive cost from potential aggressors, especially the United States and U.S. regional allies. Among other things, Iran combines official statements, well-publicized parades, set-piece exercises and shows of force, and tests of advanced systems such as intermediate-range ballistic missiles to deter adversaries from initiating conflict. Iran's reliance on deterrence—as well as its acknowledged military inferiority vis-à-vis its main adversary, the United States—provide the impetus for Iran to seek nuclear weapons.

Third, if aggression occurs, Iran's military forces would seek to vigorously defend the homeland and resort to what former IRGC commander Major General Yahya Rahim Safavi describes as an "offensive strategy with devastating effects."[3] Countering invasion constitutes a primary focus of Iran's defense strategy; despite Iranian statements that the U.S. entanglement in Iraq diminishes the threat of U.S. invasion, Iranian strategy emphasizes defense of the homeland in depth.[4] Short of invasion, Iran would seek to protect key targets and complicate an adversary's efforts by using asymmetric means to threaten or strike its

lic's Military Doctrine," OSC IAP20021113000150, January 1, 2001, pp. 600–604.

[3] On September 1, 2007, the Supreme Leader replaced Major General Safavi as IRGC head with Mohammad Ali Ja'fari, a career IRGC commander. See "'Routine' Change of Commander Consolidates Iran's IRGC," BBC Monitoring, OSC Feature FEA20070903303187, September 3, 2007. For Safavi's comments, see "Iran to Resort to Offensive Strategy If Attacked," Iranian Mehr News Agency via BBC Worldwide Monitoring, November 17, 2006. *Artesh* commander Major General Mohammad Salimi assured the nation at one point that the military forces are on standby in case of an attack on Iran's nuclear facilities: "All our forces, including land forces, anti-aircraft and radar tactics are protecting the nuclear sites and attacking them will not be simple" (Mohammad Salimi, comments in *Iran Daily*, No. 2196, January 22, 2005).

[4] This indicates an apparent duality in Iranian treatment of the threat of invasion. On one hand, the emphasis on the United States being "bogged down" in Iraq and on the relatively more secure position of the Islamic Republic could serve propaganda efforts in the region and among some Iranian factional constituencies. Conversely, the emphasis on homeland defense provides the government with a nationalist theme that it can exploit to unify the populace.

forces and interests. Iran would seek to execute a "peripheral" strategy that provides strategic depth to Iran's homeland defense by drawing on both lethal and popular support from non-state Islamists and the Arab public. Tehran sees this as a form of forward defense.

Finally, Iran uses its armed forces to extend its influence through operations aimed at intimidation, dissuasion, and coercion of other nations in the region as well as the United States. Tehran's aim is to gain status and prestige, which are much more important in Iran's geo-political outlook than acquiring territory. Iran also uses arms exports to extend its influence, countering U.S. influence and burnishing its status as a global power. Hezbollah, Venezuela, and various African nations benefit from military relationships with Iran.

According to the International Institute for Strategic Studies, Iran spends about $6.6 billion annually on defense.[5] While this represents a near doubling of defense expenditures since 2001, it remains equivalent to about 3 percent of Iranian gross domestic product (GDP). As Figure 3.1 reveals, Iran's spending does not exceed regional norms and pales in comparison with that of Saudi Arabia and even Israel and Turkey.

Moreover, Iran is well below the regional average on defense expenditures as a percent of GDP and per capita. Based on such comparisons, Iran does not appear to be a nation on the verge of becoming a regional hegemon.[6] And in light of the economic challenges facing Iran, it is unlikely that the Iranian government will seek to maintain recent rates of growth in defense spending over the long term.

Iran's Security Forces: Overlapping Missions Create Friction
Informal decisionmaking processes and overlapping missions are defining features of the security structures responsible for implement-

---

[5]   As of 2006, in constant 2005 dollars. International Institute for Strategic Studies, *The Military Balance 2007*, London: Routledge, 2006, p. 224.

[6]   Iran does not publish its defense budget, and information on its expenditures is scarce. The budget estimates for Iran may exclude such important elements as subsidies to the domestic defense industry, costs of the nuclear program, research and development, and paramilitary forces. But even if actual spending is double that of reported figures, Iran would be average among the highest spenders in the Middle East in expenditure as a percentage of GDP and would remain well below average in per capita defense spending.

Figure 3.1
Comparison of Defense Expenditures Among Highest Spenders in the Middle East

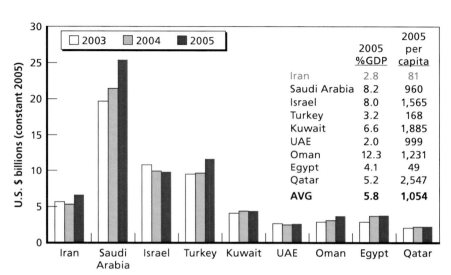

	2005 %GDP	2005 per capita
Iran	2.8	81
Saudi Arabia	8.2	960
Israel	8.0	1,565
Turkey	3.2	168
Kuwait	6.6	1,885
UAE	2.0	999
Oman	12.3	1,231
Egypt	4.1	49
Qatar	5.2	2,547
AVG	**5.8**	**1,054**

SOURCE: International Institute for Strategic Studies, *The Military Balance 2007*, London: Routledge, Table 36, pp. 407–408.
RAND *MG781-3.1*

ing Iran's defense strategy, and these features engender both strengths and weaknesses for Tehran. Figure 3.2 depicts a formal organizational structure of Iran's security establishment; note, however, that this depiction offers an incomplete picture of the intra- and inter-organizational relationships because of the informal networks that characterize Iran's bureaucracy.

To many Americans, President Ahmadinejad is the face of Iran and, in part because of his headline-grabbing, strident public remarks, appears to hold the reigns of power in Tehran. But despite his chairmanship of the SCNS, he has little authority in matters of defense. The Supreme Leader, Ayatollah 'Ali Khamenei, wields ultimate authority, and, as commander-in-chief of the armed forces, his weight on security matters is second to none. He formally exercises that authority through the SCNS, the security ministries, and the security forces themselves, although he also has more-direct, though less-formal, chains of com-

Figure 3.2
Formal Structure of Iran's Security Establishment

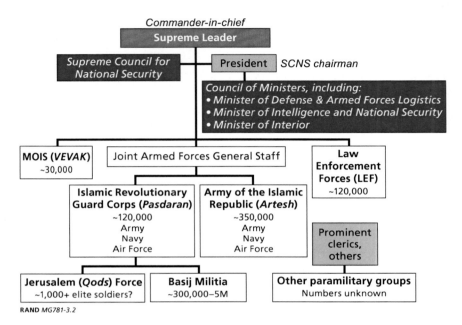

RAND MG781-3.2

mand to components of the security forces through representatives or personal relationships with key decisionmakers.[7]

Iranian armed forces are bifurcated between the IRGC and the regular armed forces. Reflecting the revolutionary regime's early concerns about the loyalty of the Shah's armed forces, this structure presents both strengths and vulnerabilities. On one hand, by assigning overlapping, redundant responsibilities to various institutions and by tacitly encouraging competition for resources, the regime has secured a degree of insulation from a potential coup d'etat.[8] At the same time, however, the parallel chains of command and the lingering ambiguity

---

[7]   See Buchta, 2000, pp. 47–52.

[8]   This organizational feature is present in many Middle Eastern militaries. See James T. Quinlivan, "Coup-Proofing: Its Practice and Consequences in the Middle East," *International Security*, Vol. 24, No. 2, Autumn 1999, pp. 131–165.

over roles create numerous friction points and impede joint military operations.

The IRGC's estimated 120,000 personnel fulfill a number of functions related to internal security, external defense, and regime survival, and it fields an army, a navy, and an air force. Reflecting its original charter of defending the revolution, there are IRGC installations in all of Iran's major cities organized into Quick Reaction Groups that serve as a reserve against unrest.[9] In rural regions, the IRGC operates with other security forces in missions that include border control, counter-narcotics, and disaster relief. The IRGC has primacy over Iranian unconventional warfare options: It maintains tight control over the development and deployment of Iran's ballistic missiles, and it wields an external terrorism capability through its elite Qods Force.[10] Were Iran to develop and field nuclear weapons, oversight of their storage, training, and deployment infrastructure would likely fall to the IRGC.

Significantly, the IRGC is heavily invested in both the political and economic spheres. Current and former officers are members of the political leadership, including President Ahmadinejad, Saeed Jalili (secretary of the SCNS), Ezzatolah Zarghami (head of the Islamic Republic of Iran Broadcasting Corporation), and Mohsen Rezai (secretary of the Expediency Council), as well as other cabinet ministers, *Majlis* members, and heads of economic foundations (or *bonyads*).[11] Moreover, the IRGC oversees or owns important interests in the oil, construction, and defense sectors of the economy. In a 2006 interview with the Iranian newspaper *Sharq*, the acting commander of the IRGC's *Khatam-ol-Anbiya* engineering firm stated that about 30 percent of the IRGC's engineering capability is engaged in construction efforts and that 1,220 projects had been completed since 1990, with 247 currently

---

[9] Samii, 2002. Also, Michael Eisenstadt, "The Armed Forces of the Islamic Republic of Iran," *Middle East Review of International Affairs,* Vol. 5, No. 1, March 2001.

[10] Anthony H. Cordesman, *Iran's Developing Military Capabilities,* Washington, D.C.: The Center for Strategic and International Studies, 2005, pp. 45–48.

[11] Mehdi Khalaji, "Iran's Revolutionary Guard Corps, Inc.," Washington Institute for Near East Policy, PolicyWatch No. 1273, August 17, 2007.

under way.[12] In 2006, the Oil Ministry awarded no-bid contracts total-ing several billion dollars to *Khatam-ol-Anbiya* to implement the 15th and 16th expansion phases of the South Pars oil field.[13] IRGC pen-etration of important sectors of the Iranian polity is considerable and growing, lending power to the corps in national-level decisionmaking while providing leverage to high officials with an IRGC pedigree.

Iran's regular military, or *Artesh*, also encompasses ground, naval, and air forces and comprises roughly 350,000 personnel. The consti-tutional mission of *Artesh* is to defend Iran against external aggres-sion. As such, while the regular forces have little capability for internal policing or experience in expeditionary warfare, there is considerable overlap with the IRGC in defending the nation against attack or inva-sion. This overlap breeds competition for resources to modernize, with the IRGC often receiving priority for new, high-end systems, especially from such external arms suppliers as Russia and China.[14] And despite improvements in *Artesh*-IRGC combined training and exercises, there is continued resentment within the *Artesh* over the superior pay, faster promotions, and better retirement benefits of the IRGC. The domi-nance of IRGC officers in the Ahmadinejad government, combined with their pervasive presence in Iran's commercial and industrial realm, will probably intensify this antagonism over the long term.[15]

The IRGC-QF, the MOIS, and other elements of the IRGC all play a role in collecting intelligence, intimidating dissidents, and nurtur-ing pro-Iranian "proxies" in foreign nations. Subordinate to the IRGC commander, the tiny Qods Force engenders Iran's overseas unconven-tional warfare capability. Reportedly comprised of 1,000 highly trained soldiers, the force specializes in training foreign insurgents and terror-

---

[12] "Iran Press: General Discusses IRGC Role in Engineering, Economic Contracts," *Sharq* (Tehran), in Persian, OSC AP20060702011002, June 26, 2006, pp. 1, 11.

[13] "Iran Press: General Discusses IRGC Role in Engineering, Economic Contracts," pp. 1, 11.

[14] For example, Iran's newest surface-to-air missile (SAM) system, the Russian Tor-M1 (SA-15 "Gauntlet"), is being operated by the IRGC. See Robin Hughes, "Tehran Fires Tor-M1," *Jane's Defence Weekly*, February 14, 2007.

[15] Cordesman, 2005, pp. 19–44; Buchta, 2004, pp. 7–8.

ists, political warfare, and propaganda. Its diverse portfolio includes support to Hezbollah and other Levantine terrorist groups, as well as Shi'ite militants in Iraq, Afghanistan, and the Persian Gulf states. As part of its larger defense strategy, the regime wields the IRGC-QF and its terrorist network as a retaliatory capability against an attack on the Iranian homeland.[16]

Comprised of an estimated 30,000 personnel, the MOIS has constitutional responsibility for foreign intelligence collection and espionage. Prior to 1999, the organization was widely feared because of its assassinations of dissident activists abroad and in Iran. During the presidency of Mohammad Khatami, however, the MOIS was purged of many hardliners, and it has largely abandoned its policy of assassination.[17] Overseas, the MOIS reportedly liaises with several foreign Shi'ite militant groups and insurgent organizations and would likely play an important role as a retaliatory tool in the event of an attack on Iran. These relationships probably bring the MOIS into competition with the Qods Force.[18]

The MOIS shares its domestic security responsibilities with other institutions: the *Basij* militia, the Law Enforcement Forces (LEF), and some paramilitary groups. The *Basij* Resistance Force (*Niru-yi Moqavaemat-i Basij*) is a popular reserve force headed by an IRGC general with an active strength of 300,000 and a claimed mobilization capacity of 5 million. The organization emerged during the Iran-Iraq War as an ideologically motivated body of urban shock troops that act as a vanguard for popular resistance against invasion. The regime regards *Basij* training, especially for youth and part-time reservists, as an important vehicle for indoctrination and enforcement of Islamic norms in society. The *Basij* are present in virtually all sectors of Iranian society; there are specially organized *Basij* units for university students, local tribes

---

[16] Yet, as will be discussed in Chapter Four, the effectiveness of the Qods Force's "proxy" strategy depends upon the availability of local allies who are willing to act in Tehran's interests. These groups often have their own agendas, and their receptiveness to Iranian direction is more ambiguous than conventional wisdom suggests.

[17] Buchta, 2004, pp. 13–16.

[18] *Radio Free Europe/Radio Liberty Iran Report*, August 8, 2005.

and villages, factory workers, and so forth. The *Basij* also play a role in nationwide domestic reconstruction projects, medical assistance, and disaster relief.[19]

Subordinate to the Ministry of Interior, the LEF is Iran's national gendarmerie and includes roughly 120,000 personnel. This institution's diverse responsibilities include counter-narcotics, riot control, border protection, morals enforcement, and anticorruption.[20] Finally, there are a number of ultraconservative vigilantes or "pressure groups." These quasi-official bodies, such as the notorious *Ansar-e Hezbollah*, are an additional layer of protection against anti-regime dissent. Comprised in many cases of poorly educated hooligans, they have operated as the shadowy shock troops for prominent clerics, particularly in the Council of Guardians, and attack protestors, intimidate dissident intellectuals, and help mobilize electoral support for conservative candidates.[21]

To summarize, the multiple security organs and overlapping missions that characterize the Islamic Republic's national security structure are features of the Iranian landscape dating back to the earliest periods of the revolution and the Iran-Iraq War. Competing interests and informal relationships help insulate the regime against internal threats to stability and to its own survival. But, as we will see, this same competition creates inefficiencies that inhibit Iran's pursuit of military

---

[19] Anthony Cordesman and Martin Kleiber, *Iran's Military Forces and Warfighting Capabilities: The Threat in the Northern Gulf*, Washington, D.C.: Center for Strategic and International Studies, 2007, pp. 81–82, 132. See also Buchta, 2004, pp. 12–13; Byman et al., 2001, pp. 38–39; Michael G. Knapp, "The *Basij* Resistance Force," in *How They Fight: Armies of the World*, National Ground Intelligence Center, NGIC-1122-0204-98, 1998; Naser Shabani, "The *Basij* and National Security," *Military Knowledge*, in Persian, Summer–Fall 1996, FBIS 19970711001453, July 15, 2007.

[20] Buchta, 2004, pp. 11–12.

[21] "Ansar-i Hizbullah: Followers of the Party of God," Globalsecurity.org, Web page, n.d. See also "Iran: Political Figures Comment on Violent Groups, Elections, Other Issues," *Yas-e Now*, in Persian, FBIS IAP 2003121600005, December 8, 2005. *Ansar-e Hezbollah* members also helped the IRGC stage the so-called recruitment drive of Iranian suicide bombers for Iraq (*Radio Free Europe/Radio Liberty Iran Report*, December 7, 2004; also, Byman et al., 2001, p. 39; International Crisis Group, "Iran: The Struggle for the Revolution's Soul," Middle East Report No. 5, Tehran and Brussels, August 2002, p. 11).

power to the fullest extent and retards its ability to present the most severe threats to U.S. and allied interests.

Iranian Doctrine Aligns Well with Military Strategy

Iran fought a costly war with Saddam Hussein's Iraq from 1980 to 1988, a war that left a deep impression on Iran's decisionmakers and the planners of its military strategy, doctrine, and capabilities. The war proved to Iranian leaders that they could not rely on outside assistance, not even when Iran was a victim of unprovoked aggression. It served to provide many other lessons that the national security establishment would apply toward formulating Iranian defense doctrine, developing major CONOPs, and acquiring military capabilities. Since that conflict and the "tanker war" Iran fought with the United States in the late 1980s, the Iranians have acquired little direct military experience.[22] But they have been interested observers of important events in their region. Figure 3.3 summarizes important events and the lessons Iran learned from them; we incorporate these lessons into our discussion of major themes in Iranian military doctrine.

Given that the United States poses Iran's most important security challenge, major elements of Iran's doctrine and CONOPs are aimed at countering a militarily superior adversary. Having seen U.S. military prowess applied in its own neighborhood, the Iranian military is aware of its own limitations and recognizes that its conventional forces cannot compete on an equal footing with a military such as that of the United States. This realization has led the Iranian military to embrace capabilities for "asymmetric" warfare that seek to avoid direct confrontation with a superior military while exacting a high cost from the United States and its regional partners—and to tout these capabilities to deter aggression in the first place and enhance Iran's declared status as a dominant regional power. Tehran has attempted to apply asymmetric concepts to all facets of defense, and it appears to focus on implementing several key CONOPs, including impeding regional access by for-

---

[22] Iranian doctrine has benefited significantly from Iran's close military ties with Hezbollah, whose operations against Israel have served as a kind of battlefield laboratory that has strongly influenced Iranian asymmetric warfare doctrine.

Figure 3.3
Key Events and the Military Lessons Iran Has Learned

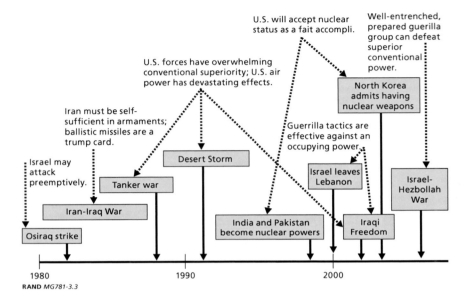

RAND MG781-3.3

eign forces, inhibiting export of energy resources, conducting warfare by "proxy" (the topic of Chapter Four), defending the homeland in depth, and pursuing popular resistance against occupation.

In practical terms, maintaining the capability to hinder the flow of U.S. forces to the region and disrupt their operations once deployed would improve Iran's ability to defend against invasion and less ambitious attacks. Iran would hope to have a direct effect on U.S. forces, but another key aim would be to convince regional governments playing host to those forces that the costs of incurring Iran's wrath would greatly outweigh the potential benefits of siding with the United States. Based on their experience in the Iran-Iraq War—during which exchanges of ballistic missiles caused modest destruction yet had great impact on civilian morale—Iranian leaders appear convinced that ballistic missiles are the most reliable means for attacking deep targets, and that they would have psychological effects disproportionate to their destructive power.[23] Iran likely would threaten other states in the region—particularly their population centers and energy infrastructure—with ballistic missile strikes if they allowed U.S. aircraft based on their territory to participate in heavy attacks on Iran. Likewise, Iran would, in certain future cases, hope to strike Israel in an attempt to draw it into a conflict that would in turn put pressure on Arab governments to curtail support of U.S. military action.

Iran may plan to conduct raids with commando forces, landing them by small craft on littorals or inserting them clandestinely to strike U.S. assets and personnel in the region, sabotage facilities critical to deployment and to energy exports, and conduct terrorist attacks. Iran also seeks to apply asymmetric tactics to operations that deny access to Iranian littoral areas and airspace and threaten maritime traffic in the Strait of Hormuz, the Persian Gulf, and the Gulf of Oman. Learning from losses its conventional naval forces suffered at the hands of the U.S. Navy during the tanker war and the ineffectiveness of its efforts to close the strait, Iran's naval doctrine emphasizes "swarming" tactics characterized by "light, mobile forces with substantial striking power, capable of rapidly concentrating to attack an enemy from multiple directions and then rapidly dispersing."[24] Such tactics could be used against both military and commercial vessels and would be supported by "camouflage, concealment, active and passive deception, the use of advanced electronic equipments [sic] and radar stations, [and] eavesdropping."[25]

Iranian strategists recognize the devastating effects of airpower that the United States demonstrated against Iraq in Operation Desert Storm and the need for "aerospace security." In a 2001 article entitled "What Will Future Wars Be Like?" a *Saff* contributor noted that "suc-

[23] For an Iranian view of the effect of the Iran-Iraq War on strategic thinking today, see Taremi, 2005a.

[24] Fariborz Haghshenass, "Iran's Doctrine of Asymmetric Naval Warfare," Washington, D.C.: Washington Institute for Near East Policy, PolicyWatch No. 1179, December 21, 2006.

[25] Mohammad 'Ali Bakhshi, "Standing on the Ship of Power," found in "Iran: Report Says Iran's Navy Executed 'Ettehad-83' Maneuver in Various Waters," *Saff* (Tehran), in Persian, OSC IAP20050103000091, June 7, 2004, pp. 21–23.

cessive bombings in Iraq finally brought an end to the nation's military capability, and its power to move on the ground was paralyzed."[26] As indicated above, Iran sees its ballistic missiles as a potent answer to U.S. airpower, both as a deterrent to regional states that would grant access to their airbases and as a hindrance to U.S. air operations.[27] In addition, Iran emphasizes passive defenses to complicate U.S. targeting through hardening, concealment, and advanced denial and deception techniques, all developed through years of observing U.S. operations and learning from Russia, China, Yugoslavia, and others.

As with other components of Iranian doctrine, Tehran seeks to use its air-attack and defense assets to complicate enemy access to Iranian airspace and to impose a high cost on enemy strike packages with the hope of denying an adversary his objectives. The Islamic Republic of Iran Air Force (IRIAF) and Islamic Revolutionary Guard Corps Air Force (IRGCAF) would employ SAM systems and air interceptors in a layered air defense of the country. It is likely that the air forces would seek to create conditions that enable them to ambush or otherwise surprise attackers by using terrain masking, advanced radar tactics, and electronic warfare techniques. Iran's ground-based air defenses would try to protect cities and critical sites with a combination of long- and short-range SAM systems and guns that would be reconfigured frequently.[28] Iranian doctrine also appears to be emphasizing air-land operations, whereby attack aircraft support ground operations and conduct longer-range strikes against military and civilian targets in the region.[29] If fully developed, this would provide Iran a third power-

[26] See "Iran: Magazine Looks at What Future Wars May Be Like," *Saff* (Tehran), in Persian, OSC IAP20010524000001, May 21, 2001, pp. 17–20. See also "Iran: Report Highlights 'Need' for Aerospace Security, 'Fourth Force'," *Saff* (Tehran), in Persian, OSC IAP20050210000086, October 1, 2004, p. 6.

[27] As will be discussed in Chapter Five, this doctrine has unsettled smaller Gulf states (RAND interview with a former commander of the UAE Air Force, February 9, 2006, Abu Dhabi, United Arab Emirates).

[28] Ward, 2005, p. 571; Michael Knights, "Iran's Conventional Forces Remain Key to Deterring Potential Threats," *Jane's Intelligence Review*, February 1, 2006.

[29] See "Iran: Report Highlights 'Need' for Aerospace Security, 'Fourth Force'," 2004, p. 6; "Iran: Magazine Looks at What Future Wars May Be Like," 2001, pp. 17–20. See also Robin

projection capability in addition to ballistic missiles and commando forces or "proxy" groups.

As mentioned previously, the Iran-Iraq War was a seminal period in the formation of the Islamic Republic and in the development of Iran's defense strategy. Having lost some 400,000 people during a war in which ideological ardor was a staple of Iranian doctrine, Tehran undertook an overhaul of its defense establishment that emphasized professionalism, access to advanced military hardware, and deterrence.[30] However, Iranian strategists also drew lessons from the war regarding the importance of mounting a capable defense in depth and mobilizing the population to resist invaders. Emphasis on these concepts has grown in recent years as Iran has observed the relative success Hezbollah and Iraqi insurgent groups have enjoyed against Israel in Lebanon and U.S. forces in Iraq. Moreover, defense in depth and popular mobilization would seem to provide President Ahmadinejad and the IRGC leadership—members of the "war generation"—platforms from which to emphasize ideological commitment to the Islamic Revolution.

In defending the homeland in depth and pursuing popular resistance against occupation, Iran would seek to impose a high cost upon an invader (namely, the United States) as a deterrent and, if invaded, to draw out the campaign to the extent that the invader loses the mettle to pursue its objectives to their conclusion. Iran envisions a "mosaic defense" and partisan warfare that presents the invader with multiple threats each step of the way to Tehran and renders any occupation of the country untenable.[31] Exercise activity suggests that Iranian armed forces would respond to invasion by employing hit-and-run tactics against enemy forces while avoiding being targeted by airpower. The

---

Hughes, "Iran Eyes Long-Range Air Strike Capability," *Jane's Defence Weekly*, February 7, 2007; Robert Hewson, "Iran Stages Large-Scale Exercises to Underline Defence Capabilities," *Jane's Defence Weekly*, September 13, 2006; Jane's Information Group, "Iran—Air Force," *Jane's Sentinel Security Assessment-Gulf States*, March 2005.

[30] Byman et al., 2001, pp. 35–36.

[31] "IRGC Commander Discusses New Strategy," *Radio Free Europe/Radio Liberty Iran Report*, September 27, 2004. The Ashura exercises in September 2004 demonstrated the concept of defense in depth. See *Radio Free Europe/Radio Liberty*, Vol. 7, No. 38, November 1, 2004.

Basij forms an important pillar in the regime's homeland defense strategy and would play a prominent role in training and mobilizing the Iranian population for countrywide partisan warfare.[32] This homeland defense doctrine is informed by observations of what Iranian strategists see as the success of guerilla warfare in negating technologically superior conventional power. Hezbollah's role in Israel's withdrawal from Lebanon in 2000, Hezbollah's "victory" against Israel in the summer of 2006, and the insurgency in Iraq are recent examples of such perceived success. Deft use of the media and other propaganda tools to influence popular sentiment would "exaggerate the weaknesses of the rival, even if they be small, and in contrast to show [one's] own victory as being larger than it is."[33] In short, the Iranian concept is to avoid protracted tactical engagements but enforce a protracted war whose cost would be so unpalatable that an invader would be compelled to abandon his objectives and withdraw.

From the invader's perspective, an invasion and occupation of Iran would be far more risky, costly, and complex than Operation Iraqi Freedom. Iran is a much larger country, with nearly three times the population of Iraq. For example, the distance from the Kuwait-Iraq border to Baghdad is about 425 km, but the distance from Bandar Abbas to Tehran exceeds 1,000 km. Moreover, the terrain in Iran is far more favorable to the defender than in Iraq. In its march on Baghdad, the U.S. 3rd Infantry Division (Mechanized) traversed mostly open terrain with very few significant obstacles until it reached the Euphrates River, just south of the city. In contrast, every axis of advance on Tehran, except those out of Afghanistan, passes through mountainous

---

[32] "Iran Revolution Guards Hold 'Asymmetric Warfare' Ashura-5 Exercises," Vision of the Islamic Republic of Iran Network, in Persian, OSC IAP20040913000110, September 13, 2004; "IRGC Ground Force Commander Speaks on Reorganization, Combat Plans," Vision of the Islamic Republic of Iran Network, in Persian, FBIS IAP20050309000087, March 9, 2005. According to former IRGC commander General Safavi, the *Basij* "have been equipped to defend the surface of the country rather like a mosaic and if any force contemplates aggression against our country, it will not be safe anywhere in this country" ("Guards C-in-C Says Iran's 'Deterrent Capability' Extends to Entire Region," BBC Monitoring International Reports, September 11, 2004).

[33] "*Saff* Article on Methods of Propaganda in Psychological Warfare," *Saff* (Tehran), in Persian, FBIS IAP20010525000001, March 1, 2001, pp. 24–26.

terrain. Starting from the Persian Gulf, an invader must pass through the Zagros Mountains and traverse long valleys between the peaks. Defending forces could exploit the rugged terrain an invader would encounter, terrain that impedes and canalizes an invading army's advance and greatly favors the defender. Moreover, cities sprawl across the axes of advance, presenting the defender with additional opportunities. In fact, the sheer scale and complexity of Iranian territory and population is so daunting that Iranian defense capabilities may be less important than the fundamental geography of Iran itself.

Four Themes Underlie Iran's Military Activities

Supporting Iran's asymmetric warfare doctrine are several underlying doctrinal themes by which its armed forces organize, train, and equip. Among these themes are building ideological fortitude in the ranks of its military forces and citizenry; attaining self-sufficiency to ensure its national security; enhancing joint force integration, training, and readiness; promoting initiative among its field officers; and incorporating modern surveillance, command and control, and mobility capabilities into the force.

Ideology. Recent shifts toward homeland defense and mass mobilization have elevated the importance of ideology and indoctrination. The IRGC in particular sees revolutionary zeal and popular will as centers of gravity on the battlefield and lays claim to "strategic superiority" in the form of "faithful, wise, brave, and revolutionary persons."[34] Thus, the role of clerical "commissars" has become increasingly important, especially for mobilizing and indoctrinating the *Basij* "five-million man army" for partisan warfare and for allegedly enabling combat units to "triple in less than 48 hours."[35] And in statements by

---

[34] "General Rahim Safavi: America's Aim Is to Prevent Iran from Becoming the First Power in the Middle East," *Keyhan* (Tehran), in "Persian Press: Revolutionary Guard Commander on Way to Fight Unequal Enemy," in Persian, OSC IAP20061231011007, December 26, 2006, p. 14.

[35] "Iran Guards' Commander Says Combat Units Can Expand Threefold in 48 Hours," Tehran Fars News Agency, Web page, BBC Worldwide Monitoring, November 12, 2006. See also "Iran: Profile of IRGC's Shahid Mahallati Theological-Political College," in Persian, OSC IAP20061208427001, December 7, 2006; Knapp, 1998.

government officials, commanders, and clerics, martyrdom in defense of Islamic Iran has been more frequently emphasized.[36]

Self-reliance. As indicated previously, a key tenet in Iran's military doctrine is self-reliance and independence in its ability to train and equip its armed forces and secure its national interests. In February 2007, Iranian Defense Minister Mostafa Mohammad Najjar stated that Iran was seeking to achieve military self-sufficiency, conduct research and development in modern industries, and develop the capability to fight in "modern and ultra-modern domains."[37] Iran is developing and expanding defense industries in virtually every area of armament to reduce its dependence on foreign suppliers, minimize the effects of sanctions, and realize its aim of becoming a modern military power that can tout major technological achievements.[38]

Joint Operations. Iran's military leaders increasingly emphasize the necessity of joint force integration, training, and readiness to improve the operational capabilities of all components. Iran conducts large joint wargames, ostensibly to evaluate the integration of its air, land, and sea forces to "face the enemy in various points of the country at once."[39] The IRGC commander recently introduced a "doctrine of

---

[36] For example, the Friday prayer imam of Orumiyeh in Azarbayjan Province stated that "the enemies of Islamic Iran should know that admirable soldiers like martyr Hoseyn Fahmideh [a 13-year-old boy who fought in the Iran-Iraq War] are ready to defend the territory of Islamic Iran" ("Iran: Provincial Cleric Urges Unity to Foil Enemy 'Threats,' 'Plots'," *Orumiyeh Vision of the Islamic Republic of Iran*, West Azarbayjan Provincial television, in Persian, OSC IAP20071026950088, October 26, 2007).

[37] "Iran Defence Doctrine Deterrent—Defence Minister," transcript of interview on Iranian television, February 13, 2007, BBC Worldwide Monitoring, February 17, 2007.

[38] For example, Mohammad Reza Naqdi, the Logistics and Industrial Research deputy in the General Staff of the Armed Forces, claims that "sanctions are an opportunity rather than a threat, and we are able to produce all sanctioned materials inside Iran by setting in motion an emergency plan." This allows Iran to set "an exceptional example for all independent countries of the world" ("Iran Press Military Says Sanctioned Equipment May Be Produced Internally," BBC Monitoring International Reports coverage of a report by Iranian newspaper *Siyasat-e Ruz*, April 23, 2007, A2007043030-14936-GNW, April 30, 2007).

[39] Iranian Ground Forces Commander Brigadier General Kiumars Heydari, quoted in Robin Hughes, "Iran Launches 'Great Prophet 2' Joint Military Exercise," *Jane's Defence Weekly*, November 8, 2006.

units" in which "every unit must, on its own and continuously, improve all aspects of its inherent readiness, including the readiness of individuals, equipment, and the unit as a whole, as well as religious and revolutionary discipline." He added, "repair and maintenance of equipment, maintenance of communications, mobility, fluidity, [and] discipline of individuals and units are among the priorities that the commanders must pay attention to."[40]

Taking Initiative. Significantly, the Iranian military encourages initiative and creativity by its junior leaders.[41] This is a key requirement for the tactical success of its operational approach that is based on independent small unit actions on land (mosaic defense) and at sea (swarming). Iran's strategists view homeland defense as a "captain's war." In this way, Iran's doctrine is more akin to Western military tradition than the rigidly hierarchical and centralized decisionmaking that characterizes Soviet/Russian military thought.

Iran's military doctrine and CONOPs are designed first and foremost to deter aggression against it and, secondly, to enhance its regional standing and strategic weight. In the same interview quoted above, Najjar noted that

> The defense doctrine of the Islamic Republic of Iran is based on deterrence. We have always announced that our policies are defensive. We in fact believe that the development of these capabilities will contribute to peace and stability in the region. It is good for the countries of the region to have a powerful neighbor rather than a weak one.[42]

Overall, Iran's doctrine aligns rather well with its national security objectives and military strategy. It remains to be seen, however, whether the forces it fields on balance provide the capabilities necessary to execute the military strategy and meet the doctrinal ambitions the

---

[40] "Iran: Guards Chief Outlines New Doctrine for Improving Combat Readiness," Tehran Fars News Agency, in Persian, Web page, OSC IAP20061217950103, December 17, 2006.

[41] "Iranian Ground Force Tactics," in *How They Fight: Armies of the World*, National Ground Intelligence Center, NGIC-1122-0097-00, August 2000.

[42] "Iran Defence Doctrine Deterrent—Defence Minister," 2007.

Islamic Republic's leaders, strategists, and tacticians have set forth. We now turn to an analysis of Iran's military capabilities.

The Operational Capabilities of Iran's Armed Forces

Iran Faces the Challenge of Modernizing a Large, Structurally Weak Force

While Iran pursues diverse military capabilities and seeks to present the armed forces of a regional military power, it has made only limited progress in modernizing its relatively large conventional force structure. The bulk of its equipment is out of date and poorly maintained, and its ground forces suffer from both personnel and equipment shortages.[43] Its ability to conduct sustained combined arms and joint operations is limited and is unlikely to improve significantly in the near term. This is because of both the country's limited resource infrastructure and the ingrained attitudes and continuing competition for resources of the *Artesh* and the IRGC.[44] The military capabilities of Iran are summarized in Table 3.1. Despite its numerous material shortcomings, the Iranian military does have important strengths. We focus on those capabilities most relevant to U.S. interests and to the USAF posture in the region.

The IRIAF fields a varied mixture of about 300 mostly older-generation Russian, Chinese, French, and U.S. fighters and reconnaissance aircraft and some 65 tanker and transport aircraft. Tehran acquired some fighters when Iraqi pilots fled to Iran during Operation Desert Storm in 1991, and a number of these remain operational. Despite efforts to modernize its front-line fleet, Iran's air capabilities remain weak in relation to those of its neighbors, much less with regard to U.S. airpower. Of note, however, is Iran's apparent interest in longer-range air strike capability. The IRIAF appears to be trying to expand

---

[43] Lowell E. Jacoby, *Current and Projected National Security Threats to the United States*, DIA Statement for the Record, Senate Select Committee on Intelligence, February 16, 2005, p. 14; Jane's Information Group, March 2005.

[44] Cordesman, 2005.

Table 3.1
Summary of Iranian Military Capabilities

Capability	System Type	Number in Service	Comments
Air forces	Combat aircraft	280	Mostly third generation, includes MiG-29, Su-24MK, Mirage F1
	Airborne early warning/reconnaissance aircraft	22	Includes P-3 MR and IL-76 AEW
	Unmanned aerial vehicles (UAVs)	?	*Ababil* and *Muhadjer* families of intelligence, surveillance, and reconnaissance (ISR); attack; communications relay UAVs
	SAMs	240+	85 SA-2, -5, -15; SA-10 on order for Bushehr; MANPADs
Naval forces	Major surface combatants	5	3 frigates, 2 corvettes
	Submarines	6+	3 Kilo, 3 Qadir (coastal), plus 3 midget subs
	Antiship cruise missiles	125+	Air-, ground-, and sea-launched, including C-801/802, *Seersucker*
	Mine layers	100s?	Small craft
	Fast attack/patrol ships	220	Includes 20 missile fast attack
Ground forces	Tanks	1,600	T-72, T-54, other—mostly decades old
	Infantry fighting vehicles/armored personnel carriers	1,250	BMP-1, BMP-2, other
	Brigades	38+	Includes 6 commando and 3 airborne brigades, 225 helicopters
	Artillery	2,400+	Mostly towed
	Multiple rocket launchers	860+	Mostly 107mm, some 122mm
Missile forces	Medium-range ballistic missiles	380	Includes 20 Shahab-3, 12–18 Transporter Erector Launches (TELs) for 350 Shahab-1/2
	Short-range ballistic missiles	1,200	Battlefield missiles
	Land-attack cruise missiles	6	Kh-55/AS-15 Kent (operability unknown)
Other	Chemical and biological warfare	?	Thought to have latent capabilities

SOURCES: Anthony Cordesman, *Iran's Developing Military Capabilities*, Washington, D.C.: Center for Strategic and Intentional Studies, 2005; International Institute for Strategic Studies, 2007, pp. 188–190; *Jane's Sentinel Country Risk Assessments: Iran* (continually updated online).

its aerial refueling capacity, especially for its Su-24MK Fencer aircraft, and there is speculation that it is exploring acquisition of Su-22M Backfire bombers from Russia.[45] In addition, the Iranians are pursuing upgrades to their surface-based air defense capabilities. Early in 2007, Iran test-fired one of its 29 short-range SA-15 (Tor-M1) SAM systems delivered from Russia, and there have been reports that it has acquired "at least two" long-range SA-10 (S-300) SAM systems.[46] These newest additions would complement older SA-5, I-Hawk, and other SAM systems, as well as a variety of air defense artillery and man-portable air defense systems (MANPADs), including the Stinger, SA-14, and SA-18. The Iranian military deploys these systems largely as point defenses to protect major cities and key sites, such as Bushehr and others associated with the nuclear program. Iran lacks the command and control, warning and tracking, and integration capabilities necessary to field a modern, national integrated air defense system.

To support its naval doctrine emphasizing "swarming," Iran's naval capabilities are centered on fast-attack craft, antiship cruise missiles, and mine-laying to enable Tehran to protect Iran's coastline, impede commercial maritime traffic in the Gulf, and harass or destroy U.S. naval assets by creating a "360-degree threat." Both the IRGC and regular navies emphasize small, fast patrol and attack boats with antiship cruise missiles, torpedoes, multiple rocket launchers, and rocket-propelled grenades. Iran also deploys land-based antiship cruise missiles, including the Chinese Seersucker and C-801/802 systems, along its considerable coastline, as well as a handful of short-range air-launched cruise missiles. Tehran is thought to have over 2,000 mines that can be deployed by naval surface vessels, helicopters, and perhaps hundreds of small military and civilian craft.[47] In addition, Iran's three

---

[45] See Hughes, February 7, 2007; "Procurement," in *Jane's Sentinel Country Risk Assessments: Iran.*

[46] "Highlights: Iranian Military Developments, 8–14 June 2007; Iran to Get SA-19 Grissom," in English, OSC Summary IAP20070615339001, June 8–14, 2007; "Iran: Commander Says New Russian-Delivered Defense System Quick, Responsive," *Keyhan* (Tehran), Web page, in Persian, OSC IAP20070221397002, February 8, 2007.

[47] Cordesman, 2007, p. 58.

recently acquired *Kilo*-class diesel-powered submarines enable its regular navy to lay mines covertly while providing an undersea torpedo threat to U.S. Navy and commercial vessels. Finally, Iran is attempting to improve its ability to track and strike targets—especially surface vessels—with the indigenously produced Ababil and Muhadjer families of UAVs.

The ground forces of the Islamic Republic are large by regional standards but, like the air force, are saddled with a substantial number of older weapon systems. Iran is attempting to upgrade and modernize its armor and antitank capabilities through both imports and indigenous production, but not at a rate that would "recapitalize" the entire army in the near future. Its force of artillery and multiple rocket launchers is large in comparison with other regional actors, but many of these are towed and more useful for static defense than maneuver warfare. More than 60 percent of the regular army's total end strength of 350,000 soldiers are conscripts, and the IRGC's ground forces are lightly manned during peacetime. Many units are only partially equipped. Generally, the Iranian ground forces are designed to defend the nation from invasion, although they may have very limited capability to conduct incursions into bordering countries, such as Iraq or Afghanistan.

Iran possesses under IRGC control an important arsenal of short- and medium-range ballistic missiles consisting of a few hundred Shahab-1 (Scud-B), Shahab-2 (Scud-C), and Tondar-69 (CSS-8) short-range ballistic missiles as well as a handful of Shahab-3 medium-range ballistic missiles.[48] The short-range ballistic missiles can reach some or most of the small Persian Gulf states and the eastern portions of Iraq and Saudi Arabia, as well as western Afghanistan, while the Shahab-3 is within range of Israel, eastern Turkey, and most of Saudi Arabia. These missiles are generally inaccurate, thus limiting their military utility in the near term, but improvements in accuracy and firing doctrine and the deployment of submunitions could enhance their effectiveness against large soft targets on military bases. An equally important limitation is the relatively small number of TELs believed to be available for the Shahab-1/2 short-range ballistic missile, as this puts

---

[48] Director of Central Intelligence, *Acquisition of Technology*, November 2004, p. 3.

important constraints on Iran's ability to mass the fire of these missiles in order to overwhelm missile defenses. This will be particularly true if the IRGC deems it necessary to disperse its missiles throughout Iran to enhance survivability or to ensure some degree of missile capability on multiple fronts. These missiles, along with the Shahab-3, are capable of damaging economic infrastructure and population centers and thus serve as an important deterrent. Moreover, the inaccuracy and relatively small payload capacity of the Shahab-3s serve as indicators that Iran could be seeking to arm them with weapons of mass destruction, including nuclear weapons.[49] Iran appears to be further extending the range of its missile forces, announcing in late 2004 that it was mass-producing a Shahab-4 with a range of 2,000 km.[50] Reports also allege that Iran is pursuing intercontinental-range missiles with the help of North Korea, although Tehran maintains it is developing such missiles for space launch.[51]

Despite Iran's signing of the Biological and Toxin Weapons Convention and the Chemical Weapons Convention, there are indications that it has active, dedicated chemical or biological weapons programs, or that it at least has a latent capability to produce and weaponize some chemicals and toxins. A CIA report to Congress in November 2003 asserts that Iran continues to "vigorously pursue" indigenous biological-weapon and chemical-weapon capabilities and seeks foreign equipment, materials, training, and know-how, focusing "particularly on entities in Russia, China, North Korea, and Europe."[52] Iranian scientific journals

---

[49] For analysis of Iranian missile developments, see Defense Threat Reduction Agency, "Special Report: Challenges of Iranian Missile Proliferation," *WMD Insights*, October 1, 2006; Taremi, 2005a; Uzi Rubin, "The Global Reach of Iran's Ballistic Missiles," Tel Aviv, Israel: Tel Aviv University, Institute for National Security Studies, Memorandum 86, November 2006.

[50] Kenneth Katzman, "Iran: Current Developments and U.S. Policy," Congressional Research Service, July 25, 2003, p. 20.

[51] Defense Threat Reduction Agency, 2006, p. 2. The report mentions a "Shahab-6" based on the North Korean Taepodong-2 with a range of 5,000–6,000 km.

[52] Central Intelligence Agency, "Attachment A: Unclassified Report to Congress on the Acquisition of Technology Relating to Weapons of Mass Destruction and Advanced Conventional Munitions," January 1–June 30, 2003.

discuss biological agents such as anthrax in the context of bioterrorism, but their research can be dual-purposed by Iran either for defensive or offensive applications.[53] As for chemical weapons, the 2003 CIA report maintains that Iran continues "to seek production technology, training, and expertise from Chinese entities that could further Tehran's efforts to achieve an indigenous capability to produce nerve agents," and that Iran likely stockpiles "blister, blood, choking, and probably nerve agents—and the bombs and artillery shells to deliver them."[54] There is, of course, ample concern in the international community that Iran's civilian nuclear program serves as a cover for a concerted effort to develop nuclear weapons.[55] We address the potential implications of Iranian nuclear weapons for Iran's defense strategy below.

Iran has developed a domestic defense industry that produces a range of weapon systems as part of its drive for self-sufficiency. The defense sector develops and manufactures, assembles, or produces under license equipment in nearly every category of military hardware. Iran is an exporter of arms to a number of countries and terrorist groups. It provides ballistic missiles and other arms to Hezbollah in Lebanon and supports the Palestinian groups Hamas and Islamic Jihad. It claims to export more than $100 million worth of military equipment to some 50 countries.[56]

---

[53] A series of relevant articles has appeared in the proceedings of an Iranian public health congress; Iran's Ministry of Health and Medical Education published the proceedings. See, for example, A. Valinejad, "Is Anthrax the Most Dangerous Biological Weapon?" *Medical and Health Aspects of Bioterrorism Panel No. 005* (Tehran), translated in "Iranian Scientists Review B. Anthracis as Biological Weapon," OSC IAP20040830000037, January 1, 2001.

[54] Central Intelligence Agency, 2003. See also Gregory F. Giles, "The Islamic Republic of Iran and Nuclear, Biological, and Chemical Weapons," in Peter R. Lavoy et al., eds., *Planning the Unthinkable: How New Powers Will Use Nuclear, Biological, and Chemical Weapons*, Ithaca and London: Cornell University Press, 2000, pp. 79–103.

[55] See, for example, Seth Elan et al., "Open-Source Research on Nuclear Doctrine and Strategy, Command and Control, and Delivery Systems in Iran and Israel," Library of Congress, Federal Research Division, Washington, D.C., December 2005, pp. 13–16. This report was prepared under an interagency agreement with the National Intelligence Council/National Intelligence Officer for Military Issues.

[56] Nasser Karimi, "Iran Unveils Locally Made Fighter in War Games," The Associated Press, September 6, 2006.

In sum, the Islamic Republic fields relatively large armed forces, by regional standards, with equipment whose level of modernity could be described as modest at best. In certain areas, including but not limited to ballistic and cruise missiles, submarines, UAVs, and SAM systems, Tehran can claim to be making strides in incorporating technologically sophisticated systems into its force structure. Given the preponderance of older equipment in its arsenal, however, Iran would require huge defense expenditures and many years before it could acquire and incorporate the equipment necessary to recapitalize its entire force. The challenges for Iranian planners and strategists are to set forth doctrine and define CONOPs that make best use of assets on hand to achieve national security and military objectives and to recommend options to the leadership for mitigating shortfalls in the future. We now assess how well Iran's military capabilities support the doctrine it has developed.

Iran's Operational Capabilities Fall Short of Doctrinal Ambitions

In light of our review of Iran's military objectives, doctrine, and force structure, how effective might its capabilities be? Do its capabilities meet its doctrinal expectations? Iran does a good job of formulating doctrine based on its objectives, its lessons learned, and the realization that it is no match for the U.S. military in a head-to-head conflict. The best it can expect to do is impose costs on U.S. action and "outlast" U.S. will to prevent Washington from achieving its objectives in a conflict with Tehran. The *Artesh* and IRGC have many military weaknesses, but in some areas they are improving substantially in ways that could pose risks to the United States and its allies in any crisis or conflict.

The Iranian leadership and military make a concerted effort in their statements, procurement patterns, and exercises to strengthen their deterrent posture in ways that give adversaries and their potential supporters pause in considering military confrontation with the Islamic Republic. Articles and discussions appear in the Iranian (and Arab) press on a continuing basis attesting to the prowess and sophistication of Iran's operational capability and technological know-how. Iranian interlocutors often exaggerate Iranian military capabilities and pepper statements with claims of capabilities heretofore unknown by external observers. And they make clear the intention of Iran to retaliate in devastating ways in response to an attack on it. For example, then–Defense Minister Ali Shamkhani stated in August 2004 that "the Islamic Republic has acquired massive military might, the dimensions of which still remain unknown, and is prepared to attack any intruder with a fearsome rain of fire and death."[57] Iran holds large and relatively frequent exercises during which it demonstrates its latest advances in equipment and tactics. Iranian state television reported during Iran's 2006 Great Prophet 2 exercise that "Shahab missiles, carrying cluster warheads . . . were fired from the desert near Qom" and that 15 missiles were salvoed simultaneously, giving Tehran "unlimited and infinite" missile launch capability.[58] Thus, while it is difficult to measure the effect of Tehran's deterrent efforts—except by observing that Iran has not been attacked since the 1980s—these efforts appear concerted, well thought out, and supported, at least nominally, by Iran's doctrine and forces.

Clearly, Iran's ballistic missile capabilities—and the implication that they could be platforms for weapons of mass destruction—serve as a potent part of the deterrent. And in the event of crisis or conflict, these weapons would be useful in attempts to dissuade U.S. allies in the Persian Gulf from fully supporting certain U.S. operations from their territories. Iran may be able to salvo these missiles, possibly overwhelming U.S. and allied missile defenses in some circumstances while making it difficult for U.S. airpower to target mobile launchers. In the near term, despite their potential utility in deterring U.S. allies from cooperating with Washington in a crisis or conflict, Iran's missiles are unlikely to possess the accuracy and payload necessary to pose an operationally meaningful conventional threat to U.S. air operations or most other military activities in the region. They could be used to harass U.S. air operations by targeting airbases on the opposite side of the Persian Gulf, but U.S. efforts to provide passive protection to

---

[57] Presumably, Shamkhani was referring to Iran's growing inventory of ballistic missiles. See "Iranian Bassij Wishes for U.S. Defeat in Iraq," Agence France Presse, Arab News, December 1, 2003; also reported by Al-Muqtada.

[58] Quoted in Hughes, 2006.

assets on the ground should minimize the missiles' effect at this level of threat. However, as Iran improves the accuracy and payload of its ballistic missile inventory over time, its ability to destroy U.S. air assets and cause casualties on the ground and ultimately disrupt sortie generation likely will become more serious. Of course, mating nuclear warheads with its ballistic missiles would give Tehran a much more effective counterforce capability. But even improvements in guidance systems and conventional warheads and submunitions in the future could provide Iran missiles with operational military utility. In light of weaknesses in other components of its military, Tehran will continue to rely on its ballistic missiles as one of its few tools for maintaining strategic reach and impeding U.S. access to the region and to Iranian territory and airspace.

Iran is applying its doctrinal emphasis on asymmetric warfare across the board, but with mixed results. Iranian security forces remain fundamentally oriented to the defense of Iranian territory and to the deterrence of a foreign invasion. Given the size and terrain of Iran, Iranian ground forces appear adequately equipped and trained to make the cost of invasion and occupation of the country exorbitant, especially in relation to the U.S. and coalition experience in Iraq.[59] How effective the *Basij* would be in a conflict is open to question. *Basij* units are lightly armed, and most *Basij* personnel do not receive significant military training. What the *Basij* do provide, however, is a large pool of manpower familiar with the use of light infantry weapons; these militia forces can form the nucleus of regional resistance movements. If only a fraction of the estimated three to six million individuals on the *Basij* payroll remain loyal to the Iranian clerical regime and take up arms, there would be a significant post-conflict resistance movement in Iran.[60]

---

[59] As we noted in earlier, Iran is about three times the size of Iraq in population and area, and its terrain is much more rugged.

[60] The *Basij* generally recruit young volunteers (11–17 years of age) from rural areas or the poorer sectors of larger cities. Some appear to be ideologically motivated and deeply religious, but many are poorly educated. In many areas, particularly in the countryside and small towns, the *Basij* are little more than a civic/social group, and some of its members are

While Iran's air forces have tried to modernize (especially in the area of surface-to-air defenses), improve proficiency, and adopt asymmetric tactics, their ability to counter air operations in Iranian airspace by the USAF and U.S. Navy seems rather limited. It is unclear how third- and fourth-generation IRIAF air interceptors could "ambush" U.S. F-22s, B-2As, and F/A-18s, which would have superior situational awareness and concepts of employment. On the other hand, acquisition of increasingly sophisticated SAM systems such as the SA-10 and, in the future, the SA-20 would complicate U.S. air attacks on key Iranian targets and could threaten U.S. strike, command and control, and ISR aircraft. But limitations in surveillance and command and control capabilities likely will continue to hamper the integration—and hence full exploitation—of these systems into a functional integrated air defense system.

Iran's most effective option for protecting critical assets is likely to be passive defense. Over time, Iran has been concealing, dispersing, and hardening potential targets of a U.S. attack and would step up its passive defense efforts in camouflage, concealment, and deception as the United States built up forces in the region and an attack appeared imminent. Iran might also hide assets in civilian facilities (such as hospitals, schools, and mosques) and populate key sites with civilian "volunteers" (such as *Basij* militia members) to deter U.S. strikes. These modes of passive defense would prove extremely challenging to U.S. intelligence and targeting capacities, which might mischaracterize potential targets or even fail to identify and track key Iranian assets.

Of the land, sea, and air components of Iran's armed forces, its navies appear to have made the most headway in adopting asymmetric tactics to protect the coastline, conduct sea denial operations (particularly in the Strait of Hormuz), and damage U.S. forces. Setting aside for a moment the efficacy of trying to close the strait, Iran's mining, anti-ship cruise missile, and fast-attack capabilities could create very difficult conditions for passage of tankers through this critical waterway—even under U.S. convoy. Even if such Iranian efforts did not stop traffic

---

apparently motivated primarily by the monthly stipend provided by membership (International Crisis Group, 2002).

altogether, they would still have a profound effect on global energy markets. This is one of the few ways in which Iran can impose *strategic* costs on the United States. These efforts could internationalize the conflict in ways that would bring severe pressure on the United States to terminate hostilities before it had achieved its objectives. Moreover, well-executed swarming tactics could take some toll on U.S. naval vessels in the Persian Gulf, Strait of Hormuz, and Gulf of Oman. However, though it is slowly improving its capabilities, Iran's ability to find and target vessels over the horizon is quite limited; this presents a major challenge to effective use of its cruise missiles, except in the narrow strait. And because Iran's military relies extensively on mobilization of reserves, it is not clear how many of the small-boat crews have the training necessary to properly execute the precise coordination required to surprise and overwhelm U.S. ship defenses. Still, success is possible for Iran's navies, especially in the beginning of a shooting conflict.

In other doctrinal areas, grandiose statements by Iranian leaders and commentators mask shortfalls in implementation. The military is beset with institutional friction that prevents it from achieving jointness and integration. For example, after years of animosity dating back to the Iran-Iraq War, there appears to be little coordination between the IRIAF and the IRGCAF, a situation that could have dire consequences for aircraft operating in the same airspace.[61] Despite "joint exercises" ostensibly arranged to improve coordination between the IRGC and the *Artesh*, the armed forces are poorly integrated. Moreover, the Iranian military establishment has only very slowly mitigated its command and control, readiness, logistics, and ISR shortfalls, which remain substantial and render much of Iran's military second-rate.

While Iran emphasizes ideology and indoctrination in training, there are some indications that it is meeting widespread cynicism and ambivalence in the ranks—especially among the *Basij*, many of whom are drawn from the ranks of Iran's disaffected youth. As stated by one 24-year-old member in a 2005 interview: "The only reason I stay in the *Basij* is for the money . . . many of my friends in the *Basij* are unhappy

---

[61] See Fariborz Haghshenass, "Iran's Air Forces: Struggling to Maintain Readiness," Washington Institute for Near East Policy, PolicyWatch No. 1066, December 28, 2005.

with the government."[62] The *Basij* appear to be divided between those who are true believers in the revolution and those who serve primarily because of the substantial subsidy they receive.[63] In addition, the changing demographics of the *Basij* could degrade its revolutionary ardor: The growing influx of retired IRGC officers and elderly pensioners into the force may create generational friction with younger, discontented members.

Iran's defense industry does not appear to be able to produce equipment of the quality and quantity that the Iranian military requires.[64] Iran has not funded the development of a research and development establishment that will allow it to indigenously design, develop, and produce a broad range of modern military systems.[65] In fact, Iran's modernization program may have been slowed by its emphasis on the indigenous production of weapons. As part of its self-sufficiency initiative, it has focused on developing reverse-engineered weapon systems that are built to different standards. In addition to exacerbating existing logistics and supply problems within the Iranian military, this also dilutes the effect of Iran's investments in its arms industry.[66] Former Defense Minister Shamkhani noted in 2002 that

> We regard modernization as a key element of a comprehensive plan for the Iranian defense structure over the current decade. However, the main trend in Iran's defense procurement strategy is to rely on domestic manufacture to the maximum possible extent, and this has led to some delays in our modernization pro-

[62] International Crisis Group, "Update Briefing—Iran: What Does Ahmadi-Nejad's Victory Mean?" Tehran/Brussels, August 2005.

[63] International Crisis Group, 2002, p. 8; International Crisis Group, "Update Briefing—Iran," 2005, p. 6.

[64] Cordesman, 2005, p. 9; Enrico Po, "Iran (Almost) Does It Alone," *Bergamo Rivista, Italiana Drefesa*, in Italian, translated by FBIS, FBIS EUP20030407000354, January 2, 2003.

[65] See Ali Ghafuri, "An Interview with General Tavakoli, Deputy Commander of the Army in Charge of Self Sufficiency Jihad," *Iran Daily Newspaper*, Vol. 9, No. 2734, February 25, 2004, p. 15.

[66] Iran, for instance, produces small arms and artillery systems to both Western and Russian standards (Po, 2003).

cess. Because of existing limitations and restrictions on our access to advanced technologies, we are not in the position to quickly improve on our material. So, we try to use alternative solutions, such as strengthening civil and popular resistance, in order to achieve a balanced defense structure.[67]

In sum, Iran has succeeded in enhancing—and will continue to improve—its deterrent posture in some important fields, particularly in its ability to counter invasion and occupation, to reduce its vulnerability through passive defenses, to threaten or mete out punishment on other states and foreign forces in the region through ballistic missile and unconventional attacks, and to impede military and commercial maritime operations in contiguous waters. Overall, however, while Iran's military doctrine is designed to mitigate its inferiority in the face of more-powerful adversaries such as the United States and to exploit perceived enemy weaknesses, there are many areas where Iran's military capabilities do not meet doctrinal expectations. It is in light of these weaknesses—coupled with the belief that the United States poses an existential threat to the revolution—that Iranian leaders may seek to acquire nuclear weapons. It is this topic to which we now turn.

---

[67] "Interview with Adm. Ali Shamkhani, (former) Minister of Defense of the Islamic Republic of Iran," *Military Technology*, No. 7, 2002, p. 36. The existence of the *Basij* also exacerbates existing difficulties in modernizing the Iranian military. While exact figures are not available, personnel costs for the *Basij*, even at relatively modest pay scales, are likely to be a significant drain on Iran's defense budget. These costs could easily be in the range of $1 billion or more a year. The stipend for some *Basij* members is 95,000 toman (950,000 rials) a month. This amounts to $1,323 a year at the 2004 official exchange rate. Were the average *Basij* member on the *Basij* payroll to receive a stipend equal to 15 percent of this amount, *Basij* personnel costs would be in the range of $0.6–$1.2 billion a year (International Crisis Group, "Update Briefing—Iran," 2005). The magnitude of these potential costs is reflected by the decision of the *Majlis* in late 2004 to vote for the withdrawal of $350 million from Iran's Foreign Exchange Reserve Fund to pay for *Basij* expenses (Samaneh Ekvan, "Reserve Fund Rivalry," *Iran Daily*, December 13, 2004, p. 6).

The Impact of Nuclear Weapons on Iranian Military Strategy Remains Uncertain

While our discussion in Chapter Two sets forth the rationale for Iranian acquisition of nuclear weapons, what is less clear is the Iranian leadership's own thinking about how such weapons could be deployed and employed to bolster the country's defense and protect the regime. Aside from the routine denials by Iranian officials about the military purpose of their nuclear program, reading Tehran's intentions is especially difficult given its strategic culture and decisionmaking processes.[68] Opacity, indirectness, and parallelism would appear to inform much of Iranian strategy on critical policy issues, and the incorporation of a nuclear arsenal into its defense doctrine is likely to follow similar precepts.

Available military literature in Iran has touched on the subject of nuclear weapons at both the strategic and operational levels. One Iranian writer noted their deterrent value:

> Through the effective implementation of nuclear deterrence, governments will attain the stage of security measures and trust building that we have baptized as the international security regime . . . . [G]overnments that accept voluntarily to be among the have-nots would expose themselves to uncertainty and enjoy no guarantee or support for their survival.[69]

In asking "What will future wars be like?" a writer in the Iranian military journal *Saff* answers, "In the future, tactical doctrine is likely to emphasize [the element of] surprise, an understanding of defense, superior firepower, nuclear weapons, and communications."[70]

---

[68] For example, Ali Larijani, then–Secretary of the SNSC and a negotiator on nuclear matters, said in February 2007 that "repeatedly and frankly we have announced that in Iran's national security doctrine there is no room for atomic and chemical weapons as we consider them against Islamic laws" ("No Room for WMDs in Iran's National Security Doctrine, Says Larijani," IRNA, distributed by United Press International, February 11, 2007).

[69] Khan, 1998.

[70] "Iran: Magazine Looks at What Future Wars May Be Like," 2001, pp. 17–20.

Recent RAND research on nuclear-armed regional adversaries suggests that such regimes may believe that nuclear weapons could deter the United States from intervening or projecting power in their region, blunt U.S. military operations if deterrence fails, intimidate U.S. regional partners into denying the United States access to bases, and limit U.S. objectives (especially dissuading the United States from seeking to impose regime change).[71] Assuming that Tehran is indeed striving for nuclear weapons, how might Iranian acquisition unfold? And how might Iranian military doctrine evolve in the presence of these weapons?

Paths for Crossing the Nuclear Threshold Carry Risks for Tehran

Based on its perceptions of the security environment and its domestic legitimacy, Tehran could take a path to join the nuclear club that lies along a continuum between transparency (open acknowledgment that it has acquired a nuclear weapons capability) and opacity (secretly acquiring the capability and denying or slowly leaking that Tehran possesses it). Each method confers both costs and benefits for Iran in terms of diplomatic standing and deterrence value.

Transparency. Tehran might undertake a full declaration of its nuclear arsenal through open testing if it sensed an imminent threat to its survival or a drastic decline in relations with regional states. In these cases, the regime would calculate that the need to unambiguously convey a nuclear capability would outweigh the probable international criticism Iran would incur for breaking its obligations under the Nuclear Non-Proliferation Treaty. Additionally, Tehran might choose this path in times of domestic crisis, believing that an open test would produce an outpouring of nationalistic fervor and popular support for the regime.

---

[71] This research also suggests that Iran's conventional military weaknesses could make it more dangerous in a conflict in which its leaders perceive regime survival to be at risk. These leaders may be more prone to see the brandishing or use of nuclear weapons as their only means of changing the military situation in their favor. See David Ochmanek and Lowell Schwartz, *The Challenge of Nuclear-Armed Regional Adversaries*, Santa Monica, Calif.: RAND Corporation, MG-671-AF, 2008.

Opacity. A strategy of opacity would be taken by a regime that is relatively confident of its regional posture and enjoys good relations with neighboring states, yet seeks an additional layer of deterrence. Taking this path, Tehran would subtly reveal the existence of its nuclear weapon in a less confrontational manner to avoid forcing an explicit security dilemma on GCC and other neighboring states. Iran might continue flight tests and public displays of an extended-range Shahab while at the same time leaking evidence of its nuclear warhead capability. Tehran may believe that without detonation testing and full acknowledgement, regional states would feel less threatened and be less inclined to cut ties with Iran and join a U.S. security umbrella. Additionally, this path may allow Iranian leaders to preserve at least the fiction of adherence to the Nuclear Non-Proliferation Treaty. As noted in Chapter Two, such an option is consistent with Tehran's strategic culture and previous policies: opening multiple, seemingly contradictory avenues of influence, using both inducements and threats, and cloaking them in subtle ambiguity. One major drawback, however, is that without open testing, Tehran's planners might be uncertain of the weapon's reliability.[72]

On the other hand, Tehran may adopt "opacity" as a means of concealing the limitations of its program while conveying to the outside world some capability "heretofore unknown" that could be unleashed if Iran is attacked. In this way, the Islamic Republic could create a perceptual, or "virtual," deterrent even when its actual progress toward a nuclear weapon capability may be marginal. However, over-emphasizing this in a threatening way may have the effect of increasing U.S. influence with Iran's Persian Gulf Arab neighbors at a time when Iran lacks the capabilities to back up its rhetoric.

The choice between transparency and opacity will ultimately hinge on Tehran's reading of regional threats and U.S. strategic intent as reflected by the U.S. military posture in the region. Certainly, the regime's understanding of these issues is fraught with paranoia and sus-

---

[72] For a discussion of transparency and opacity, see Kori N. Schake and Judith S. Yaphe, "The Strategic Implications of a Nuclear-Armed Iran," McNair Paper 64, Washington, D.C.: National Defense University, 2001, pp. 13–14.

ceptible to distortion and miscalculation. A lingering U.S. presence in Iraq, a military buildup in Central Asia and the Caucuses, the threat of sanctions or interruption of oil trade, or an increasingly assertive U.S. naval presence in the Persian Gulf could all stir Iranian fears of encirclement, bolstering the conclusion that an open test is the most expeditious deterrent. Conversely, Tehran's perception of robust trade and diplomatic ties with the GCC and Central Asia; healthy relations with the European Union, Russia, and China; and an American military preoccupied with Afghanistan and Iraq might push the regime toward a less blatant revelation or even a full deferment of acknowledging Iran's nuclear capability. However, it is reasonable to speculate that transparency may be the greater risk for Tehran with violation of the Nuclear Non-Proliferation Treaty potentially leading to economically devastating sanctions and, possibly, preventive war against it.

Nuclear Weapons Are Unlikely to Supplant Other Iranian Deterrent Options

If Tehran does cross the nuclear threshold, how might Iranian planners integrate nuclear weapons into a larger defense strategy, and how would this new capability affect Iranian conventional forces and warfighting doctrine? On the issue of nuclear command and control, there are many unknowns, and it is quite possible that Iranian leaders have not fully thought through specific procedures.[73] An article from *Saff* does gives some indication of Iranian thinking on nuclear command and control by stating that "the control of nuclear weapons on the battlefield requires that under the necessary conditions one must have rapid and reliable communications, and one must also use modern, rehearsed and swift methods."[74]

Others have argued that Iran will seek to challenge the prevailing orthodoxies on deploying, posturing, and targeting nuclear weapons, believing that the mere acquisition of the bomb (or even nuclear technology itself) will be a sufficient psychological deterrent. Press statements, writings in military journals, and other glimpses into Iranian

[73] Cordesman, 2005, p. 139.

[74] "Iran: Magazine Looks at What Future Wars May Be Like," 2001, pp. 17–20.

thinking on this issue appear to support the conclusion that Tehran regards nuclear weapons as powerful psychological assets but poor warfighting tools. For example, in an April 2003 press interview, a senior Iranian air force commander noted,

> In today's wars, the most important instruments of military power are nuclear, chemical and electronic. The first two because of the damage to generations and the residue in international communities, have limited application.[75]

Despite these unknowns, however, one can speculate about nuclear command and control and the associated military activity that would accompany this weapon. Given the IRGC's current control of Iran's strategic missile forces and any chemical weapons in its inventory, it is likely that the management of nuclear weapon storage, launch facilities, command and control, and delivery systems would also fall to this elite force.[76] However, it is also possible that the Iranian leadership's penchant for bureaucratic counterbalancing could play out in relation to such a critical capability. Namely, the Supreme Leader could create a parallel, IRGC-competitor institution charged specifically with oversight of nuclear weapons and associated command, control, communications, computers, and intelligence capabilities. This would prevent the IRGC from controlling both paramilitary operations and terrorism *and* the regime's strategic deterrence options. Likewise, the leadership could task separate organizations to control dual-purpose delivery means, such as ballistic missiles and certain strike aircraft (e.g., the Fencer or, if acquired, the Backfire).

To protect the nuclear infrastructure, Iran would put heavy emphasis on conventional forces required to defend it from threats ranging from special operations through conventional strike to nuclear attack. The IRGC would likely direct an intense denial and deception effort, expanding the construction of underground shelters, decoys,

---

[75] Lt. Col. Rahmatollah Salmani Mahini, interview with Brig. Gen. Naser Ma'sumarast, "Electronic Warfare Past and Present," *Saff* (Tehran), in Persian, FBIS IAP2003042000149, April 28, 2003, pp. 16–18.

[76] See Giles, 2000.

and camouflaged TELs, as well as focused improvements in active defenses. A major effort would also be required to develop survivable, redundant communications to ensure positive control of nuclear weapons and delivery means during crisis and conflict. Iran would also want to acquire adequate targeting, tactical warning, and attack assessment capabilities, which may nudge it toward an accelerated space effort, deployment of satellites, and cooperation with other space powers.

The IRGCAF and IRIAF would bolster Iran's nationwide air defenses, focusing on point defense, low-altitude radar coverage, and the integration of disparate systems from different countries. It is unlikely, however, that the IRGCAF would devolve any measure of authority or operational control over nuclear-related air defenses to the regular air force, given the sensitivity of these sites and the current state of rivalry between the two services. The advent of a nuclear weapon capability could therefore shift greater resources and funding to the IRGCAF (especially for surface-based air defenses), resulting in a corresponding atrophy of the regular air force. This has the potential to be a severe source of tension between the two organizations, especially if it involves transferring existing assets to the IRGC.

At first glance, a nuclear-armed Iran that feels reasonably confident of its deterrent posture might be expected to reduce its reliance on conventional forces, some parts of its doctrine related to asymmetric warfare in homeland defense, or its sea denial capabilities in the Strait of Hormuz. Despite this temptation, however, the regime is likely to retain multiple layers of deterrence, continuing to modernize its conventional military even at the expense of other priorities. First, Tehran would need to address the multitude of challenges involved in developing a credible deterrent and understanding the factors that underpin it, and conventional forces will remain an important part of that deterrent. Iran will continue to face uncertainty regarding its neighbors, to include Iraq, over the long term. For many contingencies, it would continue to need conventional or non-nuclear asymmetric capabilities both to deter invasion and to conduct combat operations. In many contingencies, nuclear weapons might be inappropriate or lack credibility as a deterrent or military instrument. And related to the credibility issue, even when confronting the United States—indeed, especially when confronting the United States given the vast disparity between U.S. and Iranian nuclear capabilities—Iran's existential nuclear deterrent may suffer from severe credibility problems except in those cases in which regime survival is directly threatened or in which Iran faces catastrophic losses. If Tehran assumes that the most likely future is one involving long-term competition with the United States, it must have robust alternatives to the use of nuclear weapons. Otherwise, it becomes hostage to a narrow set of responses. Finally, in the event of some version of a U.S. invasion, the most credible nuclear threat may be one that is made while U.S. and Iranian conventional forces are engaged.

Second, a number of other factors may drive Tehran to continue to develop and sustain its conventional forces even if it were to acquire nuclear weapons. There are sufficient bureaucratic impulses within the military to convince key decisionmakers that Tehran's external procurement and domestic modernization program should continue unabated. Moreover, Tehran is seeking to become a major arms exporter to the Third World, and the addition of the bomb to its arsenal is unlikely to derail this effort.[77] And finally, Tehran would likely maintain a desire to project the image of a "first power" in the Middle East, and this would include the capacity to field a more modern, multifaceted military. However, Iran's future military modernization efforts could suffer if the acquisition of nuclear weapons spurs outside arms suppliers to halt shipments and technical assistance as part of a larger sanctions regime; they may also suffer if the development, maintenance, defense, and improvement of a nuclear weapon infrastructure and delivery means siphoned resources away from indigenous production of conventional armaments.

---

[77] Iranian Student News Agency, FBIS IAP20050722011019, July 22, 2005. In this report, Shamkhani states that military exports themselves are an important foundation of Iran's deterrence strategy.

Conclusions

Iran's strategy is largely defensive, but with some offensive elements. Iran's strategy of protecting the regime against internal threats, deterring aggression, safeguarding the homeland if aggression occurs, and extending influence is in large part a defensive one that also serves some aggressive tendencies when coupled with expressions of Iranian regional aspirations. It is in part a response to U.S. policy pronouncements and posture in the region, especially since the terrorist attacks of September 11, 2001. The Iranian leadership takes very seriously the threat of invasion given the open discussion in the United States of regime change, speeches defining Iran as part of the "axis of evil," and efforts by U.S. forces to secure base access in states surrounding Iran. However, this threat has diminished somewhat in the minds of Iranian planners—at least for now—in light of the new administration in Washington and the demands U.S. involvement in Iraq and Afghanistan have placed on U.S. combat forces.

Iran seeks to attain and enhance capabilities at the low and high ends of the spectrum of conflict. At the low end, Iran focuses on support for terrorist groups, subversion, agitation of external Shi'ite communities, and asymmetric tactics against invasion. At the high end, Iran pursues ballistic and cruise missile capabilities and, probably, nuclear weapons. In addition, Iranian leaders seek to deter the United States and Israel and intimidate U.S. allies by emphasizing Iran's ability to exact an enormous cost for aggression against it based on many of these capabilities (nuclear weapons excepted) and some additional ones it claims are unknown to the outside world.

Iran's military doctrine is well suited to its defense strategy. Iran's military doctrine and major CONOPs are formulated to support its defense strategy. Iran fields some capabilities that are well suited to implementing these concepts. Iran's ballistic missile forces hold at risk assets the United States and its regional allies value and could constitute a psychological factor in any conflict. As Iran's missile force becomes bigger and more capable, it will pose a growing threat to military forces and bases in the region. These missiles, along with antimaritime capabilities, could enable Iran to impede U.S. access to the region and disrupt the exploitation, refining, and export of Persian Gulf energy resources. Finally, Iranian forces have formidable capabilities to greatly complicate any invasion and occupation of the country.

However, Iran faces severe shortcomings in its military capabilities, which fall short doctrinally and operationally. Despite a major emphasis on asymmetric warfare in its military doctrine, Iran's ability to support this doctrine still falls short in some areas due to conventional inertia, decrepitude in a number of components (such as its air forces), procurement patterns, and shortfalls in training. Moreover, although Tehran's layered and overlapping security structures are key pillars of the regime's survivability in the face of potential unrest, the redundancy of roles and competition for resources between the different security organs creates friction, ambiguity, and institutional rivalry. These conditions, despite the regime's best attempts to overcome them through exercises and training, are damaging to battlefield performance and multiservice operations. Thus, the very sources of Iran's *internal* security may degrade its capability against an *external* threat. There is little sign that Iran will soon acquire meaningful numbers of late-generation conventional systems or greatly improve readiness, command and control, and other hallmarks of a modern army. While the ballistic missile force is certainly a psychological tool to be reckoned with in regard to U.S. allies in the region, it will be difficult for Iran to seriously disrupt U.S. deployments and operations without significant increases in accuracy and payload provided the United States and its GCC partners continue to harden key facilities.[78]

Despite existing weaknesses, Tehran is enhancing some capabilities that in future years could present challenges to U.S. military operations in the region. Iran will continue to emphasize doctrine and capabilities at both ends of the spectrum of conflict, but it will also pursue a wide range of conventional means if only because of bureaucratic inertia and vested interests that will exert pressure on the government to improve these capabilities even if they are doctrinally unrealistic. Iran will also continue to seek ways to threaten U.S. power projection oper-

---

[78] The introduction of Iranian nuclear-armed ballistic missiles would require a reassessment of U.S. concepts for power projection.

ations—including the deployment and employment of airpower using bases in the region—and likely will improve these capabilities as long as animosity forms the foundation of the long-term U.S.-Iranian relationship. In the near term, weaknesses in Iranian CONOPs, military equipment, and infrastructure will limit the Islamic Republic's options in a crisis or conflict with the United States. Although important areas of its military capability are in disrepair and show few signs of improving quickly, Iran could potentially field capabilities that could challenge U.S. interests, influence, and force posture in the region. Future enhancements to Iran's arsenal of ballistic missiles and in its asymmetrically oriented naval operations could be among the most promising areas of emphasis for Iranian planners. And, of course, a future arsenal of nuclear weapons and associated delivery means could be a key element in Iran's quest to threaten the ability of U.S. commanders to deploy and employ military power effectively to protect U.S. interests in the region.

CHAPTER FOUR

Iran and Its Non-State Partners: Assessing Linkages and Control

As noted in Chapter One, support to non-state Islamist actors around the globe forms an important component of Iran's power projection, deterrence, and retaliatory strategy. With Iran's perceived encirclement following the U.S.-backed toppling of the regimes of the Taliban and Saddam Hussein, this strategy has grown in importance, albeit not for the same aims that defined Tehran's early support to Shi'ite militants following the revolution.

In the early years of the Islamic Republic, the main objective of Iranian foreign policy was to export the revolution, most significantly to areas marked by Shi'ite marginalization in the Persian Gulf states and Lebanon. Iran sought ties with existing Islamist organizations, both Sunni and Shi'ite, and created some new ones as part of an effort to challenge ruling regimes throughout the Middle East. In more recent years, though, Iranian foreign policy has moved away from this revolutionary objective and back to a more traditional emphasis on state-to-state power politics—dealing with regimes as they are rather than trying to violently overturn them.

Nevertheless, Iran continues to provide lethal support to regional terrorists and paramilitaries for a variety of reasons. In the case of Palestinian groups and Hezbollah, this rejectionist strategy buys Iran enormous symbolic currency among Arab publics who are frustrated with the seemingly status quo approach of their authoritarian regimes. Together with Syria, Tehran has calculated that its lethal support to Hezbollah, the Palestinian Islamic Jihad (PIJ), and Hamas will enable it to play a spoiler role in the peace process at critical junctures. As will be discussed in depth below, however, this expectation is ultimately subject to the calculations of these local groups, who often act or abstain from action independently from Tehran's wishes.

Aside from the Palestinian cause, Tehran supports terrorists and paramilitaries as agents of political influence who can exert pressure on unfriendly regional governments at critical moments. As noted above, the goal is not to overthrow these regimes but to "make the pot boil," as one scholar described Iran's paramilitary strategy in Iraq.[1] More importantly, though, lethal support to terrorists gives Tehran a retaliatory capability against U.S. assets and allied regimes in regional states, should hostilities erupt. Finally, in light of regional sectarian tensions stemming from Iraq, Iran also intends for its military support to Shi'ite militants to empower local Shi'ites against the threat from Sunni radicals and militias. While Iran does not actively seek to create a civil war in Iraq or elsewhere, it will nonetheless exploit sectarian strife to bolster its position as a regional patron of the Shi'ites and to block the expansion of Sunni Arab, particularly Saudi, influence.

This chapter addresses the dynamics of Iranian patronage to violent non-state actors, focusing specifically on three groups of critical importance to long-term U.S./DoD and USAF interests in the region: the Lebanese Hezbollah and, in Iraq, the SCIRI (now the ISCI) and the followers of Iraqi cleric Muqtada al-Sadr. We first identify the mechanisms through which Iran provides support to these groups, drawing from some general observations about Iranian support to non-state partners worldwide. We then examine in greater depth the history and evolution of Tehran's relationship with Hezbollah, the ISCI, and the Sadr movement, as well as shifts in how these groups perceive Iran as a spiritual mentor, reliable supplier of weapons, political advisor, or overly demanding patron. In all three cases, Iran's influence is circumscribed by a host of factors—most significantly, these groups' own calculations about whether Iranian aid advances their own domestic agendas.

---

[1]   Comments by a scholar of Iran at a Washington, D.C., conference on regional Shi'ite dynamics, September 30, 2004.

Based on these limitations, we assess that Iran will never reliably *control* these groups and that, even in the case of Hezbollah, Iran's expenditure of financial resources and military aid has not translated into unquestioned loyalty by a group it essentially founded. Thus, the use of the term "proxy" to define the relationship between Iran and its regional militant allies is overstated and inaccurate, with important implications for U.S. strategy. Most significantly, Tehran's support to these groups appears quite cynical and calculated—Iran would not hesitate to barter or terminate its patronage if it perceived that the state's broader strategic aims would be better served. This dynamic is most evident in Tehran's May 2003 offer to the United States to effectively disarm Hezbollah.

In addition, the willingness of these organizations to act as retaliatory agents for Tehran during an open conflict between the United States and Iran should not be taken as a priori. Instead, the decision to employ violence on Tehran's behalf will be based on a complex set of calculations that are rooted in these groups' perception of their domestic standing, their fear of a direct threat from the United States due to their affiliation with Iran, and, possibly, their calculations about whether the Islamic Republic would survive a U.S. attack. Fractionalization and splintering within these groups may occur between pro-Iranian and neutral wings, possibly with the tacit approval of Tehran. Alternately, the leadership of these groups may decide to secretly subcontract retaliatory attacks to a spin-off or "rogue" element to preserve deniability and ensure the continued political survival of the mainstream body.

By focusing on these variables and not categorizing these groups as Tehran's automatons, the menu of policy options available to the United States expands, with important implications for exploiting fissures and disagreements.

Iran Exerts Influence Through Various Kinds of Support

Iran provides many different types of support to its non-state partners, ranging from materiel and technical assistance to spiritual guidance. This support can be categorized as follows:

- **Financial support.** Iran supplies many of its partners with cash payments that can be used to support all of their various activities. These funds are used to pay recruits and new members, purchase armaments, sustain logistics networks, and otherwise underwrite their activities. Such financial assistance enables group members to focus on the substance of their activities rather than on fund-raising. Furthermore, financial assistance can help make groups self-sustaining: Groups with more resources can do more things than poorly funded rivals and can in turn attract more recruits and more funds for more activities.[2]
- **Military assistance.** Iran provides many different forms of military assistance to its non-state partners. It provides weapons ranging from small arms to heavy weaponry and advanced technologies that non-state groups often cannot develop or procure on their own. Iran also provides the training that is the vital link in turning weaponry into true military capability. As discussed in Chapter Three, the elite Qods Force specializes in training foreign partners. It often brings members of its partner groups to Iran for training and, in some cases, will provide training opportunities in the groups' home countries.
- **Social services.** Iran often provides the funding and organizational capacity that enables its partners to build social service networks. These have proven particularly important in conflict zones where the government has stopped providing basic educational, medical, and humanitarian services. Groups that can step in and provide for these basic human needs are likely to gain loyalty and support, even among people who do not have a natural ideological affinity for the groups' goals.

---

[2]   Byman, *Deadly Connections*, 2005, pp. 60–61.

- **Ideological influences.** As the country with the largest Shi'ite population and the birthplace of the Islamic Revolution, Iran sees itself as a natural religious leader.[3] It provides financial and spiritual support to Shi'ite scholars and clerics throughout the Muslim world, and it promotes the Iranian city of Qom as one of the main centers of Shi'ite scholarship.

Iran provides a wide range of assistance to its non-state partners to maximize its influence. These different forms of assistance reinforce each other and ensure that the groups cannot easily switch loyalties. A group might easily decide to reject Iranian military assistance if it could get weapons from another source, for example, but it would be much less likely to receive the same levels of training, financial resources, and ideological justification that Iran currently provides. Thus the multi-faceted nature of assistance is part of an Iranian strategy to make Iran's support indispensable and thereby increase Tehran's influence over its partners' activities.

This strategy has its limits, however. Influence is not the same as control. Many of Iran's partners have other sources of support—most commonly, revenues from smuggling routes and criminal behavior—which means that they can afford to run against Iranian interests without risking their own survival. Groups that receive significant assistance from Iran, especially across multiple issue areas, are likely to accommodate Iranian interests when they can. But Tehran's assistance does not buy unconditional loyalty; these groups may be willing to act independently when their own organizational interests and agendas are at stake.

The rest of this chapter examines how these support mechanisms function in two cases that are particularly important to the United States: Hezbollah in Lebanon and Shi'ite groups in Iraq. Though the historical background and context of these two cases vary considerably,

---

[3] Iran's population includes 61.8 million Shi'ites, which is approximately 90 percent of the total population. Pakistan ranks second, with 33.2 million Shi'ites (about 20 percent of the total population), and Iraq ranks third, with 17.4 million Shi'ites (about 65 percent of the total population). (Vali Nasr, "When the Shi'ites Rise," *Foreign Affairs*, Vol. 85, No. 4, July/August 2006, p. 65.)

they share some important common features that allow us to make a broader assessment about Tehran's relationship with its militant partners worldwide—namely, that Iranian support does not automatically lead to Iranian control.

Lebanon: Iran Maintains Strategic Influence Over, But Not Control of, Hezbollah

Iran has pursued its multifaceted relationship with Hezbollah in the pursuit of several strategic objectives. First, Lebanon remains one of the few places to which Iran can claim to have successfully exported its revolutionary agenda. While it is arguable that this objective had greater resonance in the 1980s than it does today, one should not underestimate its importance to hardliners within the Iranian regime, especially within the IRGC. Second, Iran's support for Hezbollah provides an opportunity to strengthen its influence within Syria and Lebanon. Similarly, Iran has derived collateral acclaim from Arab publics for its role in sponsoring Hezbollah as an anti-Israeli force. And third, Hezbollah remains an asset for Iran because of the threat and distraction it poses to U.S. forces in Iraq and elsewhere in the region.[4] As part of its strategy of deterring the United States, Iran points to Hezbollah's 2006 war with Israel as a validation of its own asymmetric strategy, with the warning that the United States can expect a similarly lethal guerilla opponent in the form of *Basij* paramilitary units.[5]

Historical Ties Between Iran and Hezbollah

The historical relationship between Hezbollah and Iran can be traced back to the 1960s and the Shi'ite city of Najaf in Iraq. Figure 4.1 shows

---

[4]   Indeed, Chapter Two argues that Iran uses its relationship with Hezbollah and Islamic Jihad as an instrument of deterrence, especially in the aftermath of the 2006 conflict with Israel.

[5]   For an overview of Iran-Hezbollah relations and the role of Syria, see Abbas William Samii, "A Stable Structure on Shifting Sands: Assessing the Hizbullah-Iran-Syria Relationship," *The Middle East Journal*, Vol. 62, No. 1, Winter 2008, pp. 32–53. For the strategic utility of Iran's support, see Chubin, 2002, pp. 88–95.

Figure 4.1
Key Events in the Relationship Between Iran and Hezbollah Since the 1960s

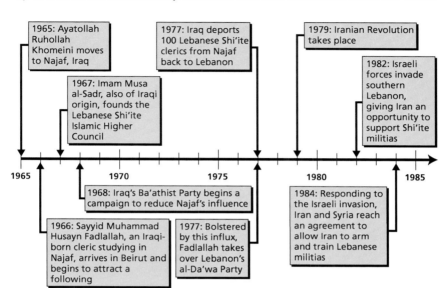

RAND *MG781-4.1*

key events in the evolution of this relationship. Many Lebanese clerics traveled to Najaf to study with well-respected Shi'ite intellectuals in the seminaries there, such as Ayatollahs Muhsin al-Hakim and Muhammad Baqir al-Sadr. Ayatollah Ruhollah Khomeini also resided in Najaf between 1965 and 1978, allowing the development of strong personal ties between leading Iraqi, Iranian, and Lebanese Shi'ite clerics.[6] One of these clerics was Sayyid Muhammad Husayn Fadlallah, who some experts now believe functions as Hezbollah's spiritual guide, while others contend that the relationship is unclear.[7] Regardless of whether

---

[6] For more information, see Martin Kramer, "Muslim Statecraft and Subversion," *Middle East Contemporary Survey, 1983–84*, Vol. 8, 1986, pp. 170–173.

[7] Magnus Ranstorp, for example, attributes Fadlallah as Hezbollah's spiritual guide, while Amal Saad-Ghorayeb argues otherwise. See Magnus Ranstorp, *Hezbollah in Lebanon*, New York: St. Martin's Press, 1997; Amal Saad-Ghorayeb, *Hizbullah: Politics and Religion*, London: Pluto Press, 2002.

or not Fadlallah has a direct relationship with Hezbollah, most experts agree that his beliefs have made an impact on the organization.[8]

Upon assuming power in 1968, Iraq's Ba'ath Party began a campaign to suppress Najaf's influence. This campaign included the 1977 deportation of approximately 100 Lebanese Shi'ite clerics studying in Najaf back to Lebanon.[9] Fadlallah, who had traveled to Beirut in 1966, found his modest group of Lebanese followers bolstered by this influx from Iraq. This proved critical in allowing him to take control of the fledgling al-Da'wa Party in Lebanon.

At its establishment, the purpose of al-Da'wa was to reform Lebanon's more secular political establishment from within. But al-Da'wa was confronted with a significant contender for Shi'ite support in Lebanon in the form of another revolutionary movement, the *Afwaj al-Muqawama al-Lubnaniya* (AMAL). AMAL had been active, particularly in southern Lebanon, since the mid-1970s. AMAL also had strong ties with Iran. In 1959, an Iranian-born Lebanese cleric, Musa al-Sadr, was invited to act as the religious leader of the Shi'ites in Lebanon. As part of this role, Sadr subsequently founded the Lebanese Shi'ite Islamic Higher Council in 1967 as well as a series of militias, including AMAL in 1975.[10] The purpose of these militias was to protect Shi'ite residents of southern Lebanon from Israeli forces, Lebanese Christian militias, and, to a certain extent, Palestinian guerillas. Al-Da'wa was able to recruit members away from AMAL, apparently due to their opposition to AMAL's more secular nature.[11]

Notably, some of AMAL's leaders also disagreed with its more secular nature. In particular, AMAL's deputy leader, Abbas al-Musawi, championed an Islamic agenda for AMAL. Al-Musawi also expressed some concern over Syria's growing influence over AMAL. Therefore, al-Musawi pushed AMAL into a situation where its leaders essentially

---

[8]   Ranstorp, 1997; Saad-Ghorayeb, 2002.

[9]   Saad-Ghorayeb, 2002, p. 13.

[10] These militias were established as part of a wider conflict, and indeed civil war, that began in April 1975 and continued for approximately 15 years (Hala Jaber, *Hezbollah: Born with a Vengeance*, New York: Columbia University Press, 1997, pp. 11–12).

[11] Saad-Ghorayeb, 2002, p. 14.

had to choose between a more secular (Syria) or religious (Iran) strategy. AMAL's leaders chose to pursue a more secular revolution, which eventually resulted in Iran's public denunciation of AMAL in the early 1980s.[12] This denunciation coincided with al-Musawi's departure from the AMAL movement and his creation of "Islamic AMAL."

Following the 1979 Iranian Revolution, Iran's leaders also began to encourage the more radical members of al-Da'wa to leave the party. According to Magnus Ranstorp, Iran encouraged this defection because it viewed Lebanon as an excellent prospect for the exportation of the revolution.[13] Martin Kramer also observes in his research that in the early 1980s, Fadlallah publicly disagreed with Iran on Lebanon's place in the revolution, believing that an Islamic Republic in Lebanon would emerge gradually and over a longer period of time.[14] Iran encouraged the defection of al-Da'wa members in response to this disagreement, thus reinforcing a pattern in which Iran has encouraged splinter groups in situations where disagreement exists. Several notable Hezbollah leaders were part of this defection, including current leader Hassan Nasrallah. Most of these individuals joined with al-Musawi in forming the Islamic AMAL. The leadership of Islamic AMAL, soon to be known as Hezbollah, therefore drew its members from both the more militant-minded AMAL activists and the more spiritual-minded al-Da'wa Party. In both cases—al-Da'wa and AMAL—Tehran exacerbated fissures within the organizations as their leadership began to adopt a strategy counter to Iranian interests.[15]

The Israeli invasion of Lebanon in 1982 provided a critical opening for Iran to expand its influence with the Shi'ite militias through military training and financial support. Yet at the same time and somewhat ironically, Israel's eventual occupation of southern Lebanon dis-

---

[12] Ranstorp, 1997, pp. 31–32.

[13] Ranstorp, 1997, p. 30.

[14] Martin Kramer, "The Moral Logic of Hezbollah," in Walter Reich, ed., *Origins of Terrorism: Psychologies, Ideologies, Theologies, States of Mind,* Washington, D.C.: Woodrow Wilson Center Press, 1998, p. 138.

[15] Iran's strategy of exploiting fissures within organizations it supports may also be repeated in Iraq, as discussed in the following section.

tracted Hezbollah from its pursuit of Iran's ideological revolution in favor of removing Israeli forces. In March 1984, responding to the Israeli invasion, Iran and Syria reached an agreement that would allow Iran to arm and train Lebanese militias.[16] Iran initially sent 800 IRGC members into Lebanon to train Islamic AMAL members, in particular, to fight against Israeli soldiers. Soon thereafter, Iran sent approximately 700 additional IRGC personnel to establish six camps in the Beka'a Valley and participate in training activities. Trainees received stipends of $150–200 per month in the camps.[17] In addition to the IRGC, it is worth noting that Iran reportedly also sent approximately 30 to 40 clerics to Lebanon in an effort to strengthen ties and pursue its revolutionary agenda. According to one source, Iran spent approximately $50 million in aid to the militias in the mid-1980s.[18]

In this initial period, several factors laid the foundation for a strong future partnership between Hezbollah and Iran. Primarily, Hezbollah and Iran shared personal, religious, financial, and military ties. Yet beyond these personal and organizational ties, Hezbollah's leaders observed, from very early on, an Iranian tendency to denounce and even fracture those allies that choose an alternative path. For example, Iran encouraged members of AMAL to defect as its leaders developed a closer relationship with Syria. Iran also encouraged members to defect from al-Da'wa when its leaders expressed hesitation in applying Iran's revolution to Lebanon. Based on these experiences, it seems likely that Hezbollah's leaders believed the internal cohesion—and even survival—of their organization rested on maintaining close ties to Tehran. This belief may continue to a certain extent even today.

---

[16] "Baalbek Seen as Staging Area for Terrorism," *Washington Post*, January 9, 1984; Anthony Wege, "Hizbollah Organization," *Studies in Conflict and Terrorism*, Vol. 17, No. 2, 1994, pp. 151–164; Jerry Green, "Terrorism and Politics in Iran," in Martha Crenshaw, ed., *Terrorism in Context*, University Park, Pa.: Pennsylvania State University Press, 1995, pp. 553–594.

[17] "Baalbek Seen As Staging Area for Terrorism," 1984; Wege, 1994; Green, 1995, pp. 553–594.

[18] Green, 1995, pp. 553–594.

Iran Has Tried to Strengthen Its Influence Over Hezbollah

Tehran's initial hold over Hezbollah can be most readily discerned in the group's founding charter, which clearly defined the relationship between the Lebanese militia and its state patron. In February 1985, Hezbollah officially announced its existence in a document titled "Open Message from Hezbollah to the Downtrodden in Lebanon and the World." In this charter, Hezbollah described itself as follows:

> We, the sons of Hezbollah's nation in Lebanon, whose vanguard God has given victory in Iran and which established the nucleus of the world's central Islamic state, abide by the orders of the single wise and just command currently embodied in the supreme example of Ayatollah Khomeini.[19]

The statement indicates that Hezbollah leaders viewed themselves as part of a global Iranian revolution and answerable to Khomeini's authority. Indeed, at the time of this announcement, Iran had begun to use several mechanisms to exert influence over Hezbollah. Primarily, the IRGC provided guerrilla warfare training to Hezbollah leaders, members, and recruits. Officials in the Iranian embassy to Lebanon also interacted with Hezbollah.[20] Money and equipment traveled from Iran to the leaders of the Shi'ite militias, primarily via Syria.

Similarly, close parallels existed between Iran's and Hezbollah's interests in the mid- to late 1980s. Both Iran and Hezbollah wanted to remove multinational forces, particularly those including U.S. troops, from Lebanon. Both Iran and Hezbollah also wanted to repel Israeli interests in Lebanon. This parallel was reflected in Hezbollah's activities. For example, Hezbollah attacks during the mid-1980s can be grouped into two basic categories: suicide attacks on Israeli and mul-

---

[19] John Kelsay, *Islam and War: A Study in Comparative Ethics*, Louisville, Ky.: Westminister/John Knox Press, 1993, pp. 77–110.

[20] In *Pity the Nation*, Robert Fisk described a trip to the Iranian Embassy in 1985, noting that the guards outside the embassy were part of Hezbollah (Robert Fisk, *Pity the Nation*, 3rd ed., Oxford: Oxford University Press, 2001, p. 609). See also Magnus Ranstorp, "Hezbollah's Command Leadership," *Terrorism and Political Violence,* Vol. 6, No. 3, August 1994.

tinational forces and the kidnapping of Western hostages.[21] Figure 4.2
shows key Hezbollah attacks during the 1980s.

Interestingly, according to Martin Kramer and Magnus Ranstorp,
Hezbollah's leadership began to question the utility and morality of
hostage-taking and suicide attacks in the late 1980s.[22] The appropriate
role for suicide attacks was contentious because Ayatollah Khomeini
apparently did not provide any specific guidance on this tactic. Similarly, Fadlallah reportedly provided a justification for these attacks in
1983, but then subsequently retracted it.[23] The fact that Hezbollah

Figure 4.2
Hezbollah Attacks During the 1980s

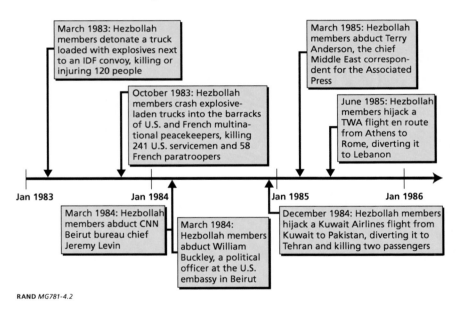

RAND MG781-4.2

---

[21]   For more information on Hezbollah tactics during this period, see Brian A. Jackson, John
C. Baker, Peter Chalk, Kim Cragin, John V. Parachini, and Horacio R. Trujillo, *Aptitude
for Destruction,* Santa Monica, Calif.: RAND Corporation, MG-331-NIJ and MG332-NIJ,
2005; Ranstorp, 1997; Jaber, 1997.

[22]   Magnus Ranstorp, "The Strategy and Tactics of Hezbollah's Current 'Lebanonization
Process,'" *Mediterranean Politics,* Vol. 3, No. 1, Summer 1998, pp. 103–134; Kramer, 1998.

[23]   Ranstorp, 1998; Kramer, 1998. See also Amal Saad-Ghorayeb, 2002, pp. 127–133.

leaders turned to Iran, as well as a closely associated cleric, for guidance on this issue further underscores the strength of the relationship between Iran and Hezbollah. It also indicates a willingness on the part of Hezbollah leaders to defer to Iran's judgment, at the very least in situations for which they do not have a strong opinion or when they need to maintain internal unity. Although the issue of suicide bombings was never fully resolved, the lack of direction from Iran and the ongoing internal Hezbollah debate apparently contributed to a decrease in the use of suicide attacks by 1986.

Iran also sought to maintain influence in Lebanon as a means to pursue both partnership and competition with Syria. Hezbollah thus became an impetus for cooperation between the two states, as well as a source of friction. Competition between Iran and Syria peaked in the late 1980s, which saw a significant increase in internecine violence between the various Lebanese militias—AMAL, Hezbollah, Lebanese Christian militias, and Palestinian guerrillas—in Lebanon. This violence was magnified by the militias' various nation-state proxies, namely Syria, Iran, and Israel.[24] The civil war finally reached its peak in 1989 and was resolved to a certain extent through the Taif Accords. The accords established a power-sharing arrangement among Christians, Sunnis, and Shi'ites in Lebanon; they also required all militias to decommission their weapons.[25] The one exception to this disarming was Hezbollah. In an agreement facilitated by Iran, Hezbollah was allowed to keep its weapons as long as it focused its attacks on Israeli rather than Lebanese targets.[26]

Iran solidified its ties with the Hezbollah leadership and cadre throughout the 1990s. For example, in 1992, Israeli forces assassinated then–Hezbollah leader Abbas al-Musawi.[27] Al-Musawi was succeeded

---

[24] For more information, see Robert Fisk, 2001; Ian Black and Benny Morris, *Israel's Secret Wars*, New York: Grove Weidenfeld, 1991.

[25] "Syrian Troops Enforce South Beirut Truce; Inter-Shiite Fighting Ends," *World News Digest*, June 3, 1988; "Baalbek Seen as Staging Area for Terrorism," 1984; Wege, 1994, pp. 151–164.

[26] "Syrian Troops Enforce South Beirut Truce," 1988; Wege, 1994, pp. 151–164.

[27] Peter Hirshberg, "Getting Smart," *Jerusalem Post*, December 17, 1992.

by Nasrallah, the current leader of Hezbollah. Nasrallah had responded to Iran's encouragement and defected from the al-Da'wa Party in the early 1980s; he also trained with IRGC members. Under Nasrallah's guidance, Hezbollah retaliated for the assassination of al-Musawi by attacking the Israeli embassy (1992) and a Jewish cultural center (1994) in Argentina. According to evidence revealed in the Argentina trials, individuals at the Iranian embassy there housed the responsible bombers and conveyed messages to and from Hezbollah leadership in Lebanon.[28] In fact, some evidence suggests that Hezbollah requested permission from Iran before actually conducting the attacks.[29] These attacks led to a tacit status quo between Hezbollah and Israel—Israel would not assassinate top Hezbollah leaders and Hezbollah would not attack Jewish targets outside of the Levant.

Similarly, in the mid-1990s, Nasrallah began to expand Hezbollah's presence in southern Lebanon to better access and infiltrate Israeli targets.[30] Israel responded by bombing villages sympathetic to Hezbollah. Once again, Hezbollah turned to Iran for help in its attempts to bolster popular support in southern Lebanon. Iran therefore increased its aid to Hezbollah significantly (to approximately $200 million annually).[31] Hezbollah used this money to establish *Jihad al-Bina'*, an organization that rebuilt homes destroyed by Israeli attacks. Hezbollah also created *al-Imdad*, which provides health workers and clinics

---

[28] "Focus on Hezbollah," *The Lebanon Report*, Vol. 4, No. 3, March 1993, pp. 6–7; "Buenos Aires: A Prime Target for Pro-Iranian Terror," *Jerusalem Post*, August 11, 1994; Israeli Ministry of Foreign Affairs, "Special Survey: Bombing of the AMIA Building in Buenos Aires," July 19, 1994; Katzman, 2003.

[29] According to Matthew Levitt, Argentina's intelligence service believes that Khamenei issued a *fatwa* permitting this attack (Matthew Levitt, "Iranian State Sponsorship of Terror: Threatening U.S. Security, Global Stability, and Regional Peace," Testimony Before the House International Relations Committee, February 16, 2005).

[30] For more information on Hezbollah's expansion in southern Lebanon, see Ranstorp, 1998, pp. 103–134; Sami Hajjar, "Hezbollah: Terrorism, National Liberation or Menace?" thesis, Carlisle Barracks, Pa.: U.S. Army War College, Strategic Studies Institute, August 2002.

[31] Ranstorp, 1998, pp. 103–134; Hajjar, 2002.

to Hezbollah sympathizers.[32] With regard to military technology, Iran also continued to provide Hezbollah with *katyusha* rockets so that it had the ability to launch attacks on Israeli towns in northern Israel. By 1996, with Iran's aid, Hezbollah was once again able to negotiate a status quo agreement with Israel—Israel would not bomb Hezbollah villages and Hezbollah would not launch *katyusha* rockets into northern Israel.[33]

This pattern—Hezbollah turning to Iran for help with its offensives/counteroffensives against Israel—continued throughout the 1990s until Israel's eventual withdrawal from southern Lebanon in May 2000. Indeed, Iran allegedly provided Hezbollah with numerous technologies that allowed this group to continue to inflict casualties on Israeli forces. Some of these technologies included night vision goggles, UAV technologies, remote-detonated IEDs, and BGM-71 tube-launched, optically tracked, wire-guided (TOW) missiles.[34] It is therefore arguable that Hezbollah was able to force Israel's withdrawal from southern Lebanon because of Iran's patronage.[35]

Experts believe that between May 2000 and August 2006, Iran maintained approximately 150 IRGC personnel in Lebanon, primarily to help Hezbollah with the acquisition and deployment of new

---

[32] Ranstorp, 1998, pp. 103–134; Jaber, 1997; Naim Qassam, *Hezbollah: The Story from Within*, London: Saqi Books, 2005.

[33] Such a status quo agreement is not beyond belief and, in fact, had precedent in the Hezbollah-Israel conflict. For example, in 1993 Israel Defense Forces Chief of Staff Ehud Barak made a public statement to this effect, which was reprinted in the September edition of *The Lebanon Report* ("What Security for the South?" *The Lebanon Report*, Vol. 4, No. 9, September 1993, p. 5).

[34] "Hezbollah and Israeli Wage Electronic War in South Lebanon," *Jane's Intelligence Review*, February 1, 1995; Leslie Susser, "Hezbollah Masters the TOW," *Jerusalem Report*, March 13, 2000, p. 18; and "Recognizing Iran as a Strategic Threat: An Intelligence Challenge for the United States," Staff Report of the House Permanent Select Committee on Intelligence, August 23, 2006.

[35] On August 15, 2006, al-Muqtadah aired a documentary on the life of Nasrallah. In this documentary, Nasrallah credited aid from Syria and Iran for Hezbollah's success against Israel in southern Lebanon that forced the May 2000 withdrawal ("Al-Jazirah TV Airs Documentary on Life, Rise of Hezbollah's Hasan Nasrallah," OpenSource.gov, GMP20060816637002, August 15, 2006).

weapon systems.[36] These weapons were transported from Iran by air or sea to Damascus and then overland to Lebanon in trucks.[37] For example, a *Jane's Intelligence Digest* article reported that in July 2006, Iran loaded eight Chinese-designed C-802 antiship cruise missiles and three launchers onto a transport plane at the military section of Mahrebad airport outside Tehran for shipment to Hezbollah via Syria.[38]

In addition to the weapon systems described above, the 2006 conflict revealed new information about Hezbollah's guerrilla warfare capabilities. According to experts, Hezbollah's strategy was to retain the capability to launch rockets into Israel over the course of the conflict, in effect waging a psychological campaign against the Israeli populace.[39] To do this, it used mobile rocket launchers, as seen in past confrontations with Israel. Hezbollah also placed some launchers on platforms that could be raised and lowered from holes in the ground. After the rockets were fired, Hezbollah teams would then lower the platforms and place fire-retardant blankets over the launchers to lessen their infrared signatures.[40] Israeli military reports also suggest that 45 percent of Israel's main battle tanks hit by Hezbollah antitank guided missiles were penetrated.[41]

Finally, it appears that Hezbollah became concerned enough about Israel's air capabilities in the summer of 2006 that it began to pursue countermeasures through Iran. Since August 14, 2006, some reports have suggested that flights originating in Tehran have been landing at Lebanon's al-Qusayr airport on a daily basis.[42] Most of these shipments appear to be aimed at resupplying Hezbollah's rocket stockpiles. But

---

[36] Katzman, 2003; "Arming Hizbullah," *Jane's Intelligence Digest*, October 20, 2006.

[37] Katzman, 2003; "Arming Hizbullah," 2006.

[38] Katzman, 2003; "Arming Hizbullah," 2006.

[39] "Deconstructing Hezbollah's Surprise Military Prowess," *Jane's Intelligence Review*, November 1, 2006.

[40] "Deconstructing Hezbollah's Surprise Military Prowess," 2006.

[41] "Israeli Armor Fails to Protect MBTs [Main Battle Tanks] from ATGMs [Antitank Guided Missiles]," *Jane's Defence Weekly*, August 30, 2006.

[42] "Arming Hizbullah," 2006

Hezbollah also has turned to Iran for newer technologies. For example, in September 2006, Cypriot authorities seized a freighter bound for Syria from Iran that was carrying 18 truck-mounted air-defense radars and three command vehicles.[43]

Iran Also Has Expectations of Hezbollah

Given Iran's continued support for Hezbollah over a period of 20 years, it is reasonable for Iran to expect something in return. For example, most experts agree that Iran expects Hezbollah to continue to pursue its revolutionary agenda in Lebanon, allowing Iranian clerics to teach in Hezbollah mosques, and advocating for an Islamic state in Lebanon.[44] It is difficult to determine how significant a priority this revolution is for Iran; it is likely more important for some components of the Iranian regime than others. But the continued emphasis on religious ties suggests that some expectation still exists.

Additionally, Iran apparently hopes that Hezbollah will regulate its own attacks against Israel in such a way that Iran will not get dragged into a direct confrontation with Israel or the United States.[45] This expectation might require that Hezbollah at least notify Iran before conducting a significant attack or making another strategic decision, such as the kidnapping of Israeli soldiers in the summer of 2006. But it might also suggest at least some degree of "permission" for strategic attacks, as was suggested by the Argentina bombings.

Finally, some U.S. government officials believe that Iran expects to be able to use Hezbollah as an extension of its military apparatus and more clandestine foreign policy.[46] That is, Iran might expect Hezbollah to conduct attacks ordered by the regime and yet still provide Iran with a certain degree of plausible deniability. One often-cited example is Hezbollah's alleged training of Shi'ite militias in Iraq. For example,

---

[43] "Arming Hizbullah," 2006

[44] Vali Nasr, "After Lebanon, There's Iran," *Christian Science Monitor*, August 9, 2006.

[45] Robert Grace and Andrew Mandelbaum, "Understanding the Iran-Hezbollah Connection," United States Institute of Peace Briefing, September 2006.

[46] U.S. Counterterrorism Coordinator Henry Crumpton, cited in "Recognizing Iran as a Strategic Threat: An Intelligence Challenge for the United States," 2006.

in November 2006, the *New York Times* cited a U.S. intelligence official who claimed that Hezbollah was providing training and assistance to the Mahdi Army in Iraq, including information on how to make shaped charges that have proven effective against armored vehicles.[47]

In sum, it is clear that Iran has worked to strengthen and expand its influence over Hezbollah over the past 24 years. Moreover, this relationship thus far has served Iran's strategic interests in the region, mainly its promotion of a revolutionary agenda, its animosity toward Israel, and its influence within Lebanon and Syria. Iran also likely perceives its relationship with Hezbollah as a potential counterweight against the United States should tensions rise further between the two countries. Just because the ongoing relationship furthers Iran's interests, however, does not necessarily mean that Hezbollah will always act in Iran's strategic interests.

Hezbollah's Commitment to Iran Fluctuates

At its inception, Hezbollah's leaders apparently viewed themselves as a vanguard of Iran's revolution in Lebanon and under the command of Ayatollah Khomeini, according to the aforementioned "Open Message from Hezbollah to the Downtrodden in Lebanon and the World." This statement was a clear departure from the position taken by Fadlallah and the al-Da'wa Party, who believed that an Islamic revolution would take place much more slowly in Lebanon than in Iran. Moreover, it was apparently reinforced by Iranian clerics sent to Hezbollah mosques in Lebanon, as well as trainers from the IRGC. Since that time, however, Hezbollah's interests with respect to its relationship with Iran have evolved as the group has matured and become a regional actor in its own right.

It is arguable that the first true shift in Hezbollah's interests came with the end of the Lebanese civil war and the 1989 Taif Accords. With Iran's acquiescence, these accords shifted Hezbollah's focus away from internal activities toward the fight against Israel. Indeed, as a result of the brokering of this agreement among Lebanese factions, Hezbollah

---

[47] Michael Gordan and Dexter Filkins, "Hezbollah Said to Help Shiite Army in Iraq," *New York Times*, November 28, 2006.

was forced to concentrate its efforts on a guerrilla campaign against Israeli forces in southern Lebanon, as opposed to attacking Western and Lebanese targets. As Hezbollah's efforts expanded in southern Lebanon, it needed to improve its local intelligence collection and so, similarly, it increased its social services and recruitment activities in the south. The expansion of Hezbollah's intelligence apparatus, of course, has been viewed and much discussed by experts as a significant contributing factor to its success against Israel.[48] Equally important, however, Hezbollah's recruitment efforts in southern Lebanon also helped direct its interests away from an Islamic revolution and toward national liberation.

Throughout the 1990s, Hezbollah's message to audiences—and, thus, potential recruits—in southern Lebanon reflected much less Islamic revolutionary goals than Lebanese nationalism. For example, according to Ron Schleifer from Bar Ilan University in Israel, Hezbollah's messages between 1991 and 2000 incorporated a mix of Shi'ite fundamentalism and national liberation rhetoric.[49] Schleifer's study of Hezbollah propaganda revealed an emphasis on the following themes: (1) unity within Lebanon—Shi'ite, Christian, Sunni, and Druze, (2) Israel's occupation of Jerusalem, (3) the justness of Hezbollah's use of violence, (4) determination in the face of a long struggle against Israel, (5) opposition to Israel's bombardment of Lebanese and Palestinian villages, and (6) God's will to expel Jews from southern Lebanon.

Given these broader goals, it appears that as Hezbollah's leaders felt the need to expand their pool of supporters and potential recruits, their messages similarly broadened: Hezbollah leaders believed that messages of Lebanese nationalism would hold greater appeal with its support communities in southern Lebanon. Of course, it is likely that, if asked, Hezbollah leaders would have argued that in order to pursue

---

[48] "Hezbollah's Intelligence Apparatus," *Jane's Terrorism and Security Monitor*, September 13, 2006; Ranstorp, 1997; Jaber, 1997; Ron Schleifer, "Psychological Operations: A New Variation of an Age Old Art: Hezbollah Versus Israel," *Studies in Conflict and Terrorism*, Vol. 29, 2006, pp. 1–19.

[49] Schleifer, 2006.

an Islamic revolution within Lebanon, Israeli forces first had to be evicted. But Schleifer's study reinforces the view that, in the 1990s, Hezbollah shifted its emphasis away from an Islamic revolution and toward Lebanese nationalism in an effort to broaden its appeal, representing at least a short-term change in its interests.

This shift subsequently affected Hezbollah's perception of its relationship with Iran. Iran apparently became much less directive of Hezbollah's activities and more of a facilitator of Hezbollah's fight against Israel. At that time, Hezbollah's own interests took precedence over Iran's in Hezbollah's activities. The most striking example is the aforementioned 1996 status quo negotiation between Hezbollah and Israel on the use of *katyusha* rockets on targets in northern Israel. It was clearly in Hezbollah's interest to halt Israeli military attacks on Hezbollah villages in southern Lebanon; likewise, it was in Israel's best interest to halt Hezbollah *katyusha* attacks on Israeli towns in Galilee. But this status quo agreement seems to have constrained one of Iran's more significant means of pressuring Israel.

Indeed, Hezbollah's overwhelming identification with ending the Israeli occupation of southern Lebanon meant that the May 2000 withdrawal represented both a victory and a dilemma for the organization. How could Hezbollah justify its existence once Israel withdrew from Lebanon? In response to this challenge, Hezbollah began to transform itself into a political party rather than a resistance movement.[50] To do this, it attempted to expand its presence into Christian-dominated areas of Lebanon and run on its history of social services and its nationalistic agenda. This approach gained Hezbollah nine affiliated and three non-affiliated seats in the Lebanese parliament.

One wonders if perhaps Iran and other revolutionaries quietly criticized Hezbollah for this outreach and, arguably, political moderation. The defensive tone of key Hezbollah officials certainly conveys this impression. For example, in his 2005 book, *Hezbollah: The Story from Within*, Naim Qassam, the deputy secretary of Hezbollah, attempted to justify his organization's alliance with other parties as follows:

---

[50] Rodger Shanahan, "Hezbollah's Dilemma," *Mideast Monitor,* February 2006.

> [Hezbollah's] commitment to the Jurist-Theologian [the Supreme Leader] and his jurisprudence does not limit the scope of internal work at the level of forging relations with the various powers and constituents of Lebanon. It further does not limit the sphere of regional and international cooperation with groups with whom the Party's strategic direction or concerns meet.[51]

In this statement, Qassam seems both to be taking a further step back from Iran and its authority over Hezbollah's day-to-day decisions, especially with regard to Lebanon's internal dynamics, and to be reaffirming Hezbollah's acceptance of Supreme Leader Khamenei's spiritual authority. It is clearly a difficult balance to achieve, but most experts seem to have interpreted this balance as mostly an assertion of independence on the part of Hezbollah between May 2000 and August 2006.[52]

Of course, Hezbollah's ability to assert its independence was eroded to a certain extent after the August 2006 ceasefire between Hezbollah and Israel. As mentioned previously, Hezbollah has turned to Iran for support in rebuilding its infrastructure, including financial aid to rebuild support services and direct weapon transfers to rebuild caches of *katyusha* rockets in particular. This reliance on Iran (as well as Syria) makes it difficult for Hezbollah to assert its independence, even when it comes to internal domestic politics in Lebanon. Even beyond Hezbollah's own interest in achieving a certain degree of independence from Iran, a perception of independence is important for its own internal struggle for legitimacy. Increasingly, Lebanese politicians opposed to Hezbollah have used its association with Iran as leverage and a means of criticism.[53]

Indeed, this domestic pressure has been increasingly evident in Hezbollah's own rhetoric as it has attempted to respond to accusations that it pursues Syria's and Iran's interests, not those of the Lebanese

---

[51] Qassam, 2005.

[52] Grace and Mandelbaum, 2006.

[53] One such politician is Walid Jumblatt, who has waged a continuous campaign against Hezbollah since August 2006.

people. For example, in a January 2007 speech given to residents of neighborhoods in southern Beirut, Nasrallah once again attempted to place some distance between Hezbollah and Iran:

> Nowadays, there is talk of reviving new initiatives, of Saudi-Iranian moves, of Arab moves. We bless any endeavor, and bless whoever seeks to help Lebanon. But to dispel any delusion, any . . . [changes thought] . . . I know the brothers in Iran, and based on what we heard from the brothers in the Kingdom of Saudi Arabia—neither Saudi Arabia nor Iran is entertaining the notion of embarrassing its friends in Lebanon or forcing their hands. This is the first point. I am being polite here. Second, it goes without saying that any agreement that could be achieved between any two world states or governments, even if they are held in high esteem and enjoy respect, cannot be binding to the Lebanese, who should pursue their real national interests.[54]

In sum, Hezbollah statements suggest that it does not consider its interests to be in perfect alignment with those of Iran, and its behavior reaffirms this assessment—Hezbollah continues to focus its energies on internal Lebanese politics. Although this divergence in interests between Hezbollah and Iran has yet to play itself out, it seems clear that the instability in Lebanon and tensions between the United States and Iran have the potential to force these two entities apart or forge an even stronger alliance between them. U.S. planners should carefully consider how to account for the Hezbollah threat, therefore, if tensions rise between Iran and the United States. In this context, rather than viewing Hezbollah as a proxy for Tehran, U.S. planners should attempt to weigh and anticipate Hezbollah's own interests. Our research findings suggest that Hezbollah likely will feel obliged to help Iran should it confront the Unites States, given Iran's continued support to Hezbollah in its conflict with Israel. But Hezbollah may only feel this obligation under certain circumstances.

---

[54] Speech given by Hasan Nasrallah, live televised speech given in the southern neighborhoods of Beirut, al-Manar television, January 24, 2007.

The most likely circumstance would be in response to U.S. aggression against Iran, whether preemptive or after an escalation of tensions.[55] If Iran asks Hezbollah to attack U.S. interests under these circumstances, it may feel as if it has no option but to attack. Given Hezbollah's past history, this support for Iran could manifest itself in attacks against U.S. forces in the region. But Hezbollah could also attack U.S. civilians in retaliation, as it did to Jewish targets in Argentina. Attacks against U.S. civilians would not necessarily take place in the U.S. homeland, but Hezbollah might choose instead to attack softer, more easily accessible targets in the Middle East, Latin America, or even Western Europe. Beyond U.S. aggression, U.S. military planners should also expect Hezbollah to feel obliged to assist Iran with terrorist attacks against Western targets should a stringent and economically punishing UN embargo be placed on Iran.

In contrast, Hezbollah is less likely to respond positively to Iran's requests for help if Iran escalates any tensions with the United States to the point of aggression. Hezbollah leaders might feel, in these circumstances, that it would be risking local popular support within Lebanon if it paralleled Iranian aggression against the United States with its own. Similarly, despite Hezbollah's alleged presence in Iraq, it is less likely to initiate attacks against the United States—particularly U.S. civilians—in response to arguments between Iran and the United States over the fate of Iraq. Of course, these suppositions still could be explored much more thoroughly, perhaps in scenarios and exercises. Fundamentally, the key finding from our research is that Hezbollah does pursue its own interests and, therefore, will not always do Iran's bidding.

---

[55] When asked about Hezbollah's reaction to a strike on Iran, the party's deputy secretary general, Na'im Qassem, stated in September 2007, "The state that comes under attack is responsible for responding to the attack and defending itself" (Interview with Naim Qassem, al-Watan, September 23, 2007, cited in Samii, 2008 p. 53). On the issue of Hezbollah retaliation, Samii writes, "Hizbullah's willingness to put itself at risk on Iran's behalf under current circumstances is questionable. Hizbullah may act if the survival of Iran's Shi'a regime is at stake—if a war against Iran is launched, for example" (Samii, 2008, p. 53).

Iraq: Iran's Strategic Interests Drive It to Partner with Multiple Groups

Iran has several important strategic interests at stake in Iraq. Proximity alone means that Iran will be directly affected by future developments in Iraq. The two countries share a border that extends over more than 900 miles of mountainous terrain; this border is virtually impossible to control, which means that Iran remains vulnerable to smuggling, crime, and refugee flows out of Iraq. This vulnerability is compounded by the memory of the bloody eight-year Iran-Iraq War, which resulted in hundreds of thousands of casualties on both sides. Iran therefore wants to ensure, above all else, that the Iraq which ultimately emerges has peaceful intentions toward its neighbors. As one former Iranian official explained, chaos in Iraq "does not help Iranian national interest[s]. If your neighbor's house is on fire, it means your home is also in danger."[56] To this end, Iran seeks a future Iraq that is

- Territorially intact. The breakup of Iraq into any number of smaller states would create massive refugee problems. It could also embolden the secessionist desires of Iran's many minority populations, especially among the 4.5 million Iranian Kurds.
- Ruled by a central government. A central Iraqi government, even one that is weak, will be more capable of mitigating sectarian tensions and secessionist desires than any alternative form of government. It will also be the most likely to constrain Sunni extremist sentiment, which poses a direct threat to Iran and its predominantly Shi'ite population.
- Diplomatically friendly to Iran. Iran would prefer to see Iraq ruled by pro-Iranian Shi'ites, ideally under the Iranian model of *velayat-e faqih*, or clerical rule. But Iran could tolerate alternatives, as long as the Iraqi government maintained good diplomatic relations with Iran and did not pursue policies that consistently undermined Iranian political, economic, and religious interests.

---

[56] Former Iranian Deputy Foreign Minister Abbas Maleki, as quoted in Nasr, 2006, p. 69.

- Unable to pose a military threat to Iran. Iran wants to prevent Iraq from ever being able to invade its territory again, as it did at the start of the Iran-Iraq War in 1980.[57]

Iran's objectives are fairly straightforward, but it faces a difficult calculation to identify the best strategy to achieve those objectives. This strategic challenge stems from the uncertainty of Iraq's future. There is no way to predict how events will unfold in the next couple of years as the United States starts to draw down its military forces. Even the relevant actors keep changing because of continual infighting and splintering within religious and extremist groups. Picking winners and losers is a risky proposition in such an uncertain and fluid environment.

Iran's solution to this strategic challenge has been to support as many different Iraqi groups as possible. This is akin to the strategy that investors use in assembling diversified portfolios: Over the long term, investing in a wide range of stocks and bonds is much less risky than investing in one or two individual stocks that may do well but that may also become worthless. Similarly, Iran has chosen to support a wide range of Iraqi parties and groups—even some Sunni and Kurdish groups—because doing so enables Tehran to try to influence events as they unfold and maximizes the chances that whoever ultimately gains power in Iraq will already have a cooperative working relationship with Iran.

This strategy also has two important additional benefits. First, it helps Iran achieve its strategic objectives vis-à-vis the United States. Iran feels threatened by the large U.S. military presence on its border, particularly given perceived U.S. pursuit of regime change in Iran. By supporting some groups that attack U.S. forces in Iraq, Iran helps keep the United States bogged down in Iraq and makes it less likely that Washington will pursue regime change in Iran through force. Second, this strategy may enable Iran to avoid a very divisive internal debate about which Iraqi groups to support. The Iranian political structure

---

[57] Nasr, 2006, p. 66, notes that most of Iran's current leaders are veterans of the Iran-Iraq War, and he argues that they "see the pacification of Iraq as the fulfillment of a strategic objective that they missed during that conflict."

is extremely complicated and decentralized, with many different factions and power centers.[58] The diversified portfolio strategy enables the Iranian regime to avoid forcing all of those factions into an internal consensus regarding which Iraqi groups to support. This strategy does entail some risks. Groups that Iran supports may turn on it or on other Shi'ite groups in the future, as occurred with Iranian support to Kurdish paramilitary groups. It also risks exacerbating existing divides within Iran about which groups deserve the most support. A number of Iranian commentators, officials, and clerics for example, have denounced Muqtada al-Sadr and have criticized Iran's continuing support for his actions.[59]

Perhaps the most important thing to note about the Iranian strategy regarding Iraq is that it is driven by national interests and not ideology and is consistent with the traditional principles of realpolitik: It seeks to protect the security and stability of the Iranian state by forestalling massive refugee flows, preventing domestic secessionist movements, and lessening the ability of the United States to pursue forcible regime change. More broadly, Iran also seeks to take advantage of U.S. difficulties in Iraq to reduce U.S. influence in the region and around the world. Iran would like to build a long-term partnership with Iraq that would complement, and perhaps offset some of the risks of, its traditional alliance with Syria. Iran would also like to use its leverage over Iraq to build closer relations with Russia and China, ideally at the expense of these nations' relations with the United States.

None of these policy goals are driven by a desire to export the Islamic revolution beyond Iran's own borders. Iran would certainly prefer to see Iraq governed according to *velayat-e faqih*, but this can be explained by realpolitik calculations as much as by ideology. Iranian-style clerical rule in Iraq would make the country more likely to align itself with Iran and pursue cooperative policies that benefit the Iranian regime. The diversified portfolio strategy seeks to ensure that Iranian

---

[58] Buchta, 2000.

[59] RAND interviews in Washington, D.C., 2007, and Baghdad, 2008. See, for example, "Iran: Conservative Cleric Criticizes al-Sadr for Making Karbala, Najaf U.S. Targets," 2004; "Iran: Commentator Says Shi'i Scholars Should 'Boycott' Al-Sadr," 2004.

strategic interests will be protected regardless of whether clerical rule is ever established in Iraq.

Iran Maintains Ties with Many Iraqi Actors

Iran has ties to a wide range of Iraqi actors, both official and unofficial. Official ties exist between the two governments, which include standard diplomatic exchanges and security cooperation agreements. Iran has struck numerous trade deals, including deals on exporting electricity to Iraq and trading Iraqi crude oil for refined oil products. Iran has also agreed to provide more than $1 billion in aid packages. Private investments and commercial ties are significant and increasing, particularly as Iranians invest in land, construction, and hospitality for pilgrims in the Shi'ite holy cities of Najaf and Karbala.[60]

These official ties are dwarfed, however, by the extent of unofficial ties between the two countries. Iran has direct links with many different non-state actors in Iraq, including political parties, militias, insurgent groups, and terrorist networks. Iran also maintains a direct, and often covert, presence in Iraq. Iranian officials from the MOIS and the IRGC-QF are operating throughout the country, particularly in the south.[61] In July 2007, U.S. military officials announced that operatives from the Qods Force have been training secret cells designed to mirror the structure of Lebanese Hezbollah,[62] and in August 2007, a U.S. general publicly stated that 50 members of the IRGC have been training Shi'ite militias in the area south of Baghdad.[63] There are also

---

[60] Nasr, 2006, p. 60.

[61] International Crisis Group, "Where Is Iraq Heading? Lessons from Basra," Middle East Report No. 67, June 25, 2007, p. 8. One source also reports that many members of Iranian intelligence were naturalized as Iraqi citizens during the past few years, and that Iranian agents have bought real estate and businesses in Baghdad, Basra, Najaf, and Karbala to serve as command centers and living quarters (Mounir Elkhamri, "Iran's Contribution to the Civil War in Iraq," *The Jamestown Foundation Occasional Paper*, January 2007, p. 6).

[62] Brigadier General Kevin Bergner, Spokesman, Multi-National Force-Iraq, press briefing, July 2, 2007. See also Michael Knights, "Shiite Backlash–Anti-Coalition Sadrist Factions in Iraq," *Jane's Intelligence Review*, July 2007b.

[63] Megan Greenwell, "Iran Trains Militiamen Inside Iraq, U.S. Says," *Washington Post*, August 20, 2007.

108 Dangerous But Not Omnipotent

widespread personal ties between the populations of the two countries. Many of the Iraqi Shi'ites exiled by Saddam Hussein during his reign went to Iran, and some became senior clerics and IRGC commanders despite their Iraqi citizenship.[64]

Through these official and unofficial links, Iran provides a number of different types of support to Iraqi actors:

- Financial support. Iran provides considerable financial support to a wide range of groups in Iraq. Estimates of the extent of this support are difficult to find, but anecdotal evidence suggests that southern Iraq in particular is awash in Iranian money. One former U.S. government official in Iraq estimated that Iran provides between $150 million and $200 million to Iraqi actors every year.[65]
- Military assistance. The Qods Force provides Shi'ite militias with weapons, training, financing, and technical support, all of which are used for attacks on U.S. forces, Iraqi forces, and Iraqi civilians. The most lethal assistance includes EFPs, an advanced technology that can penetrate armor at long distances. Iran also provides these militias with rockets, mortars, and IEDs.[66] The extent of this support is also hard to estimate, but one officer who defected from the IRGC has claimed that the extent of Qods Force operations in Iraq is larger than it was during the Iran-Iraq War.[67] Much of this military support is intended to support attacks on U.S. forces rather than fueling internal strife among Iraq's sectarian communities.[68]

---

[64] Nasr, 2006, p. 62.

[65] RAND interviews with U.S. analysts, Washington, D.C., June 2007.

[66] James Glanz, "U.S. Says Arms Link Iranians to Iraqi Shiites," *New York Times*, February 12, 2007; Michael Knights, "Deadly Developments–Explosively Formed Projectiles in Iraq," *Jane's Intelligence Review*, March 2007a; U.S. Department of Defense, "Measuring Security and Stability in Iraq," March 2, 2007, p. 17.

[67] Elkhamri, 2007, p. 5.

[68] Knights, 2007b.

- Social services. Many Shi'ite groups have established social service networks throughout southern Iraq to provide health, education, and other local services that the Iraqi government has been unable to provide. Many of these networks were created with Iranian financial and logistical assistance in an effort to bolster public support for the groups that run them, much as has been the case with Hezbollah.[69]
- Ideological influences. Iran has sought to burnish its Islamist credentials by providing spiritual support and guidance to Shi'ite clerics and scholars in Iraq. Since 2004, Iran has reportedly sent more than 2,000 students and scholars to Najaf and Karbala—two of the holiest sites in Shi'ite Islam—and is providing cash payments to Shi'ite students and school instructors.[70]

Iranian Support of Iraqi Groups Does Not Equal Control

As with Hezbollah, Iranian support for these groups does not mean that Iran controls them. Quite to the contrary, despite Iran's considerable support for these groups, the influence that Iran wields over them remains limited for at least four reasons. First and foremost, Iranian money is not essential to the survival of the major Shi'ite political parties and organizations. Some of the smaller groups might not be able to survive if Iran cut off financial assistance, but all of the major groups have other important sources of revenue that would continue uninterrupted. Members of the Iraqi government have used their ministries as sources of patronage, providing jobs and distributing services to supporters of their own parties.[71] This means that the government payroll essentially functions as a major source of financial support to nonstate actors—a source that will likely become institutionalized because even ministers from a different political party who are appointed in the future will find it difficult to purge the ministries of large numbers of civil servants. Beyond the government, many Shi'ite groups also have

---

[69] Nasr, 1997, pp. 145–168.

[70] Elkhamri, 2007, p. 5.

[71] Sometimes different groups control different parts of single ministries. See Ned Parker, "Interior Ministry Mirrors Chaos of a Fractured Iraq," *Los Angeles Times*, July 30, 2007.

long-standing real estate and business interests along pilgrimage routes to Najaf and Karbala that provide a continual revenue stream. Iranian financial support certainly enables the recipients to undertake activities and gain support from the population that they might not otherwise be able to, but it does not buy the degree of loyalty and influence that follows from complete financial dependence.[72]

Second, the Shi'ite militias generally do not depend on military assistance from Iran. EFPs are one very important exception; no Iraqi militias possess the technology to manufacture the specially shaped charges that make EFPs so lethal to U.S. forces.[73] But the rockets, mortars, and other armaments that Iran provides are all largely available in Iraq. Iraq is awash in conventional armaments of all shapes and sizes, in part because of the looting of the country's plentiful arms caches that occurred after the U.S. invasion in 2003. Also, with the subsequent dissolution of the Iraqi army, many people with weapon skills blended back into the regular population. Iranian weapons and training do provide additional capabilities for Shi'ite militias (just as Iranian money enables the political groups to pursue additional activities), but the militias have access to enough weapons and trained personnel that they could continue to operate without Iranian assistance. They might be less capable of conducting lethal attacks on U.S. forces without Iranian EFP technology, but the weapons and training available inside Iraq would most likely enable them to continue inflicting heavy casualties on U.S forces, Iraqi forces, and Iraqi civilians.[74]

Third, a degree of religious competition is emerging between Iran and Iraq. As noted earlier, Iran has the largest Shi'ite population of any country in the world and promotes itself as the birthplace of the Islamic revolution, but the Iraqi cities of Najaf and Karbala are among

---

[72] RAND interview with U.S. analysts, Washington, D.C., July 2007.

[73] Attacks using EFPs are averaging about 60 incidents per month. They account for only a small percentage of IED incidents, but account for a very large percentage of U.S. soldiers killed by IEDs. See Brookings Institution, *The Brookings Institution Iraq Index*, July 30, 2007, p. 31.

[74] RAND interviews with U.S. analysts, Washington, D.C., June and July 2007.

the holiest cities in Shi'ite Islam.[75] Both cities have enjoyed a renaissance since the fall of Saddam Hussein, and pilgrims are flocking to these cities to visit sites that had long been inaccessible. Najaf has also historically been the main center for Shi'ite scholarship, reaching back to the early 8th century. It lost its preeminent scholarly position to the Iranian city of Qom as the repression of the Iraqi Shi'ites worsened and as Qom flourished as a center of scholarship after the Islamic Revolution. Yet now that Najaf is open and accessible once again, it is slowly regaining its place of prominence. Furthermore, Iraqi Shi'ism and Iranian Shi'ism differ significantly.[76] In particular, Najaf and Qom have advanced different views of the role of clerics in governance. The Najaf school promotes what is often called a *quietist* approach, which holds that clerics should not hold political office but should instead exert indirect influence and oversight, while the Qom school, in general, has tended to favor direct clerical rule.[77] Thus, Iranian efforts to provide spiritual support and guidance to Iraqi Shi'ite groups are motivated by the politics of influence as much as by religion. Iran wants to make sure that Iranian clerics and scholars, and the principle of direct clerical rule, are not eclipsed by Iraqi clerics and scholars as Najaf and Karbala reemerge from their isolation.

Fourth, Iraqi nationalism is intensified by a pervasive distrust of Iran and its intentions. There is a long history of tensions and conflict between the two territories reaching back as far as the Persian empire and vividly reinforced by the devastation of the Iran-Iraq War in the

---

[75] Najaf is the location of the tomb of the prophet's son-in-law Ali, whom the Shi'ites believe to be the rightful leader of the Islamic faith. Karbala is the site of the famous battle that is commemorated on the holiday of Ashura, and is where the prophet's grandson was martyred and buried. For more on the significance of these cities, see Marshall Hodgson, *The Venture of Islam*, Vol. 1, Chicago: The University of Chicago Press, 1977.

[76] Qom gained prominence as a center for scholarship in the 16th century, making it a relative newcomer compared to Najaf (al-Qazwini, "The School of Qum" and "The School of Najaf," in Abd al-Jabar, 2002, pp. 245–281).

[77] It should be noted, however, that even in Qom there is sharp divergence over *velayat-e faqih*; Grand Ayatollah Sistani's network is run from Qom and includes a vast array of libraries and seminaries. See Barbara Slavin, *Mullahs, Money and Militias: How Iran Exerts Its Influence in the Middle East*, Washington, D.C.: The United States Institute for Peace, June 2008.

1980s. Direct ties to Iran are a political liability for Iraqi Shi'ite leaders, and Iraqis who are perceived as being too close to Iran are often derogatorily dismissed as "Persians."[78] This distrust is perhaps best exemplified by the attacks against the Iranian consulate in Basra, despite that city's economic and cultural ties to Iran and deliberate efforts by Tehran to build alliances with local leaders.[79]

These factors suggest that Iranian support for Shi'ite groups in Iraq does not automatically lead to Iranian control over their actions. By providing many different forms of assistance to numerous different Iraqi groups, Iran is clearly seeking to influence their future activities and direction. Yet these groups have their own interests and agendas, which they will continue to pursue regardless of how much Iranian support they receive.

ISCI and the Sadrists Are Iraq's Key Shi'ite Groups

The two largest and most influential Shi'ite groups in Iraq today are ISCI (formerly SCIRI) and the organization of Muqtada al-Sadr. The families that lead these groups have been competing for the leadership of the Iraqi Shi'ites for decades. The formation of the al-Da'wa Party in 1959 ignited a rivalry between Ayatollah Baqir al-Sadr and Ayatollah Muhammad Baqir al-Hakim. Baqir al-Sadr emerged as the party leader, and he inspired a deeply devoted following that continued after his assassination in 1980 by Saddam Hussein's regime. In 1982 in exile in Tehran, Baqir al-Hakim established SCIRI, which was devoted to overthrowing Saddam Hussein. It built an armed wing called the Badr Brigades with assistance from the Iranian IRGC, but the Sadrists and many others saw this as an unacceptable degree of Iranian intervention in Iraqi Shi'ite politics. Popular support for SCIRI decreased after the failed uprisings against Saddam Hussein in 1991, and Ayatollah Sadeq al-Sadr emerged as an alternative leader. He built a power base among

---

[78] Phebe Marr, "Who Are Iraq's New Leaders? What Do They Want?" United States Institute of Peace, Special Report 160, March 2006, p. 16; Peter Harling and Hamid Yasin, "Iraq's Diverse Shiite," *Le Monde Diplomatique*, September 2006.

[79] Babak Rahimi, "The Militia Politics of Basra," *Terrorism Monitor*, The Jamestown Foundation, Vol. 5, No. 13, July 6, 2007e.

poor Shi'ites, particularly in Baghdad, and he continued to gain popularity until he was assassinated in 1999.[80]

After the U.S. invasion in 2003, the two families began an open struggle for leadership of the Iraqi Shi'ite community. Baqir al-Hakim was killed by a car bomb in Najaf in August 2003, soon after returning to Iraq from Iran. Leadership of SCIRI then passed to his brother, Abdul Aziz al-Hakim. Meanwhile, Sadeq al-Sadr's son Muqtada started to build a following based on his father's popularity and quickly emerged as ISCI's main political rival.

ISCI Is Iran's Most Powerful Iraqi Ally. ISCI is the leading Shi'ite political party in Iraq today and shares many of Iran's objectives for the future of Iraq. It is the only major Shi'ite party to support *velayat-e faqih*, the Iranian model of clerical rule. It also supports the concept of a strong Shi'ite region within a weak federal government structure, and al-Hakim has suggested that nine provinces in Iraq's south should join together to constitute that region.[81] Iran provides considerable financial support for the party and material support for its militia (the Badr Organization, renamed from the Badr Brigades). Al-Hakim has ties to many Iranian leaders, including Supreme Leader Khamenei, which reportedly enables him to bypass the leadership of the IRGC when needed and go straight to the top of the Iranian political system.[82]

Yet ISCI has also proven itself to be independent of Iran in many ways. It is seen as a moderate, not radical, Islamist party, despite its longstanding, if increasingly rhetorical, support for *velayat-e faqih*.[83] It has cooperated quite extensively with the United States both politically and militarily and has strongly opposed the establishment of a deadline

---

[80] Faleh Abd al-Jabbar, ed., *Ayatollahs, Sufis, and Ideologues: State, Religion, and Social Movements in Iraq*, London: Al-Saqi Books, 2002, pp. 164–169; Babak Rahimi, "A Shiite Storm Looms on the Horizon: Sadr and ISCI Relations," *Terrorism Monitor*, The Jamestown Foundation, Vol. 5, No. 10, May 24, 2007b, p. 2.

[81] Marr, 2006, p. 15.

[82] RAND interview with a U.S. analyst, Washington, D.C., July 2007.

[83] Some analysts have argued that ISCI has all but jettisoned *velayat-e faqih* in practice. See Slavin, 2008; International Crisis Group, "Shi'ite Politics in Iraq: The Role of the Supreme Council," Middle East Report No. 70, November 15, 2007, p. 16.

for the withdrawal of U.S. troops from Iraq. This is almost certainly a result of pragmatic political calculations because ISCI benefits greatly from the status quo.

Since 2007, the party has actively sought to distance itself from Iran. The most obvious effort was changing its name so that it would no longer contain the word "revolution." ISCI officials explained that the word was a reference to fighting Saddam Hussein and was therefore no longer needed, but there are many signs that the name change also signifies a move away from support for an Iranian-style Islamic revolution. The party has also changed its platform to be more closely aligned with the views of Iraq's top Shi'ite cleric, Grand Ayatollah Ali al-Sistani, instead of Iranian Supreme Leader Khamenei. And a senior ISCI official explicitly stated that these changes were "a step to the Iraqisation of the Islamic parties in Iraq."[84] Some analysts speculate that these moves do not represent a real break with Iran and that Iran actually supported these moves as part of an effort to appeal to Iraqi Sunnis and to move toward a new national power-sharing agreement.[85] Nevertheless, these are very significant developments that fundamentally change some of the party's basic principles and that may well shape its political program for years to come.

ISCI faces an uncertain future. Abdul Aziz al-Hakim was diagnosed with lung cancer in May 2007 and traveled to Iran for chemotherapy.[86] The next leader of the party is likely to be his son, Amar al-Hakim, who is widely seen as more charismatic than his father. Although he also has close ties to Iran, he may be more independent because he is younger and more removed from the Iranian support that launched the party a quarter century ago. He has also promoted himself as the "unifier," in his words, of the Hakims and Sadrs—his mother is from the Sadr family—as a way to bolster his claim to lead-

---

[84] Mariam Karouny, "Iraq's SCIRI Party to Change Platform, Officials," Reuters, May 11, 2007.

[85] "Iraq: Transforming Iran's Shiite Proxy, Assisting the United States," Web page, Stratfor. com, May 11, 2007.

[86] Robin Wright and John Ward Anderson, "Son of Ailing Shiite Leader Steps Forward," *Washington Post*, July 1, 2007.

ership of the Iraqi Shi'ite community.[87] But successions are not always smooth, and the illness of the elder Hakim may reduce public support for ISCI and provide an opening for its political rivals. Real questions remain as to whether ISCI can remain the dominant Iraqi political party and whether it will continue to receive a great deal of support from Iran.[88]

The Organization of Muqtada al-Sadr Has Grown in Recent Years. Muqtada al-Sadr has staked a claim to leadership of the Iraqi Shi'ite community by building on his father's legacy.[89] As noted above, Ayatollah Muhammed Sadiq al-Sadr built a strong following in the 1990s. He promoted a political program for the poor and dispossessed and established charitable networks in Baghdad and the Shi'ite south. He remained so popular after his assassination in 1999 that four years later, after the fall of Saddam Hussein, the Shi'ites living in the Baghdad slum known as Saddam City renamed it Sadr City. Muqtada al-Sadr inherited his father's political organization and charitable networks and continues to promote his father's ideas and agenda. Sadr's power base consists primarily of support from poor city residents, especially in Baghdad, and the lower ranks of the religious establishment.[90] His critics view him as too young, too unpredictable, and lacking in religious credentials.[91] His organization is not nearly as cohesive as ISCI; it lacks centralized control and the organizational structure needed to bind together the wide range of disparate groups that support his ideas.[92] Yet his party and his militia, the Mahdi Army, have grown stronger since 2003, and they pose the major challenge to ISCI's predominance.

---

[87] Wright and Anderson, 2007.

[88] ISCI candidates fared poorly in the January 2009 provincial elections.

[89] Nimrod Raphaeli argues that al-Sadr's followers see him as "the symbol and the personification" of his father's legitimacy. See Nimrod Raphaeli, "Understanding Muqtada al-Sadr," *Middle East Quarterly*, Vol. 11, No. 4, Fall 2004.

[90] Toby Dodge, *Iraq's Future: The Aftermath of Regime Change*, London: International Institute for Strategic Studies, Adelphi Paper 372, 2005, pp. 48–49.

[91] Muqtada al-Sadr has not reached the rank of Ayatollah, which means that he cannot be considered a religious authority.

[92] Knights, 2007b.

Sadr's political platform is primarily based on Iraqi nationalism, not ideology or theology. He rejects the principle of federalism and has denounced Hakim's proposal for a nine-province Shi'ite region within a federal Iraq. Instead, he promotes a single unitary government for the entire country without any regions. He has sought cooperation with Sunnis and secular nationalists, promoting what he calls a "reform and reconciliation project" among all Iraqis.[93] After the second bombing of the al-Askari mosque in Samarra in June 2007, he even suggested that his militia would be willing to protect Sunni mosques against any Shi'ite reprisal attacks.[94] He favors developing a strong Shi'ite identity in Iraq, but he emphasizes that it must be independent from Iran. He also strongly opposes the U.S. troop presence in Iraq and argues that U.S. forces should be withdrawn as soon as possible.[95]

Nationalism is an extremely practical strategy for Sadr. His power base is concentrated in Baghdad, not in the Shi'ite south, so anything short of a unitary government would dilute his power and influence. Devolving power to the regions would give ISCI an advantage because most of its supporters are spread throughout the south, and under such a government, Baghdad would become increasingly isolated from the rest of the country. Sadr has sought to diversify his power base by building increased support in Iraq's central and southern provinces, but Baghdad is likely to remain the center of his power for the foreseeable future.[96] Nationalism appeals to his base and has helped Sadr to emerge as a symbol of hope for poor and disenfranchised Shi'ites.[97]

---

[93] Rahimi, 2007b, p. 1.

[94] Babak Rahimi, "Second Samarra Bombing Strengthens Status of Muqtada al-Sadr," *Terrorism Focus*, The Jamestown Foundation, Vol. 4, No. 20, June 26, 2007d.

[95] Sadr has even described his movement in the following terms: "We are Iraqis opposed to the occupation." See "Inside the Mahdi Army Death Squads," *Jane's Terrorism and Security Monitor*, February 14, 2007.

[96] Babak Rahimi, "Muqtada al-Sadr Stepping into the Power Vacuum," *Terrorism Focus*, The Jamestown Foundation, Vol. 4, No. 19, June 19, 2007c.

[97] Robert Malley and Peter Harling describe Sadr's appeal:

> Because he was one of them, Sadr found ready support among poor Shiites. They identified with his subordinate family status and the vexations he endured, while his lack of

Despite some fundamentally different long-term objectives, Sadr and Iran maintain a tactical alliance with each other. As Sadr's power has grown, Tehran has sought closer cooperation with his movement, providing it with as much as $80 million a month in financial support. Iran also provides weapons, communications, and logistics support to the Mahdi Army, and the Qods Force has reportedly established training camps in Iran to train members of the militia.[98] Iran sees Sadr as a potentially useful partner against the United States, especially given his increasingly outspoken opposition to the U.S. troop presence in Iraq.[99] Sadr has been quoted as having pledged to help defend Iran if it were attacked by the United States, though there is some dispute about whether Sadr was referring specifically to military assistance from the Mahdi Army or to broader political support from Iraq as a whole.[100]

Yet despite such pledges and assistance, mutual distrust between Sadr and Tehran remains high. Tehran sees Sadr as often rash, unpredictable, and out to serve his own interests.[101] Sadr believes that Iranian intelligence has infiltrated the Mahdi Army as a way to exert increased

---

education made them feel better about their own. Based in popular aspirations more than clerical tradition, the Sadrist movement is more social than religious. It articulates the frustrations, hopes, and demands of many who have no other representative and who remain marginalized in the post-Hussein order.

See Robert Malley and Peter Harling, "Containing a Shiite Symbol of Hope," *Christian Science Monitor*, October 24, 2006.

[98] According to Raphaeli, 2004, one former Qods Force member estimated in 2004 that between 800 and 1,200 Sadr supporters had already been trained at these camps. See also Babak Rahimi, "Muqtada al-Sadr's New Alliance with Tehran," *Terrorism Monitor*, The Jamestown Foundation, Vol. 5, No. 4, March 1, 2007a; Nasr, "When the Shiites Rise," 2006, p. 61.

[99] In April 2007, Sadr ordered the six government ministers from his party to withdraw from the Iraqi government, partly to protest the prime minister's failure to develop a timetable for the withdrawal of U.S. forces from Iraq ("Iraq: Al-Sadr Orders His 6 Cabinet Ministers to Withdraw from Government," *International Herald Tribune*, April 15, 2007).

[100] Ellen Knickmeyer and Omar Fekeiki, "Iraqi Shiite Cleric Pledges to Defend Iran," *Washington Post*, January 24, 2006.

[101] RAND interview, July 2007.

control over its activities.[102] Tehran promotes its own tactical interests by assisting Sadr: In the short term, it keeps ISCI and Sadr fighting each other for supremacy, and in the long term, it ensures some sort of relationship with whichever group wins that battle.[103] Sadr also benefits tactically from this relationship, since Iranian financial and military assistance enables the militants in his nationalist movement to conduct attacks against the U.S. forces that remain in Iraq. The extent to which this tactical alliance will continue to benefit Sadr after U.S. forces withdraw remains unclear.[104]

Sadr's organization suffers from a number of serious internal fissures that even Sadr himself cannot always control.[105] A heated rivalry exists between the political and military wings of the organization because both believe they are the ultimate source of Sadr's power, and the fighters have grown increasingly frustrated with the lack of tangible benefits resulting from the organization's political activities. Within the political wing, tensions exist between the religious leaders of the party, who believe that they have a natural role in politics, and the politicians and academics, who want to keep religious influences out of politics. The Mahdi Army also suffers from internal divisions, which are largely generational: The older officers, many of whom had experience in Saddam Hussein's security forces, believe that their experience entitles them to the top command positions, while the younger and more inexperienced officers claim that they should lead the organization because they are untainted by association with Saddam Hussein.[106]

These internal divisions were further exacerbated by Sadr's extended absence from Iraq in early 2007. He and his top advisors left Iraq in January 2007 as the U.S. military surge got under way. Though his whereabouts were never officially confirmed, it was widely believed

---

[102] Rahimi, 2007a.

[103] Raphaeli, 2004.

[104] International Crisis Group, "Where Is Iraq Heading? Lessons from Basra," 2007, p. 8.

[105] Several splinter groups have broken away from the Sadrist movement and now operate independently, including the Fadila Party in Basra (Knights, 2007b).

[106] "Inside the Mahdi Army Death Squads," 2007; Knights, 2007b.

that he had sought sanctuary in Iran—a problematic destination for a leader promoting a nationalist political agenda. In his absence, junior leaders within the Mahdi Army emerged into the leadership void and disobeyed his orders to halt attacks on U.S. and Iraqi forces at the start of the surge. These leaders now have experience, credibility, and, frequently, a more radical agenda than those who left the country with Sadr or went into hiding, and they may well defect from the main organization in order to pursue that agenda.[107]

Sadr moved forcefully to shore up control of his organization upon returning to Iraq in May 2007.[108] He seems to have taken advantage of the increased U.S. military presence in Baghdad to crack down on or destroy disloyal elements within the Mahdi Army. Some of this attrition has occurred as a natural result of intensified U.S. operations in the capital: Rogue Madhi Army units that continue to attack U.S. and Iraqi forces have become more likely to be arrested or destroyed. There are also some suspicions that Sadr may be deliberately feeding U.S. forces information about rogue commanders in his organization, essentially relying on the Americans to eliminate his main competitors.[109] On the political side, he does not yet seem to be suffering politically for his reported stay in Iran, and al-Hakim's illness and questions about the future of ISCI may open up a new opportunity to build public support. In the past, Sadr has proven to be a shrewd and resilient leader who can manage internal divisions while expanding his political base of support.

Yet Sadr's influence, and indeed Iran's entire "proxy" strategy in Iraq, came under increasing strain from early to mid-2008. During this period, the Maliki government launched operations against Jaysh al-Mahdi fighters and militant Sadrist splinter groups (the so-called

---

[107] Peter Harling and Joost Hiltermann, "Eyes Wide Shut," *Le Monde Diplomatique*, May 2007.

[108] Sadr went back to Iran in July, reportedly to pursue clerical training to boost his credentials.

[109] Harling and Hiltermann, 2007; Rahimi, 2007a; Anthony Cordesman, "Iraq's Sectarian and Ethnic Violence and Its Evolving Insurgency," Center for Strategic and International Studies, April 2, 2007, pp. 103–106.

Special Groups), whose presence in Basra, Sadr City, and Amarah provinces had caused increasing lawlessness and criminality.[110] On one level, the operations were an encouraging sign of resolve and competency by the hitherto timid and highly sectarian Maliki government, particularly as they resulted in the pacification of Iraq's southern provinces. At another, they can be seen as a highly politicized campaign by ISCI—which supported and aided Maliki—to discredit and eliminate the Sadrist competition in advance of the provincial elections.[111]

From Iran's perspective, the operations resulted in a precipitous decline in the Iraqi public's views of Iranian influence, which was blamed in many quarters for igniting intra-Iraqi discord. Qods Force commander Qasim Soleimani in particular was widely accused in the press and by U.S. officials of provoking and aiding the fighting through the funding and training of the Special Groups.[112] Iran initially backed the Sadrists, but then switched to supporting Maliki when it sensed the tide of Iraqi opinion turning against it. It was ultimately Soleimani himself who brokered the ceasefire in Basra.[113] Yet inside Iran, this "arsonist-and-fireman" policy provoked dissent from a broad spectrum of voices about the damage the Sadrist militants were causing to Iran's long-term standing in Iraq and across the region.[114]

In the future, this reversal of fortune is unlikely to result in any significant shift in Iran's long-standing practice of using both lethal and nonlethal tools to exert influence in Iraq. Iran will pursue the further splintering and military training of "noncompliant" Sadrists—those

[110] Michael Knights, "Rocky Road for Basra Operation," *Jane's Defence Weekly*, April 23, 2008.

[111] For an illuminating analysis, see Reidar Visser, "Maliki, Hakim, and Iran's Role in the Basra Fighting," www.historiae.org, April 9, 2003.

[112] Robert Dreyfuss, "Is Iran Winning the Iraq War?" *The Nation*, February 21, 2008; Helene Cooper, "Iran Fighting Proxy War in Iraq, U.S. Envoy Says," *New York Times*, April 12, 2008.

[113] For a short overview of Soleimani's role, see David Ignatius, "At the Tip of Iran's Spear," *Washington Post*, June 8, 2008.

[114] Vali Nasr, "Iran on Its Heels," *Washington Post*, June 19, 2008.

who dismiss Sadr's ceasefire order and refuse to move toward more political activism—as a form of leverage over Iraq's future trajectory.

Looking Ahead: Iran's Control over Iraqi Shi'ites Will Remain Limited

Iraq's future remains extremely uncertain. While the Maliki government exhibited greater resolve and military competency during the 2008 campaigns in Basra, Sadr City, and Amarah, tensions and risks remain, particularly concerning the potential for intra-Shi'ite fighting and the integration of former Sunni insurgents into Iraqi political and social life.[115] At the national level, Iran recently faced two important opportunities to preserve and bolster its influence: the November 2008 signing of the U.S.-Iraq Status of Forces Agreement (SOFA) and the January 2009 Iraqi provincial elections. While it may be too soon to accurately gauge the long-term impact of both events on Iran's standing, the initial Iranian reaction suggests strong disappointment with both outcomes.

On the SOFA, Iran had lobbied hard among Iraqi parliamentarians to reject the agreement or at least modify it to terms more favorable to Iran. In the public diplomacy realm, al-Alam and the Hezbollah-controlled al-Manar TV stations voiced extensive criticism of the agreement, while in Tehran, high-ranking officials such as *Majlis* speaker Ali Larijani attacked the SOFA as a "capitulation" of Iraqi sovereignty.[116] Clerical figures in Iran derided the SOFA as well, deploying rhetoric that closely echoed Ayatollah Khomeini's denunciation of the 1964 SOFA between the Shah of Iran and the United States—an important milestone in the Iranian leader's subsequent rise to power. Inside Iraq, Iran supported Moqtada al-Sadr's mobilization of street protests against the agreement. Iranian media also attributed extensive criticism of the SOFA to Grand Ayatollah Sistani, although Sistani's own Web sites displayed no such statements, and sources close to the cleric

---

[115] As noted earlier, Sadr pulled his ministers out of the government in April 2007, and on August 1, several Sunni ministers withdrew from the government as well. Megan Greenwell, "Sunnis Quit Cabinet Posts," *Washington Post*, August 2, 2007.

[116] "Larijani Describes SOFA as American Capitulation," IRNA, October 26, 2008; "Iran Calls on Iraqi MPs to Scrutinize Security Pact with US," Tehran Fars News Agency, OSC IAP20081126950066, in English, November 26, 2008.

told Arab media outlets that he had not expressed an opinion on the matter.[117] Despite these efforts, however, the Iraqi parliament approved the SOFA, provoking expressions of surprise and criticism from several conservative Iranian media outlets.

On the provincial elections, Iran had hoped for the retention of its ISCI allies as incumbents. Yet widespread dissatisfaction with the poor performance of these officials and their corruption, particularly in the southern provinces, led to the victory of more secular figures and unaffiliated Shi'ite blocs and the defeat of ISCI and Sadrist candidates. Iranian officials and media outlets were quick to spin the results as a validation of Shi'ite Islamist power; Iran's Fars News Agency called the results "the definite victory of Islamists," while the pro-regime newspaper *Vaten-e Emruz* hailed the elections as "a great Shiite victory."[118] Iranian commentators took further comfort in the triumph of groups allied with Iraqi Prime Minister Nouri al-Maliki, noting that the victory would empower him to pursue more independent and anti-American policies in the future.

The net effect of both events was both a demonstration of the limits of Iranian influence in Iraq and a validation of Tehran's diversified portfolio approach (i.e., backing multiple players and pursuing a broad range of policy levers as a sort of safety net). From Iran's perspective, providing support to a wide range of Iraqi actors is a much better strategy because it may provide indirect influence over their activities in the short term and it increases the chances that Tehran will have cooperative relations with whomever emerges as the political victor in Iraq over the long term. If these groups are frequently quarrelsome, so much the better for Tehran, which has frequently used mediation as a form of control and influence.

Iran cannot assume that it will automatically receive reciprocal cooperation from the Iraqi groups it supports. Many of these groups offer rhetorical support to Iran, and Muqtada al-Sadr has publicly pledged

---

[117] "Iran: Officials Largely Remain Silent on Eve of SOFA Vote," OSC Feature—Iran FEA20081125796715, November 25, 2008.

[118] "Iran Sees Emergence of Shiite Coalition After Elections in Iraq," Caversham BBC Monitoring, OSC IAP20090211950138, in English, February 11, 2009.

to help defend Iran if it were attacked by the United States.[119] But it is not clear whether such pledges would translate into direct action, even in the aftermath of a U.S. attack. Some of the smaller Shi'ite groups, particularly those with direct ties to the Qods Force, would probably follow Tehran's direction and retaliate against U.S. forces because they have no strong stake in Iraq's future. But the larger groups, especially ISCI and the organization of Muqtada al-Sadr, have so much at stake in the internal struggle for control of Iraq that they may well view an Iranian request for assistance as a secondary priority, to be filled only if it furthers their own core interests. In such a scenario, the leaders of these larger groups might tacitly encourage splinter groups to conduct attacks on U.S. forces; these attacks would enable them to maintain plausible deniability and blame "rogue elements" within their midst.

Alternatively, splinter groups might simply ignore the leadership and conduct such attacks on their own. Some analysts cast doubt on whether these groups could ratchet up attacks on U.S. forces even if they wanted to, believing that these groups are already attacking U.S. forces as much as they can.[120] In any case, Iran cannot simply assume that the wide-ranging support it provides to Iraqi Shi'ite groups will ensure loyalty and a willingness to retaliate against the United States. Much will depend on the specifics of the situation and the ways in which the larger Shi'ite groups calculate their own interests.

Tehran's control over Iraqi Shi'ites will therefore remain limited. Iraqi Shi'ite groups are unlikely to feel beholden to Iran, regardless of the degree of support they receive from Iran. They will try to accommodate Iranian interests when they can, but ultimately they will pursue their own interests and agendas.

Iran's Relationship with Hamas Has Intensified

For the most part, this chapter focuses on Iranian support to non-state actors in Lebanon and Iraq. Yet examples exist of Iranian support to

---

[119] Knickmeyer and Fekeiki, 2006.

[120] RAND interviews with U.S. analysts, Washington, D.C., June and July 2007.

other non-state militant groups in the Middle East as well. Hamas, for one, is often mentioned as a primary recipient of support from Iran. Based on news reports, this support apparently comes in the form of rhetorical advocacy, financial aid, and possibly even weapons. While not a focus of this chapter, it is perhaps worth setting Iranian support for Hamas in its appropriate context.

Arab countries in particular have an established history of providing financial and other forms of support to Palestinian resistance groups. This support, of course, predates Hamas, and most militant factions associated with the Palestine Liberation Organization (PLO) have benefited from it in one form or another. In the past, Jordan, Lebanon, Syria, and Tunisia have each hosted the leaders of Palestinian resistance groups. Historically, aid provided by Arab countries was used to provide a livelihood for the leadership of these groups, purchase weapons, and fund charitable organizations in the Palestinian territories.

Beginning with the 1991 Persian Gulf War, Hamas also began to receive a portion of these funds. Former PLO Chairman Yasser Arafat voiced his support for the Iraqi invasion of Kuwait, while Hamas opposed Saddam Hussein's action. Persian Gulf nations responded to these events by shifting their financial support away from the PLO and toward Hamas.[121] Reports from the early 1990s indicate that both Iran and Sudan also provided Hamas with financial support. Many analysts believe that Saudi Arabia and Iran used financial support to Palestinian resistance groups in a bid for leadership and credibility in the Muslim world.[122] Despite these historical ties, Hamas leaders fought to maintain their independence from Iran, Hezbollah, and other supporters between 1990 and 2007. Hamas leaders knew that financial support

---

[121] Yohanan Ramati, "Islamic Fundamentalism Gaining," *Midstream*, Vol. 39, No. 2, 1993, p. 2.

[122] Ziad Abu-Amr, "Hamas: A Historical and Political Background," *Journal of Palestinian Studies*, Vol. 23, No. 4, Summer 1993, p. 6; Hisham H. Ahmed, *Hamas from Religious Salvation to Political Transformation: The Rise of Hamas in Palestinian Society*, Jerusalem: Palestinian Academic Society for the Study of International Affairs, 1994, p. 93; Ghassan Salame, "Islam and the West," *Foreign Policy*, No. 90, Spring 1993, p. 28.

from these nations often came with obligations.[123] Indeed, during the al-Aqsa Intifada, it was well known that, despite overtures to Hamas, Hezbollah formed stronger ties with Fatah's al-Aqsa Martyr's Brigades than with Hamas.[124]

This hesitancy began to change, however, with Hamas's electoral victory in January 2006. While the international community considered how it should respond to the election, Hamas and Fatah entered into a series of negotiations in an attempt to arrive at a unity government. These negotiations failed, in part because Hamas leaders refused to renounce violence and acknowledge Israel's right to exist. After violence escalated in the Gaza Strip, Palestinian President Mahmoud Abbas, emboldened by international support, appointed an emergency government without Hamas's participation in June 2007. Hamas subsequently retained control over the Gaza Strip, while Fatah, under the leadership of President Abbas, governed the West Bank. Israel reacted to Hamas's control over the Gaza Strip by instituting closures, severely limiting the movement of people and goods.

As one might expect, these closures made it very difficult for Hamas to govern effectively. Prior to the closures, Hamas delegates approached a variety of Muslim countries, such as Malaysia, Pakistan, and Egypt, to ask for financial support to rebuild the Palestinian territories after the al-Aqsa Intifada. Malaysia, for example, pledged $16 million to a Hamas-led Palestinian Authority.[125] Saudi Arabia pledged $92 million, Qatar $50 million, Russia $10 million, and Iran $50 million.[126] Nonetheless, U.S. and European pressure made it difficult for the Hamas-led Palestinian Authority to receive these funds, and so it

---

[123] According to the U.S Treasury Department, Hamas had received several million dollars in transfers from Bank Sederat in 2005, which has been used by Iran to transfer funds to terrorist groups (U.S. Department of the Treasury, "Fact Sheet: Designation of Iranian Entities and Individuals for Proliferation Activities and Support for Terrorism," press release, October 25, 2007).

[124] For more information, see Kim Cragin, Peter Chalk, Sara A. Daly, and Brian A. Jackson, *Sharing the Dragon's Teeth: Terrorist Groups and the Exchange of Technologies*, Santa Monica, Calif.: RAND Corporation, MG-485-DHS, 2007.

[125] "Malaysia Pledges $16 Million to Palestinian Authority," *Khaleej Times*, May 21, 2006.

[126] "Saudis to Transfer $92 Million to PA," *Jerusalem Post*, April 19, 2006.

resorted to smuggling. In fact, in June 2006, Hamas-nominated Foreign Minister Mahmoud Zahhar was arrested by Fatah security forces in the Gaza Strip with a suitcase containing $26 million, supposedly acquired during a trip that took him to China, Pakistan, Egypt, and Iran.[127] Logically, once the international community agreed to boycott a Hamas-led Palestinian Authority, Hamas turned increasingly to Iran. If our analysis of Iranian influence over other non-state actors is any indication, one has to be cautious about any conclusions regarding Iranian control over Hamas. Nonetheless, it appears certain that Iranian influence in the Gaza Strip in particular has increased since 2007.

Conclusions

This chapter examined Iran's interaction with non-state actors in Lebanon and Iraq—the Lebanese Hezbollah, ISCI/SCIRI, and Muqtada al-Sadr supporters—to better understand how Iran might attempt to engage its "proxies" in other countries should tensions increase with the United States. Clearly, Hezbollah and Iraq's Shi'ite militias pose different and unique threats to the United States in and of themselves. But the purpose of this chapter was to explore how U.S. national security policymakers, including the USAF, should account for these groups in their planning with regard to Iran. As such, our research suggests some common findings across the three case studies.

Promoting an Islamic revolution is not the aim of Iran's support for terrorism. In the years immediately following the 1979 Iranian Revolution, evidence suggests that Iran's leaders initially sponsored various non-state actors as a means of spreading this revolution throughout the Muslim world. Today, Iran's various leaders might still aspire rhetorically to an Islamic revolution, but this goal does not appear to be the primary basis for its relationships with Hezbollah and with Shi'ite militias in Iraq. Instead, Iran appears to be using its relationships with

---

[127]"Hamas Minister Brings Cases of Cash into Gaza," *Independent* (London), June 15, 2006.

its allies as one of many means to achieve influence inside Iraq and Lebanon.

From an Iranian perspective, therefore, Iran's relationship with Hezbollah and Shi'ite militias in Iraq is not "state sponsorship of terrorism" in the traditional sense. Iran is not currently sponsoring its non-state allies in an effort to promote a revolutionary agenda within other countries or to overthrow those countries' governments, as was the case with its state sponsorship of such entities in the 1970s and 1980s. This observation does not diminish the potential threat posed by Iran's relationship with its non-state allies; rather, it suggests that the U.S. national security community should regard Iran's relationship with these entities as more complex than it has heretofore.

Proximity does not appear to be the primary determinant of Iranian behavior. One might expect that Iran would behave more cautiously in its relationship with Iraq's Shi'ite militias than with Hezbollah simply because it shares a border with Iraq. Iran might not want Iraq to devolve into complete chaos because of the effect that would have on Iran's own internal security. Yet our research reveals that Iran's strategy inside Iraq has been quite similar to that which it has pursued inside Lebanon over the past 20 years. For example, Iran has provided similar combinations of support in both cases: financial support, military assistance, social services, and religious influence. The fact that this pattern of support contributed to significant upheaval in Lebanon during the 1980s does not appear to have deterred Iran from following the same pattern in Iraq.

Iran's non-state partners do not behave as proxies. The characterization of Hezbollah and Iraq's Shi'ite militias as Shi'ite proxies is inaccurate. Our research suggests that local partners do not see themselves as promoting Iran's revolutionary agenda in their respective countries. Instead, these non-state allies apparently view their relationship with Iran as promoting their own self-interests within Lebanon and Iraq. Fractures between Iran's self-interest and its allies' self-interest, therefore, likely would cause reluctance on the part of Shi'ite militias and Hezbollah to pursue Iran's interests at the expense of their own.

Iran's non-state partner organizations may splinter if their leaders deviate from Iran's interests. Our research suggests that, in the event of an open U.S.-Iran conflict, U.S. policymakers should be prepared for splinter groups to act on behalf of Iran even if the majority of the members of its non-state allies do not. For example, Iran clearly encouraged its supporters to leave AMAL and al-Da'wa in Lebanon when the leaders of these groups pursued goals different from Iranian interests. This experience suggests that Iran may attempt a similar approach with reluctant allies in the future in order to pressure them to attack U.S. interests or to identify new collaborators. Divisions among Shi'ite groups in Iraq, particularly within the organization of Muqtada al-Sadr, may be a tempting target for Iran to exploit.

CHAPTER FIVE

Arab Perceptions of the Iranian Threat

Aside from its support to non-state actors, Tehran also views Arab public opinion as an important vector of power projection, one that can be used to exert pressure on unfriendly Arab regimes, as well as their Western allies. Employing both indigenous media as well as its own Arabic-language media outlets, Iran has played to the major sources of Arab discontent, portraying itself variously as

- a populist challenger of the status quo political order in the Middle East
- a steadfast champion of the Palestinian cause
- the state sponsor of the only Arab military body (Hezbollah) to have successfully liberated Arab soil from Israeli control
- a beleaguered victim of Western double standards that is attempting to assert its rightful claim to nuclear energy in the service of Muslims everywhere.

As we noted in Chapter Two, this appeal to Arab public opinion and Iran's ability to speak over the heads of local regimes can be a powerful driver for assertiveness and bravado in its behavior. According to an op-ed in the prominent pan-Arab newspaper *al-Quds al-Arabi*,

> Tehran felt it could indulge in brinksmanship because it knew it had the sympathy of Arab public opinion, whatever the views of

Arab governments. This is the bleeding wound that Iran is able to exploit.[1]

At the same time, Iran's outreach to Arab opinion can be a source of caution in its foreign policy. As noted by Ray Takeyh, President Ahmadinejad's populist, grassroots appeal may have initially achieved greater resonance in Cairo and Damascus than in Tehran.[2] Yet his posturing on the Holocaust and nuclear brinksmanship—which appear calculated in part to reach regional audiences—have caused a backlash at home, both from within his own camp and from factional rivals such as former President Rafsanjani. Similarly, Arab public support for Iran often fluctuates rapidly during events that are beyond Tehran's control. The regional applause for Iran's support to Hezbollah during the summer 2006 Lebanon war quickly evaporated after the execution of Saddam Hussein by Iraq's Shi'ite-dominated government—an event that was widely perceived by regional audiences as a humiliating, Iranian-sponsored rebuke to Arab identity.

Understanding these dynamics is necessary to assess the reliability of Arab public opinion as a resource in Iran's larger regional strategy. This chapter therefore surveys shifting Arab perceptions of Iran since the election of President Ahmadinejad. First, we describe Iran's major instrument of strategic communication, assessing its resonance among Arab audiences and offering reasons for the popular acclaim for President Ahmadinejad. Next, we highlight recent fluctuations in Arab opinion toward Iran, offering an explanation by way of two key examples. Then, we highlight the major anti-Iranian themes we encountered in our survey of the Arab media. Iran's nuclear ambitions form an important topic in Arab media deliberations, yet popular views on this issue are often ambiguous; we explore the reasons for this and its implications for gauging Arab reactions to a U.S. strike on Iran.

---

[1] "Iran Seeks to Allay Sunni Anxieties in Saudi Arabia," in English, Caversham BBC Monitoring, OSC GMP20070302950043, March 2, 2007.

[2] Ray Takeyh, *Hidden Iran: Paradox and Power in the Islamic Republic*, New York: Henry Holt and Company, 2006, p. 213.

Our research indicates that Arab public opinion can be a powerful driver of Iranian assertiveness and "soft-power projection," one that is not easily contained through traditional military, diplomatic, or economic means. At the same time, its capriciousness makes it a liability for Tehran and a source of caution and pragmatism. And as we argue in the conclusion to this chapter, future U.S. policies toward the Islamic Republic may ultimately determine the extent to which Tehran is able to exploit Arab public opinion.

Tehran's Arab Media Ambitions Have Fallen Short

The centerpiece of Tehran's strategic communication strategy in the Arab world is its 24-hour Arabic-language satellite TV channel, al-Alam. Al-Alam falls under Iran's state-run media body, Islamic Republic of Iran Broadcasting (IRIB), whose chief, currently a former IRGC commander, is personally appointed by the Supreme Leader.[3] According to its first managing director, Hassan Beheshtipour, al-Alam's founding charter was "to present the view points of the Islamic world and to counter the monopolization of Western news channels."[4] Consciously emulating the presentation style of its principal Arab competitors, al-Jazeera and al-Arabiya, it began broadcasting shortly before the U.S. invasion of Iraq. Although initially focused on reaching Arab Shi'ites in southern and eastern Iraq from a terrestrial station in western Iran, it subsequently expanded to broadcasting from six satellites, and its signal can now be received throughout the Middle East, the Pacific, South Asia, Europe, and the United States.[5] Its regional news coverage focuses on Lebanon, the Palestinian territories, and Iraq, and it maintains bureaus and correspondents throughout the Arab world.

---

[3] "Analysis: Survey of Iran's Arabic Satellite TV al-Alam," Iran–OSC Analysis GMF20070703684001, July 3, 2007. Aside from al-Alam, Iran utilizes Al-Kawthar TV (which until February 2006 was called al-Sahar). This religiously oriented channel broadcasts 18 hours a day in Arabic with the aim of advancing Iran's interpretation of Shi'ite Islam, although it also includes news bulletins.

[4] Analysis: Survey of Iran's Arabic Satellite TV, al-Alam," 2007.

[5] "Analysis: Survey of Iran's Arabic Satellite TV, al-Alam," 2007.

On Iraq, al-Alam's tone frequently mirrors that of other Arab outlets, referring to insurgents who attack U.S. forces as "fighters" and the killing of Iraqi civilians as "massacres" and "terrorism." Elsewhere in the region, it adopts a predictably anti-Israeli line in its coverage of the Palestinian territories and has been sympathetic to Shi'ite causes in the Persian Gulf region, particularly during its coverage of the May 2007 clashes between Bahraini security forces and Shi'ite activists.[6]

The station's actual resonance on Arab public opinion appears to have fallen short of its founders' expectations. For example, its bias on Iraq has not gone unchallenged by Iraqi audiences; even in the Shi'ite bastion of Najaf, al-Alam faced criticism from a Shi'ite prayer leader who criticized its use of the term "resistance fighter" to describe Iraqi insurgents—an appellation that al-Alam promptly denied using.[7] Moreover, recent surveys conducted inside Iraq have consistently shown that it is not as widely watched as its pan-Arab competitors, al-Jazeera and al-Arabiya, nor is it viewed as being as reliable a news source.[8] Iran's own IRIB Research Center conducted a poll of 1,400 adults in Beirut and southern Lebanon following the Israel-Hezbollah conflict and noted that only 22 percent of respondents stated they watched al-Alam. RAND fieldwork in 2007 among Shi'ite communities in Saudi

[6]   "Analysis: Survey of Iran's Arabic Satellite TV, al-Alam," 2007.

[7]   "BBC Monitoring: Iran's Al-Alam TV Plays Role in Arab Media Scene," in English, Caversham BBC Monitoring, OSC GMP20070115950064, January 15, 2007; "Al-Alam TV News Director Responds to Al-Najaf Prayer Leader's Criticism," *Iranian Labor News Agency* (Tehran), Web page, in Persian, OSC IAP20040605000076, 0935 GMT June 5, 2004.

[8]   "BBC Monitoring: Iran's Al-Alam TV Plays Role in Arab Media Scene," 2007; "BBC Monitoring: Iran Media Guide," in English, Caversham BBC Monitoring, OSC IAP20070327950024, March 27, 2007. However, in the months following the fall of Saddam Hussein, a U.S. State Department poll noted that "al-Alam was the most trusted and watched television station in Iraq, behind the Iraq Media Network (IMN) and the religious Najaf channel." This probably stemmed from al-Alam's availability as the only non-Iraqi terrestrial station whose signal can be received without a satellite dish. By 2004, however, an Intermedia survey reported that 78 percent of Iraqi viewers had access to satellite dishes and that al-Alam's total audience reach was 15 percent (compared to over 60 percent for the most popular channels, al-Arabiya and al-Jazeera). Moreover, the station received only single digits for reliability and importance as a source of information. See "BBC Monitoring: Iran Media Guide," 2007; U.S. Department of State, Office of Intelligence and Research, "Iraq Television Viewership Poll," October 16, 2003.

Arabia's Eastern Province revealed a general distrust of the channel; those surveyed saw it as too ideological and overbearing in its promotion of Iranian policies.[9] Nonetheless, al-Alam appears to have scored at least one major public relations coup among Arab audiences in the wake of Iran's seizure of 15 British sailors and marines from the H.M.S. *Cornwall* in March 2007 (see below).

Arab Public Opinion on Iran Fluctuates But Is Generally Not Alarmist

If Arab publics appear unreceptive to Iranian media, they also do not view Iran as the hegemonic, seemingly existential threat, as sometimes portrayed by both official Arab regime outlets and the United States. A 2006 Zogby/University of Maryland poll following the 2006 Lebanon war asked 3,850 respondents in Egypt, Jordan, Lebanon, Morocco, Saudi Arabia, and the United Arab Emirates to identify the two countries that posed the greatest threat to their security; only 11 percent identified Iran, while 85 percent listed Israel and 72 percent cited the United States. Among world leaders most admired by respondents, Hezbollah leader Hasan Nasrallah came in first, while President Ahmadinejad came in third (after French president Jacques Chirac).[10] In contrast, polling conducted by the Pew Global Attitudes

---

[9] RAND interviews with Shi'ite religious leaders and activists in Qatif, Dammam, and al-Ahsa, Eastern Province, Saudi Arabia, March 15–20, 2007. According to one respondent, a noted Shi'ite intellectual, even the Hezbollah television station al-Manar is not popular among Saudi Shi'ites because it consistently adopts a tone critical of Iraqi Shi'ite parties, such as SCIRI/ISCI, toward whom the Saudi Shi'ites showed a strong affinity. It was not until the 2006 Lebanon war that al-Manar's resonance increased, largely due to its compelling battlefield footage.

[10] Saudi Arabia and Lebanon were the only countries surveyed where Nasrallah did not rank number one—probably due to Riyadh's effort to cultivate anti-Shi'ite sentiment through its vast media network and the communal ambivalence in Lebanon to Hezbollah's domestic ascendancy (Zogby International, "Middle East Opinion: Iran Fears Aren't Hitting the Arab Street," 2006). As the scholar of Arab media Marc Lynch has noted, the absence of strong anti-Iranian popular sentiment is especially noteworthy given "the months of anti-Iranian agitation in much of the Arab media and a concerted American effort to midwife a 'coalition of moderate Sunnis' against Iran." See Marc Lynch, Middle East blog, February 9, 2007.

Project prior to the summer 2006 Lebanon fighting showed implicit distrust of President Ahmadinejad, with 68 percent and 65 percent of respondents in Egypt and Jordan, respectively, saying they had little or no confidence in President Ahmadinejad to "do the right thing" in world affairs.

The subsequent surge in acclaim for President Ahmadinejad shows Iran's ability to quickly derive collateral popular support from the brazen actions of its militant allies in the Levant, rather than from its political system or ideology per se. Added to this dynamic are the populist, grassroots charisma of President Ahmadinejad and his fiery, anti–status quo rhetoric. For Sunni Arab publics, the Iranian president's unabashed hostility to Israel, war credentials, modest dress, and humble origins contrast sharply with the cautious posturing and lavish lifestyles of their septuagenarian rulers. Persian-Shi'ite identity distinctions appear to fade in the face of President Ahamdinejad's appealing challenge to the stagnant political order. "I consider Ahmadinejad a leader of the Arab people. He has the confidence. It upsets me that we don't have such a leader," noted a 20-year-old student in Cairo interviewed by a Western journalist in mid-2007.[11] Similar sentiments were observed by RAND in the United Arab Emirates during President Ahmadinejad's visit in May 2007, which included a rally in a Dubai soccer stadium, where the 3,000-strong audience cheered Iran's nuclear ambitions.[12] It is important to note, however, that this acclaim does not represent a sustained endorsement of the Islamic Republic as a model for emulation—even among Shi'ite populations in Bahrain and Saudi Arabia, which largely reject the Iranian system of clerical rule.[13] As Karim Sadjapour has aptly noted,

---

[11] Andrew England, "Arab Street Warms to Showman Ahmadi-Nejad," *Financial Times*, April 6, 2007.

[12] RAND interviews with Emirati analysts and officials, Dubai, United Arab Emirates, May 2007. See also "President's Trip to Emirate Thwarted American Plans for Regional Discord," *Tehran* (Iran), Web page, in Persian, OSC IAP20070516950068, 0000 GMT May 15, 2007.

[13] RAND fieldwork among leading Shiite clerics and activists in Manama, Bahrain, and the Eastern Province of Saudi Arabia, November 2006 and March 2007, respectively.

There is reason to believe the Arab masses admire Iran's Islamic Republic much in the same way the Latin American street once romanticized Fidel Castro's Cuba. They praise the defiant political order from afar, but do not wish it for themselves.[14]

Moreover, pro-Iranian applause is fickle. Arab opinion has fluctuated periodically toward violently anti-Iranian views, demonstrating that Arab opinion remains an unstable strategic commodity for Tehran. By 2007, available polling and media surveys revealed a noticeable drop in support for Iran, stemming principally from worsening sectarian violence in Iraq. Zogby's 2007 polling of 3,400 Arab respondents in Egypt, Saudi Arabia, Jordan, the United Arab Emirates, and Lebanon showed that a majority believed Iran's role in Iraq was unhelpful, although there was broad consensus that U.S. actions were similarly detrimental.[15] A February 2007 al-Arabiya poll of Arab viewers in the Levant, Egypt, the Gulf, and North Africa revealed similar discomfort with Iran. Fifty percent of those polled believed Iran was a threat to the Arab world, while 58 percent saw Iran as aiming to bring the Arab world under its military and political hegemony. In the Persian Gulf region alone, 53 percent of respondents did not believe Iran's nuclear ambitions to be peaceful.[16]

Rapid shifts in public opinion toward Iran appear to hinge on pivotal events that are in some cases the direct result of Iranian policies and in other instances beyond its control. For example, the hanging of Saddam Hussein in December 2006 marked a rapid reversal of the

---

[14] Karim Sadjadpour, "How Relevant Is the Iranian Street?" *The Washington Quarterly*, Vol. 30, No. 1, Winter 2006–2007, pp. 151–162.

[15] When asked about their greatest regional worry, respondents were split, with U.S. permanence in the region, the fragmentation of Iraq, and the spillover of the Iraq war generally outweighing the direct threat of Iranian hegemony (James Zogby, "Four Years Later: Arab Opinion Troubled by Consequences of Iraq War," Washington, D.C.: Arab American Institute, n.d.).

[16] The polling results are available at "Kayfa Yandhuru al-Arab ila Iran? [How Do Arabs View Iran?]," *Panorama*, al-Arabiya television, February 26, 2007. Among the 1,221 Arabs surveyed, most of whom under the age of 30, 36 percent were from the Levant, 21 percent were from the Persian Gulf region, 14 percent were from North Africa, and 29 percent were from Egypt.

pro-Iranian Arab sentiment that followed the summer 2006 Lebanon fighting. Regional commentators and officials alike saw the execution as a humiliating blow to Arab identity and part of an Iranian and U.S. plot to marginalize the Sunnis. The backlash was especially strong in Jordan, whose population has traditionally expressed pro-Saddam sentiments and where a number of former officials of Saddam Hussein's regime have taken refuge. Here, the independent press appears to have outpaced official outlets in its condemnation of Iran—an unusual development given the aforementioned animosity by Arab regimes toward Tehran's assertiveness.[17]

This anti-Iranian trend was reversed following Iran's release of the 15 British sailors and marines in April 2007. This event is significant because, like Iran's defiance on the nuclear issue, it shows how anti-Western posturing can garner applause from Arab audiences while dampening their fears of Shi'ite ascendancy in Iraq. Indeed, Tehran may have partially conceived of the seizure as a strategic communication effort to Arab audiences; its coverage of the event was initially broadcast on its Arabic-language satellite TV station al-Alam.[18] The tactic appears to have been at least partially effective. Arab commentators throughout the region interpreted the conclusion of the crisis as an Iranian diplomatic and military gain, portraying Iranian actions as magnanimous while condemning the illegitimacy of the U.S./UK naval presence in the Gulf.[19] U.S. Naval Forces Central Command's (NAVCENT's) monitoring of Arab media noted that for the first time since its monitoring began in December 2006, pan-Arab coverage had moved to a more pro-Iranian slant, with assertions that Iran was not a

[17] "Saddam Execution Stokes Arab Anti-Iran, Anti-Shiite Sentiment," Middle East—OSC Analysis GMF20070111222001, January 10, 2007; "FYI—Iran's Al-Alam TV Discusses Arab Reaction to Saddam's Execution," Al-Alam Television (Tehran), in Arabic, OSC IAP20070102950094, 1330 GMT January 2, 2007.

[18] "BBC Monitoring Analysis: Arab Press Sees Iranian Gains in British Detainees Affair," BBC Monitoring, OSC EUP20070406950039, April 6, 2007.

[19] "BBC Monitoring Analysis: Arab Press Sees Iranian Gains in British Detainees Affair," 2007.

dangerous neighbor.[20] Moreover, NAVCENT observed that although the coalition initially seized the media initiative, subsequent Iranian messaging in the weeks following the seizure resulted in a sharp rise in the prevalence of pro-Iranian themes in the pan-Arab media.[21]

Arab Regimes Have Stoked Anti-Iranian Sentiment

Some Arab regimes deliberately cultivate anti-Iranian sentiment through the official press, and their actions create ambivalence in Arab opinion toward Iran. Arab regimes oppose Iran mostly due to their own balance-of-power calculations and fears of Iran's economic and military potential and its (often inflated) ability to wreak havoc inside Arab states. Surprisingly, Arab states, particularly those in the GCC, also fear eventual U.S.-Iranian strategic collusion, which would drastically erode the privileged positions they have enjoyed as a result of Washington's two-decade-long policy of isolating and containing Iran. "We can all agree on one issue without any debate," noted a prominent Lebanese commentator and academic, "any Iranian-American agreement will be at the expense of Arabs because both countries will exert hegemony over the region."[22]

Thus, to bolster popular support for their anti-Iran policies, Arab regimes attempt to exploit the Shi'ite and Persian nature of Tehran's ambitions, which are portrayed as threatening Sunni Arabs everywhere, while downplaying its appealing challenge to the status quo and defiance of the West. The most notable examples are King 'Abdallah of Jordan's famous warning of a "Shi'ite crescent" on the eve of the Iraqi parliamentary elections and Egyptian President Hosni Mubarak's televised declaration that the Arab Shi'ites' "loyalty is always to Iran" and

---

[20] NAVCENT, "Media Analysis Report, Iran and Regional Security Quicklook," April 2007.

[21] NAVCENT, "Iran Media Analysis, Quarterly Report, January–March 2007," April 2007.

[22] Jihad al-Khazin, "Al-Maradh al-Arabi [The Arab Disease]," *Saudi in Focus*, date not available.

"not to their countries."[23] Saudi-affiliated media, including newspapers such as *al-Sharq al-Awsat* and the satellite TV station al-Arabiya, have been especially critical vectors for this strategy. In particular, prominent Saudi clerics, both inside and outside the official religious bureaucracy, have issued a stream of anti-Shi'ite and anti-Iranian religious rulings that proclaim Arab solidarity with Iraqi Sunnis and legitimate the murder of Shi'ites.[24] These decrees have elicited strong condemnation from Shi'ite clerics in Qom and other theological centers, who derided the views of the Sunni religious establishment as being out of touch with mainstream Arab sentiment.[25]

Official Arab Outlets Attack Tehran's Circumvention of Diplomatic Channels

This back-and-forth vitriol demonstrates that Arab opinion remains a contested, volatile commodity for Iran, despite Iran's appeal in regard to the Palestine issue, defiance of the West, and challenge to the status quo. To better understand this dynamic, we surveyed major Arab news outlets to identify the prominent anti-Iranian themes that have helped

---

[23] Abdullah II bin al-Hussein, King of Jordan, quoted in *al-Ra'y*, January 6, 2005; Mubarak's was carried on al-Arabiya TV, April 9, 2006. See also "Tactless Mubarak Provokes Reassertion of National Loyalties by Gulf Arab Shi'as," *Gulf States Newsletter*, Vol. 30, No. 779, April 14, 2006.

[24] Toby Craig Jones, "Saudi Arabia's Not So New Anti-Shiism," *Middle East Report 242*, Spring 2007, pp. 29–32. For examples of anti-Iranian, anti-Shiite *fatwa*, see 'Ali bin Khudayr al-Khudayr, "*Fatwa* on the Shi'a," Web page, in Arabic, date not available. Also, Nasr al-Fahd, "Letter on the Legitimacy of Swearing at the Shi'a," Web page, in Arabic, date not available; Nasr al-Fahd, "Response to the Rejectionists (Shiites) on Their Indictment of the Companions," Web page, in Arabic, date not available; al-Umar, "The Situation of the *Rafida* in the Land of Tawhed," date not available; al-Umar, "If Iran Occupies Iraq," date not available. It is important to note however, that there were significant fissures and debates within clerical circles about whether Iran and Hezbollah or the United States and Israel constituted the most immediate threat. See "Saudi Website Sunni-Shiite Reaction to Lebanon Crisis," Saudi Arabia—OSC Report, in Arabic, OSC GMP20060816862001, August 16, 2006.

[25] For an example, Middle East Media Research Institute (MEMRI), "An Eternal Curse on the Muftis of the Saudi Court and on the Pharaoh of Egypt," editorial in *Jomhouri-ye Eslami* (Tehran), July 28, 2006.

mitigate Iran's influence in the public sphere. Covering a period from September 2006 to July 2007, our canvass included major pan-Arab newspapers, such as *al-Hayat*, *Al-Sharq al-Awsat*, and *al-Elaf*, as well as local ones, such as *al-Rai* (Jordan), *al-Sha'b* (Egypt), and *al-Itihad* (United Arab Emirates). We also monitored popular television networks, such as al-Jazeera and al-Arabiya.

We encountered a prominent theme, largely in the official press, of hostility toward Iran's outreach to Arab publics and its support to internal opposition movements, both of which bypass state-to-state diplomacy by speaking "over the heads" of Arab leaders. Lebanon is a key example—the first step, according to some commentators, in Iran's plan for exerting a dominant role, not mere influence, over internal Arab affairs. For example, Walid Jumblatt, the prominent Lebanese Druze leader, stated in a live interview with al-Jazeera that Iran is responsible for destabilizing Lebanon by financing and empowering Hezbollah as a political actor.[26] Revered in 2006, Hezbollah was later attacked by numerous Lebanese voices and accused of committing "the disgraceful national sin of forming a coalition with a foreign government (Iran) and carrying out that government's agenda."[27] Hezbollah's legacy as a national resistance movement that helped liberate Lebanon from Israeli occupation in May 2000 is being replaced by a new narrative that Hezbollah is a "a state within a state"[28] serving Iranian interests. Exemplifying this critique, Sa'ad al-Hariri, the Lebanese head of the al-Mustaqbal party, gave Hezbollah an ultimatum "to choose between Iran and Lebanon."[29] Elsewhere on the Arab-Israeli front, Arab officials and commentators cite Iranian funding of Hamas

---

[26] "Lebanon Under the Current Circumstances," *Without Borders*, Al-Jazeera television, in Arabic, January 16, 2007.

[27] Al-Khedir Abd al-Aziz, "America and the Sins of Coalitions," *Al Sharq al-Awsat*, in Arabic, December 18, 2006.

[28] Jamil al-Dhiyabi, "Fa'es America wa Ghatrasat Iran [America's Ax and Iran's Arrogance]," *Al-Hayat*, June 25, 2007.

[29] Abbas Tha'ir, "Al-Hariri: Ala Hizbullah Al-Ikhtiyar bayna Lubnan wa al-Haras al-Thawri al-Irani [Hariri, Hizbullah Has to Choose Between Lebanon and the Iranian Revolutionary Guard]," *Al-Sharq al-Awsat*, July 16, 2007.

as provoking civil war among Palestinians and preventing them from forming a united front against Israel.[30]

Aside from its support to Hezbollah and specific political entities, there is a broader criticism of Iran's appropriation of Arab issues and concerns. For example, Mishari al-Zaydi, a popular Saudi columnist writing in *Al-Sharq al-Awsat*, urged his readers to

> Examine all the big Arab portfolios—Lebanon, Palestine, and Iraq. They are being stolen from Arab hands, which have traditionally handled these issues, and turned over to Iranian hands gradually.[31]

Iran's rejectionist stance on the Arab-Israeli peace process appears particularly unsettling to Arab regimes. This is especially evident in Egypt because of Cairo's signing of the 1979 peace treaty with Israel, which has exposed it to criticism that it effectively abandoned the Palestinian cause.[32] Tehran's public rejection of various Arab peace initiatives has elicited outrage from Egyptian commentators, who have argued that it is not Iran's place to take such positions, as Israel is occupying Arab and not Persian land. One Arab writer offered two interpretations of Iran's posturing. First, Iran is trying to assert that it is part of the region and thereby outmaneuver U.S. and Israeli attempts to isolate it. Second, by disagreeing with peace initiatives, Iran is proclaiming its uniqueness and steadfastness to the Palestinian cause—becoming, in effect, more Arab than the Arabs.[33]

---

[30] Hassan Haydar, "Inhinaa' Iran [Iran's Weakness]," *Free Syria*, Web site, February 8, 2007.

[31] Mishari al-Zaydi, "Uhadhir an Taqdhi Alihi al-Ama'im [Warning Against the Religious Establishment]," *Al-Sharq al-Awsat*, July 19, 2007.

[32] Egypt and Iran have had especially bitter relations stemming from Cairo's admission of the deposed Shah for medical treatment and Tehran's public homage to the assassin of Egyptian President Anwar Sadat, which is reflected in numerous postage stamps, street names, and murals.

[33] Salaah Salim, "Tajawoz al-Qati'a al-Misriya al-Iraniya [Overcoming the Egyptian-Iranian Estrangement]," *Elaph*, July 8, 2007.

Many Arabs Accuse Iran of Creating Instability, Sectarianism, and Violence

Aside from this bypassing of diplomatic channels, there are widespread accusations that Tehran cultivates Islamic extremism inside Arab states and sponsors terrorism. A representative example is Ahmad al-Rabi'i, a Kuwaiti analyst, who observed that Iranian support for violence in Arab affairs is unambiguous in the Persian Gulf and also extends to Egypt, Lebanon, and Syria.[34] Speaking more generally, *Al-Sharq al-Awsat* columnist al-Zaydi pointed out that while religious extremism has always existed in a marginalized form, "this phenomenon became a real danger to the entire Arab and Muslim worlds, and the world at large, once it reached power in Iran."[35]

In many cases, this charge appears to be a calculated tactic to shift attention away from the indigenous roots of Arab societal tensions— such as poor governance, public perceptions of regime illegitimacy, economic conditions, or the U.S. military presence—and assign blame to an external sponsor. For example, former Algerian Prime Minister Ahmad al-Ghazali cited the time-worn accusation of Iran's export of its revolution to be the primary reason for instability throughout the Arab world.[36] In a separate article, he directly accused Iran of inciting the civil war that afflicted Algeria in the 1980s and 1990s, arguing, "it was clear to us that the tensions and violence were not innate in our societies but rather are instigated from abroad."[37] This dynamic is especially evident in Yemen, where the government has pointed repeatedly to Iran's hidden hand in stoking a Zaydi Shi'ite rebellion in the north-

---

[34] "Kayfa Yandhuru al-Arab ila Iran? [How Do Arabs View Iran?]," 2007.

[35] al-Zaydi, 2007.

[36] Ahmad al-Ghasali, "Istifhal al-Azmah, Ma Hua al-Hal? [Exacerbating the Problem, What Is the Solution?]," *Al-Sharq al-Awsat*, July, 26, 2007.

[37] Ahmad al-Ghasali, "An Tajrubah: Makhatir Taqdim Ghusan al-Zaytoon LiIran [Out of Experience: The Dangers of Extending the Olive Branch to Iran]," *Al-Sharq al-Awsat*, No. 10341, March 22, 2007.

ern Sa'da province—essentially a local, center-periphery conflict that is rooted more in tribal marginalization than in any external support.[38]

Many Arabs view Iraq as the central front for Iranian aggression. An Iraqi official asserted that Tehran is "the most active terrorism sponsor in the world" and named the IRGC and other Iranian security agencies as directly involved in terrorist operations against civilians in Iraq.[39] Interviewed on al-Arabiya television, Muhammad al-Dayni, an Iraqi parliament member, pleaded to his audience,

> I am an Iraqi! I know the extent of the Iranian interference in Iraq since the Iranian Revolution. They want to spread their revolution to the Arab countries. They will fight anyone who stands in their way.[40]

Hussayn al-Mu'aid, an Iraqi Shi'ite cleric, cited the frequent refrain of Persian-Arab animosity, arguing that Iranian interference in Iraq was the first step in Iran's broader "Persian political ambitions."[41]

The warning against this drive, however, is not limited to Iraqis. An article by Moroccan writer 'Abed al-Ilah Bilqiz, for example, is representative of views in other Arab states and helps explain the aforementioned outrage over Saddam Hussein's hanging. Bilqiz argued that Hussein was ultimately transparent in his war to block Iranian expansionism, which he emphasized was Persian and Shi'ite in nature, rather than revolutionary:

> Many Arabs did not believe Saddam Hussein when he told them, a quarter century ago, about the Iranian national ambitions regard-

---

[38] The Yemeni government has accused both Iran and Libya of sponsoring a rebellion led by Zaydi Shi'ite leader 'Abd al-Malik al-Houthi, resulting in Sana'a's recall of its ambassadors from Tehran and Tripoli (Muhammad bin Sallam, "Yemen Recalls Its Ambassadors to Iran and Libya," *Yemen Times*, May 13, 2008).

[39] Al-Dhiyabi, 2007.

[40] "Kayfa Yandhuru al-Arab ila Iran? [How Do Arabs View Iran?]," 2007.

[41] "Al-Sira' al-Ta'ifi fi al-Iraq wa al-Mintaqah [The Sectarian Conflict in Iraq and the Region]," *Bila Hudud* [*Without Borders*], al-Muqtada television, January 20, 2007.

ing the Arab world. They didn't believe him when he asked them to face the Iranian ambitions with a national Arab agenda.[42]

Officials and Commentators Criticize Iran's Hegemonic Drive

Officials and Arab commentators who oppose Iran's growing influence in Iraq and elsewhere often resort to historical comparisons to provide evidence of Iran's hegemonic, territorial ambitions. For example, historian Mahmoud Sayid al-Dughaim has contended that Iran is actually a bigger source of concern to Arabs than Israel, citing the example of the Safavid Persian dynasty that competed with the Sunni Ottoman Empire for supremacy in the Middle East from the 16th through the 17th centuries. While the "Zionist project" (Israel) is a danger to Muslims because of its occupation of al-Qods (Jerusalem), he argued, the "Safavid project" (Iran) is a far more critical threat because it aims to restore Persia's former glory, dominating both the Arabian Peninsula and the entire Mediterranean. Playing on Sunni Muslim religious sensitivities, he accused Tehran of pursuing historical Persian designs to take over Mecca and Medina, which are more sacred to Muslims than Jerusalem.[43] Echoing this historical analogy, a senior Saudi diplomat told RAND researchers in March 2006 that the U.S. disbandment of the Iraqi army effectively split the Muslim world into opposing sectarian camps, recalling earlier centuries of conflict between the Sunni Ottoman Empire and the Persian Shi'ite Safavids.[44]

Because of their proximity to Iran, commentators in the GCC countries show a particular preference for this line of thinking. Most notably, they point to Tehran's disputed occupation of the Abu Musa

---

[42] Abed al-Ilah Bilqaziz, "Al-Arab wa Iran: Min al-Ummah ila al-Madhhab [The Arabs and Iran: From the Umma to the Sect]," Web page, Harakat al-Adalah al-Watania [National Justice Movement], February 20, 2007.

[43] "Al-Nufuth al-Irani fi al-Mintaqa al-Arabiya [The Iranian Influence in the Arab Region]," *Al-Ittijah al-Mu'akis* [*Opposite Direction*], al-Muqtada television, February 4, 2007.

[44] RAND interview with a senior Saudi diplomat, Manama, Bahrain, March 12, 2006.

and Tunb Islands, which are claimed by the United Arab Emirates.[45] The issue of these islands dominated the agenda of the Nineteenth Arab League Summit in 2006, resulting in a strongly worded condemnation of Iran's occupation.[46] More recently, a July 2007 article in the Iranian press by an advisor to the Iranian Supreme Leader asserted that Bahrain was rightfully a province of Iran, igniting Gulf Arab criticism of Iran's historical ambition to control Arab land.[47]

Arab Regimes Fear Iranian Nuclear Ambitions But Must Temper Their Public Criticism

As noted earlier, Arab public opinion is generally supportive or tolerant of Iranian nuclear ambitions as an indirect critique against Western interference in the region and double standards for Israel. In official circles, however, there is alarm—often conveyed more forcefully in private rather than public channels. These fears do not necessarily stem from the threat of a direct nuclear attack from Iran but rather from the "ripple effects" a nuclear-capable Iran would cause throughout the region. The potential effects include an escalating regional arms race, which could involve the acquisition of nuclear arms by major powers, such as Saudi Arabia, Egypt, or Turkey; a nuclear accident at one of Iran's reactors; and an Iran that is more aggressive in its support for terrorism and Shi'ite activism or more unyielding in its diplomacy.[48]

---

[45] Niveen Abd al-Mun'im, *Sun' al-Qarar fi Iran wa al-Alaqat al-Arabiya al-Irania* [*Decisionmaking in Iran and the Arab-Iranian Relations*], Center for Arab Unity Studies, Beirut, Lebanon, 2002, p. 247.

[46] "Al-Qimma *al-Arabiya* [The Arab Summit]," Saudi Press Agency, Web page, date not available.

[47] "Bahrain: Mudhaharat Ihtijaj ala Maqalat Kihan Bahrain [Demonstrations over Kihan's Article], *Al-Sharq al-Awsat*, Web page, date not available.

[48] This analysis is based on RAND interviews with scholars, officials, and diplomats throughout the GCC and in Egypt and Jordan in February and March 2006 and July 2007. See also Dalia Dassa Kaye and Frederic M. Wehrey, "A Nuclear Iran: The Reactions of Neighbours," *Survival*, Vol. 49, No. 2, Summer 2007, pp. 111–128; Karim Sadjadpour, "The Nuclear Players," *Journal of International Affairs,* Vol. 60, No. 2, Spring/Summer 2007,

In attempting to emphasize these concerns in the media, Arab regimes are engaged in a delicate balancing act. They are ultimately wary that Arab audiences may interpret their opposition to Iran's nuclear ambitions as an implicit endorsement of a U.S. military strike—which they fear their publics may oppose. One remedy to this dilemma is to publicly argue against a U.S. strike, make vague and somewhat anemic calls for "dialogue" with Iran on the nuclear issue, and shift the public debate to Israel by proposing a nuclear-free zone in the Middle East that would include Tel Aviv's abandonment of its own undeclared capability.[49] Even officials in Saudi Arabia, the Arab state facing the greatest threat to its status and security from a nuclear Iran, have been adamant in their public appeal for dialogue and moderation. For example, in an interview with *al-Hayat* on June 22, 2007, the Saudi foreign minister warned against the dangers of using force against Iran and stressed "the need to turn the Middle East into a nuclear-free zone."[50] Yet as noted in earlier sections, if leaders in Riyadh and other Arab capitals are hesitant to strongly criticize Iran on the nuclear issue, they have shown no such reservations in playing the "sectarian card"—exploiting fears of an Iranian-led Shi'ite crescent.

It is important to note that there are significant divisions within the Arab world regarding the type and extent of the threat posed by a nuclear Iran. For example, Egyptian commentators have not adopted the moderate and restrained tone of some of the Persian Gulf states on the Iranian nuclear issue, leading to accusations from the Persian Gulf

---

pp. 125–134; Richard L. Russell, "Peering over the Horizon: Arab Threat Perception and Security Responses to a Nuclear-Ready Iran," Non-Proliferation Policy Education Center, February 5, 2005; Judith S. Yaphe and Charles D. Lutes, "Reassessing the Implications of a Nuclear-Armed Iran," McNair Paper 69, Washington, D.C.: National Defense University, 2005; Simon Henderson, "The Elephant in the Gulf: The Arab States and Iran's Nuclear Program," Washington Institute for Near East Policy, PolicyWatch 1065, December 21, 2005; Emile el-Hokayem and Matteo Legrenzi, "The Arab Gulf States in the Shadow of the Iranian Nuclear Challenge," Washington, D.C.: The Stimson Center, May 2006.

[49] RAND interviews with foreign ministry officials, journalists, and military commanders in the United Arab Emirates, Kuwait, and Oman in March 2006 and July 2007.

[50] "BBC Monitoring Analysis: Arab Dilemma over Iran's Nuclear Program," OSC FEA20070627206546, June 27, 2007.

region that Cairo is tacitly backing a U.S. military option because it is physically removed from the consequences of an attack. Some officials from Persian Gulf states have gone so far as to suggest that Egypt is covertly backing an Iranian nuclear program to counterbalance its more immediate, proximate adversary—Israel.[51] There are even divisions within the GCC: Kuwait appears most concerned about the environmental consequences of an accident at one of Iran's nuclear facilities; Abu Dhabi has singled out increased diplomatic belligerence on the disputed islands by a nuclear Iran; and Oman appears to have fewer concerns, given its long history of interdependence and good relations with Iran.[52] Illustrating this accommodating stance, a retired Omani military commander posed this question to RAND researchers during a February 2006 meeting:

> Why should we be more afraid of a nuclear-armed Iran than a nuclear Pakistan? Prestige is driving the Pakistani nuclear program; the same holds true for Iran. Nuclear acquisition will not necessarily result in a more dangerous Iranian foreign policy.[53]

Arab Publics Fear the Consequences of a U.S. Strike Over the Nuclear Issue

Public ambivalence and fear of Iran does not necessarily translate into support for a U.S. military strike.[54] Indeed, even GCC officials who

---

[51] Kaye and Wehrey, 2007, p. 114.

[52] Kaye and Wehrey, 2007, pp. 112–120. Even within the United Arab Emirates, there are differing threat perceptions, with Dubai adopting a more accommodating stance given the heavy Iranian investment there, which may give Dubai officials a sense of immunity from an Iranian attack. In Abu Dhabi, there was fear that Iran may seek to exploit these fissures, citing the precedent of the Iran-Iraq War, which caused internal discord inside the United Arab Emirates over how to address the threat from Iran.

[53] RAND interview with a retired Omani military commander, Muscat, Oman, February 6, 2006.

[54] For regime perceptions of the consequences of a strike, see Kaye and Wehrey, 2007, pp. 115–117; Joseph A. Kechichian, "Can Conservative Arab Gulf Monarchies Endure a

expressed an uncompromising hostility toward Iran during discussions with RAND were fearful of the consequences of a U.S. strike, citing Iranian military retaliation, terrorism, public protests, and increased Shi'ite agitation inside their borders as their major concerns. Underpinning these fears is strong skepticism about the U.S. ability to conduct a short, surgical strike and concern about Iran's capacity to prolong the conflict, in turn inflicting damage on the Persian Gulf states' economies and inflaming popular Arab sentiment. During a RAND roundtable discussion on Iran with Saudi diplomatic and military officials in Riyadh, this theme emerged frequently. As summarized by the Bahraini prime minister, "the region cannot endure another war."[55]

Fear of Indiscriminate Iranian Retaliation Weighs Heavily

A major fear in public and official deliberations is the threat of direct Iranian military retaliation. A headline in the July 11, 2007, edition of *al-Sharq al-Awsat* warned, "Iran Threatens to Shower Gulf Countries Cooperating with America with Missiles."[56] A prominent Lebanese commentator echoed this alarm in his 2007 book, *America, Islam and the Nuclear Weapon*, noting that, "Iran is not Iraq . . . . It is stronger politically and militarily. One cannot attack Iran without paying a heavy price. Leaders of the West clearly realize this."[57]

Private discussions with RAND by Persian Gulf and other Arab officials revealed similar concerns. A senior Qatari Ministry of Interior official warned that Iran would "attack Qatar with ballistic and cruise missiles that can cause panic and structural damage, closure of air and

---

Fourth Gulf War in the Persian Gulf," *Middle East Journal,* Vol. 61, No. 2, Spring 2007, pp. 283–306.

[55] Salman al-Durusi, "Al-Shaykh Khalifah bin Salman: Al-Khalij La Yatahammal Harb Jadidah [Sheikh Khalifah bin Salman: The Gulf Cannot Take Another War]," *Al-Sharq al-Awsat,* July 28, 2007.

[56] "Iran Tuhadid Duwal al-Khalij al-Muta'awinah ma' America bil Sawarikh [Iran Threatens the Gulf Countries Cooperating with America with Missiles]," *Al-Sharq al-Awsat,* July 11, 2007.

[57] Isam Nu'man, *America wa al-Islam al-Silah al-Nawawi [America, Islam, and the Nuclear Weapon]*, Beirut: Al-Matbu'at Publishing House, 2007, p. 207.

sea ports, and the destruction of Qatar's oil and water installations."[58] The net effect of this retaliation, he forecasted, would be internal discord and disagreement within the government, as well as increased anti-regime activism. Officials in the United Arab Emirates pointed to their ports as a "center of gravity" for the U.S. fleets and the target of Iranian attack. Adding to this, a senior Emirati military commander opined that Iran will "not discriminate" in its targeting of GCC facilities and would attack those that are not directly connected with the U.S. war effort.[59] Even Oman did not feel immune from the consequences of a U.S. strike—an Omani government advisor and member of the GCC Consultative Council told RAND that "an attack by a single Iranian helicopter could devastate Oman's oil importing infrastructure."[60] Officials in Baghdad felt especially vulnerable, given Iraq's long border with Iran and the presence of Iranian-backed Shi'ite militants inside the country. As noted by the Iraqi vice president, a U.S. strike on Iran "would be difficult to contain because the front is wide and both sides have many resources."[61] Elsewhere in Kuwait, a retired Kuwaiti general and strategic analyst summarized the "caught in the crossfire" dilemma that prevails in the smaller GCC states. "We are stuck in the middle," he stated during an al-Jazeera talk show, "and have every right to fear the consequences."[62]

---

[58] RAND interview with a senior Qatari Ministry of Interior official, Doha, Qatar, July 2, 2007.

[59] RAND interview with a retired Emirati military commander, February 9, 2006, Abu Dhabi, United Arab Emirates.

[60] RAND interview with a senior Omani government advisor and member of the GCC Consultative Council, Muscat, Oman, February 5, 2006.

[61] Hasan Fahs, "Abd al-Hadi LilHayat: Ay Sidam Irani-Amrici Sayas'ub Dhabtuhu Li'an Sahatuhu Wasi'ah wa al-Imkanat Kabira [Abd al-Hadi to Al-Hayat Newspaper: Any American-Iranian Confrontation Would Be Difficult to Contain Because the Front Is Wide and the Resources Are Huge]," *Al-Hayat*, February 9, 2007.

[62] Comments of Dr. Sami al-Faraj on "Malaf Iran al-Nawawi wa Khayarat Majlis al-Amn [The Iranian Nuclear Portfolio and the Security Council Options]," *Akthar min Ra'i [More Than One Opinion]*, al-Muqtada television, February 17, 2006.

Some Observers Fear Militancy or Activism by Gulf Arab Shi'ites

One common refrain in the arguments against a U.S. strike by Gulf Arab officials, as well as some public commentary, is the propensity for retaliation or increased activism by Shi'ite populations within their borders. This Iranian "fifth column" argument is often taken as conventional wisdom, especially among Persian Gulf regimes but in some U.S. policy circles as well.[63] Certainly, Gulf Shi'ite populations, particularly in Bahrain and Saudi Arabia, have engaged in Iranian-assisted violence, ranging from popular street protests and coup planning to large-scale terrorist attacks, such as the 1996 Khobar Towers bombing.[64] In the event of a U.S. strike, there is the possibility that even minority Shi'ite populations in the United Arab Emirates and Kuwait (which have been relatively well-integrated and tranquil compared to their coreligionists in Bahrain and Saudi Arabia) could be inspired toward militancy.[65]

Yet as noted in our previous discussion of Iran's support to the Lebanese Hezbollah and Iraqi Shi'ite groups, Tehran's ability to exert operational control on Shi'ite organizations outside Iran's borders is curbed by those groups' own domestic agendas. In the cases of Bahrain and Saudi Arabia, RAND fieldwork revealed a strong hesitation among even the most militant Shi'ite activists and clerics to jeopar-

---

[63] RAND interviews with Bahraini foreign ministry and *Majlis al-Shura* [consultative council] officials, Manama, Bahrain, November 2006, and Saudi foreign ministry officials, Riyadh, Saudi Arabia, March 2006.

[64] In Bahrain and Saudi Arabia, Shi'ites respectively constitute 70 percent and 10–15 percent of the population. In both countries, they have suffered from political and economic marginalization and cultural repression, although in Bahrain, economic deprivation is more acute. For more on the Shi'ite populations in Bahrain and Saudi Arabia and their efforts at integration, see Nakash, 2006; International Crisis Group, "The Shiite Question in Saudi Arabia," Middle East Report No. 45, Brussels, 2005; International Crisis Group, "Bahrain's Sectarian Challenge," Middle East Report No. 40, Brussels, 2005; Fred Wehrey, "Saudi Arabia: Shi'a Pessimistic About Reform, but Seek Reconciliation," *Arab Reform Bulletin*, Vol. 5, No. 5, Washington, D.C.: Carnegie Endowment for International Peace, July 2007; Georges Malbrunot, "Golfe Alors que la tension monte entre Washington et Téhéran; Les chiites d'Arabie sous l'oeil de l'Iran," *Le Figaro* (Paris), November 17, 2007.

[65] RAND interview with United Arab Emirates foreign ministry officials and a Kuwaiti strategic analyst, Abu Dhabi and Kuwait City, respectively, March 2007. Also, Sadjadpour, "The Nuclear Players," 2006–2007, p. 130.

dize hard-won political gains by staging protests or engaging in acts of retaliatory sabotage in the service of Tehran. The possibility of sleeper cells certainly cannot be discounted. But recent RAND discussions with the leaders of the two main pro-Iranian Shi'ite organizations in Bahrain and Saudi Arabia revealed that these groups have largely jettisoned their militant tactics to pursue more-peaceful activism, such as participation in municipal and parliamentary elections.[66]

Moreover, in both countries, these pro-Iranian organizations enjoy only a limited popular following. In Saudi Arabia's Eastern Province, for example, the pro-Iranian faction failed to win a single seat in the 2005 municipal council elections. In Bahrain, Shi'ite activists argue that the ruling al-Khalifa family frequently exaggerates Iranian influence because doing so provides it a useful pretext to stall on democratization, portraying any push for reforms as "Shi'ite" or "Iranian inspired." In both countries, Shi'ite interlocutors told RAND that while they viewed Iran with spiritual and emotional affinity, there was little support for its political system or policies in the region.[67] One major explanation is the strong historical ties between Shi'ites on the Peninsula and Iraq, rather than Iran; many Bahraini and Saudi Shi'ites look to the seminaries in Najaf, particularly Grand Ayatollah 'Ali al-Sistani, instead of the Iranian Supreme Leader, for spiritual and political guidance. As a result, many argued that while there would undoubtedly be sporadic demonstrations against a U.S. strike, the notion that Tehran would be able to enlist Shi'ite diaspora populations en masse to punish their respective regimes was simply incorrect.

---

[66] RAND interviews with senior Islamic Action Society and *Khat al-Imam* [Imam's Line] clerics, Manama, Bahrain, and Dammam, Saudi Arabia, November 2006 and March 2007, respectively. The Islamic Action Society is the successor to the Islamic Front for the Liberation of Bahrain, which attempted a 1981 coup d'etat against the Bahraini regime, with Iranian backing. In Saudi Arabia, Shi'ite interlocutors and Saudi officials argued that the Saudi Shi'ite Hezbollah organization (or Hezbollah al-Hijaz) was either dormant or had been absorbed into the *Khat al-Imam* political faction and was focused on political activism and charitable activities.

[67] RAND interviews with a Shi'ite intellectual and activist, Qatif, Eastern Province, Saudi Arabia, March 20, 2007.

Finally, it is important to note that many grassroots Shi'ite activists did indeed warn of future radicalization and anti-regime agitation, particularly among Shi'ite youth who were enamored with Hezbollah's successful defiance of Israel in the summer of 2006. However, this was largely independent of Tehran's direct influence and more deeply rooted in the activists' frustration with the pace of domestic reform, economic disenfranchisement, and cultural repression in both Saudi Arabia and Bahrain. Ironically, Shi'ites perceive this stagnation to be partially the result of decreased U.S. pressure on Riyadh and Manama to effect domestic reforms and of Washington's fixation on soliciting their diplomatic support for its anti-Iranian policies.[68]

Conclusion

As noted in Chapter Two, Tehran has long viewed the "Arab street" as a means to circumvent the pro-U.S. tendencies and hostility it encounters from Arab regimes. More recently, this vector of Iranian strategy has been strengthened by popular Arab acclaim resulting from the battlefield successes of Tehran's principal Levantine ally, Hezbollah, as well as President Ahmadinejad's charismatic, grassroots appeal and defiant posturing on the nuclear issue. The belief, whether warranted or not, that it can count on popular Arab sympathy can push Tehran toward assertiveness and even brinksmanship in its foreign policy.

Nonetheless, Arab opinion remains a fickle and unstable strategic resource, potentially impelling Iranian leaders toward greater caution. As this chapter has demonstrated, Tehran's own strategic communications to Arab audiences, most notably via its Arabic-language satellite TV station, have been outpaced by its pan-Arab competitors al-Jazeera and al-Arabiya in terms of reliability and popularity. Moreover, Arab opinion on Iran fluctuates, frequently hovering between ambivalence and fear but seldom reaching the fever pitch of alarm present in official Arab discourse. At times it can rapidly swing between wild acclaim

---

[68] RAND fieldwork in Manama, Bahrain, November 2006, and Saudi Arabia's Eastern Province, March 2007.

and demonization. This vacillation can be at least partly accounted for by the plethora of anti-Iranian themes dominating the official media. However, in criticizing Iran's nuclear drive, Arab officials are careful to avoid conveying the perception that their opposition is a de facto endorsement of U.S. military action.

Indeed, both official discourse and public opinion appear firmly opposed to a U.S. strike, citing the threat of Iranian military retaliation and a potential "fifth column" retaliation by Gulf Shi'ites. However, the threat of an outbreak of Shi'ite activism or militancy purely in the service of Tehran is grossly exaggerated due to the Gulf Shi'ites' own domestic priorities and their limited political affinity for Tehran. Thus, popular sentiment in the Arab world is both an asset and a liability for Tehran. As we discuss in the next chapter, U.S. policies toward the Islamic Republic, as well as Washington's ability to manage the reactions of Arab regimes to Iranian power, will determine the degree to which Tehran can exploit Arab public opinion.

CHAPTER SIX

Conclusion: U.S. Strategy and the Islamic Republic

In the preceding chapters, we explored the reach and limitations of principal aspects of the Iranian strategic challenge: the regime's perception of itself in the world as a regional and even global power, its conventional military buildup and aspirations for an asymmetric warfare capability, its support for paramilitaries and terrorist groups, and its ability to exploit Arab popular opinion. It is clear from our analysis that Iran will present formidable challenges to U.S. interests over the next ten to fifteen years, particularly in the realm of ballistic missiles, its naval activity in the Strait of Hormuz, and its support for certain terrorist groups. Iranian ambitions for a nuclear weapon capability are especially worrisome and demand attention. Although the November 2007 National Intelligence Estimate suggests Iran halted a covert nuclear weapons program in 2003, the report also assesses "with high confidence that Iran has the scientific, technical and industrial capacity eventually to produce nuclear weapons if it decides to do so."[1] In other words, the nuclear file is still open and a source for continued international concern. Even if the overall thrust of its foreign and security policies is oriented pragmatically and defensively, Iran has a history of dangerous miscalculation, a tendency that only exacerbates fears of a nuclear-armed Iran.

---

[1] National Intelligence Council, *Iran: Nuclear Intentions and Capabilities*, National Intelligence Estimate, November 2007.

Yet the previous chapters have also offered empirical and analytic support for the proposition that Iran's ascendancy may be more limited than conventional wisdom suggests. Iran's aspirations for influence and power projection are circumscribed by a host of regional and structural factors. As we argued in Chapter Two, Iranian strategic culture contains indigenous drivers for assertiveness and aggression, but also strong sources of caution and pragmatism. When combined with the challenges Iran faces in building its conventional military capabilities (as well as Tehran's strategic missteps), not only is Iran's regional influence more limited than many would expect, but Iran also perceives itself, and indeed is, isolated and vulnerable, both militarily and politically. As a consequence, Iran frequently inflates its geopolitical weight by creating the image of indispensability often in ways directly counter to U.S interests.

Framing Iran's recent activism as a set of liabilities and assets allows us to consider a range of U.S. strategy options. In this chapter, we first consider several of the broad themes that have emerged from the study to ground our recommendations in a realistic reading of the Iranian challenge. Next, we survey previous U.S. policy approaches toward the Islamic Republic, noting their limitations in effectively addressing Iranian power and influence. Finally, we offer a different strategic approach that is marked by a unilateral de-escalation of U.S. posture on Iran in conjunction with more-sustained multilateral pressure, particularly with respect to Iran's nuclear program.

Basing Policy on Regional Realities: Key Themes from Our Study

The United States' triumph during the Cold War ultimately resulted from policies that reflected a sober assessment of the military and ideological challenges posed by the Soviet Union. Similarly realistic thinking must inform U.S. policies vis-à-vis Tehran. To be sure, Iran is a weighty rival, but it is hardly an omnipotent or immutable one. Our previous analysis identified a range of threats from the Islamic Republic, but it also revealed important limitations.

Many within the current regime in Tehran appear to view Iran as an indispensable regional power, but not necessarily a revolutionary hegemon. There is the further belief that the Islamic Republic is a model for Islamic enlightenment everywhere and the preeminent Islamic state in the region, providing a geopolitical bridge between Asia and the Middle East. As a result of these perceived attributes, the Iranian leadership has shown a marked tendency not only to push for a greater role in regional affairs but also to exaggerate Iran's strategic profile on the world stage. Much of this "triumphalism" can be accounted for by recent changes in the Middle Eastern environment that have enhanced and amplified Iran's existing influence, rather than by any real changes in Iran's intrinsic power. These enabling factors include the U.S. invasions of Iraq and Afghanistan and the growing regional perception of diminished U.S. credibility and maneuverability. The result has been a new assertiveness in Iranian foreign policy that has alarmed Iran's Arab neighbors and elicited comparisons to the post-revolutionary period.

But Iranian rhetoric, including that of President Ahmadinejad, focuses more on nationalist themes than on revolutionary ones. Although Iran certainly seeks to reduce U.S. influence in the area while expanding its own, its behavior today is informed by a greater propensity for realpolitik than for the ideological fervor that inspired the post-revolutionary period. Even in Shi'ite-dominated Iraq, Iran is not seeking to export its ideology, in spite of the fact that Tehran would ultimately prefer clerical rule as a final outcome in Iraq. Iran realizes it cannot be the dominant player in Iraq; it is simply unwilling to be excluded from helping to shape the political trajectory of its most important neighbor. As discussed in Chapter Four, Iran is banking on the success of a number of actors in Iraq, most of which directly oppose the idea of Iraq being governed according to *velayat-e faqih*. Indeed, somewhat ironically, Tehran now perceives the United States as the revolutionary and ideologically motivated power in the region.

However, Iran's largely pragmatic and nationalist orientations do not erase its history of misreading the strategic environment and overplaying its hand. As noted below, the fractured and convoluted nature of Iranian decisionmaking significantly increases the dangers of such miscalculations.

Tehran feels vulnerable, both from outside and from within. While the perception in the West is that the aftermath of the terrorist attacks of September 11, 2001, and the Iraq war has enhanced Iranian power by eliminating two of Iran's most serious threats (the Taliban government in Afghanistan and Saddam Hussein in Iraq), a closer examination highlights a myriad of threats and vulnerabilities that challenge Iran in the current strategic environment. Sectarian violence in Iraq, for example, has in the past fueled anti-Shi'ite, anti-Persian Salafism, leading to fears among Iran's leaders of al-Qaeda–inspired terrorism in Khuzestan and Baluchestan. Tehran is also concerned about the theological (and even political) challenge stemming from seminaries in Iraq. Theologically, Najaf and Karbala outweigh Qom, and this serves as a serious concern to many of Iran's religious politicians from the Supreme Leader down. Furthermore, the possible splintering of Iraq could spur increased dissent and incite separatist activity by Ahvazi Arabs, Kurds, and Baluchis.

The potential for a breakup of Iraq also worries Tehran because of the massive refugee flow Iran would face. For example, after the disintegration of Afghanistan, Iran was forced to accept almost 1 million refugees at an enormous cost to Iran's economy and its society. Many of these refugees have been repatriated, and Iran is not eager to replace them with a comparable number of homeless Iraqis.

Finally, and of greatest concern, Iran worries about a military attack on its nuclear program, although the 2007 National Intelligence Estimate and subsequent political developments in the United States have temporarily reduced these concerns.[2] At the same time, Iran is highly sensitive to interference in internal matters, interference that it regards as often bankrolled and inspired by the United States as democracy promotion and civil-society building efforts. It is unknown what actions or statements by the United States would change the perception among Iran's leaders that its ultimate objective is regime change.

Perceptions about the visceral U.S. opposition to the Islamic Republic in its current form only enhance the Iranian leadership's concern about internal threats to the revolutionary order, particularly those posed by

---

[2]   National Intelligence Council, 2007.

opposition elements perceived to be supported by outside powers, again underscoring the blurring of the external and internal environment in the regime's mindset. For example, continued protection by coalition forces of an Iraqi camp housing the Mujahedin e-Khalq, which the U.S. government has designated as a terrorist group, convinces hyper-sensitive Iranians that Washington wishes to overthrow the Iranian regime by any means possible. Increasingly, voices from within the Iranian leadership have levied criticism against President Ahmadinejad's posturing on the nuclear issue and bellicose rhetoric.

In Iranian decisionmaking, realpolitik and strategic calculations usually trump ideology. As we described in Chapter Four, one of the most instructive examples of Iran's willingness to pursue its strategic interests over its ideological agenda is its diversified portfolio in Iraq. To protect its strategic interests in Iraq, including its territorial integrity and a central government that is Iran-friendly, and to minimize military threats, Iran is hedging by supporting a wide range of groups. Given the political uncertainties surrounding key players in Iraq, including Sunnis and Kurds, Iran has decided not to invest in only one contender for power. Moreover, Iran's policy of developing a diversified portfolio of allies extends far beyond Iraq, with Iran seeking multiple channels for support and influence elsewhere in the region and beyond. For example, through its Arab popular opinion strategy, Iran seeks to appeal directly to largely Sunni populations by indirectly highlighting the illegitimacy of their rulers and demonstrating that Iran is "more Arab than the Arabs" on Palestinian issues.

Iran's growing emphasis on the East, as evidenced by its improved and strengthened relations with China, India, Japan, and Russia (as well as its interest in the SCO), further illustrates Iran's geo-strategic interest in balancing the United States and its allies, even if this means cooperation with secular states at odds with Islamist goals.[3] For example, Russia's support for Iran's nuclear program helped overcome its anti-Islamic image in the eyes of Iranians. When it is in their interest, the Iranians are as capable of calculating nonideological policies as

---

[3]   For more information on Iran's strategic relationship with Russia, see Robert D. Blackwill, "The Three Rs: Rivalry, Russia, 'Ran," *The National Interest,* January 2008.

any state in the international system. Another example of the triumph of pragmatism over ideology is Iran's relationship with Syria, whose government is as opposed to co-mingling Islam with politics as Iran's elite is committed to the inseparability of the two. The well-known massacre promulgated in Hama in 1982 by the late Syrian President Hafiz al-Assad was in direct response to the same type of Islamic-based political opposition that Iran sponsors in places such as Lebanon. Thus, the close Iranian-Syrian tie—so lamented in Washington—has everything to do with pragmatism while defying the fundamental ideological positions of both countries.

Iran has limited leverage over "proxy" groups. One critical if imperfect tool that Iran employs to elevate its status and to enhance deterrence against external threats is its financial and military support to a variety of non-state actors, some of which embody ideologies counter to Iran's own. For example, to burnish its Islamist and pro-Palestinian/Arab credentials (and as a component of its multilayered defense posture), Iran supports both Hamas, which has ties to the Sunni Muslim Brotherhood, and Hezbollah, a more natural Shi'ite ally. But Iran's influence over even its natural allies, such as Shi'ite groups in a number of countries, is not nearly as strong as is often presumed.

In Iraq, for instance, Iranian funds and military assistance are not essential to the survival of major Shi'ite political factions, and many of these Shi'ite actors prefer to maintain as much independence from Iran as possible because the Arab-Persian split can be at least as powerful as the shared commitment to Shi'ite Islam. And even Shi'ites have very different worldviews depending on the particular community and group. Indeed, the religious rivalry between Iran and Iraq (i.e., between the groups located in Qom versus those in Najaf and Karbala), the different cultural identities of Arabs and Persians, and Iraqi nationalism as opposed to Iranian nationalism also limit Iranian influence in Iraq. It is noteworthy that during the Iran-Iraq War, Arabs in Iran supported Iran while Shi'ite Muslims in Iraq supported Iraq. Former Iranian Defense Minister Shamkhani is an Arab from Khuzestan whose loyalties lie with Tehran, not Baghdad. In short, Iraqi Shi'ite groups are unlikely to favor Iranian interests over their own regardless of the degree of Iranian support they may enjoy. Many of these same factors also limit Iran's influence over other regional non-state actors in the Levant, such as Hezbollah and Hamas, as well as among Shi'ite communities in Saudi Arabia, Bahrain, and beyond.

Iranian security decisionmaking is fractured. As Chapter Two illustrated, the Iranian system is beset with factionalism. Despite the hierarchical qualities that distinguish Shi'ite Islam from Sunni Islam, qualities that permitted a revolution in Iran unlike anything ever seen in a Sunni Arab country, the Iranian political culture is composed of concentric groups with significant overlap among them. Decisionmaking requires consensus; therefore, the number and complexity of these groups, combined with the individual reluctance and ability to make decisions, makes it very difficult for the system to rapidly change course or to make significant decisions.

Among the competing groups in Iran that are involved in the decisionmaking process are the office and circle of the Supreme Leader Khamenei who, not being Khomeini, has limits on his power. Furthermore, President Ahmadinejad has his own limitations: Despite the very limited character of Iranian democracy, he was voted into office and is vulnerable to being voted out. In addition, the Iranian military and intelligence communities also have a voice in foreign and security policies. This is particularly true with regard to the IRGC, which has seen its domestic political and economic profile expand considerably. There are many components to this community, and it is unclear how well they work together.

Furthermore, there is a very powerful group of parastatal foundations, the *bonyads,* that control as much as 40 percent of the national wealth while being completely unregulated and working outside the legal system. These foundations provide significant support for and have deep involvement with the office of the Supreme Leader as well as the IRGC, which enjoys tremendous economic influence and power through the network of businesses it owns and operates.[4] Other power centers include the religious sector, the *bazaari* business community,

---

[4] Some analysts argue that the *bonyads* have declined in relative importance, particularly since the expansion of the IRGC's business activities (RAND phone interview with an Iranian-born scholar, March 4, 2008).

the traditional bureaucracy, the *Majlis,* and certain ethnic elites in different parts of the country. Understanding decisionmaking in a system for which we lack even a reliable organizational structure is exceedingly difficult. What we do know, however, is that the overlap among these groups makes Iranian decisionmaking exceedingly convoluted and complex, including vis-à-vis policy toward the United States. The factionalized nature of the Iranian system makes it difficult for Tehran to implement a consistent policy toward the United States, and it makes the prospects for rapprochement particularly challenging.

That said, the factionalism of the Iranian system lends Iranian policy a certain dynamism and fluidity—and the country has had a propensity for affecting significant course corrections in its external behavior. All the factions agree about the necessity of preserving the Republic's existing system and Iran's sovereignty, but there is significant debate about the path and means to accomplish this. More-pragmatic currents appear to acknowledge the advisability and inevitability of normalizing relations with the United States but argue this should be achieved under circumstances that favor Iran. In contrast, a more conservative current, to include the Supreme Leader, evinces a more rigid and triumphal conception of Iran's standing; with the regional "correlation of forces" seemingly on the side of the Islamic Republic, this faction may see little incentive to negotiate.

Arabs perceive Iran as a growing threat, although perceptions vary across and within states. The fragility of Iraq and sectarian tensions there have elevated concerns about the perceived rise of Iran and growing Shi'ite power among Arab governments and populations. Anti-Iranian and anti-Shi'ite sentiments are indeed strong throughout the region, particularly within official circles and the news media outlets they control. Arab governments perceive an emboldened Iran with a hand in destabilizing Lebanon, Gaza, and, most critically, Iraq. Arab governments and elites are especially concerned by Tehran's attempt to appeal directly to ordinary Arabs, as well as to disgruntled Arab populations and opposition groups.[5] The governments view these appeals as

---

[5] See for example the *Middle East Quarterly* interview with King Abdullah of Jordan in which he discusses the fear of the Shi'ite crescent ("Iraq Is the Battleground—The West

potential threats to their authority and legitimacy and are concerned about Iran's attempts to mobilize minority Shi'ite populations in Arab countries in order to destabilize conservative Sunni regimes.

In response, Arab officials have been supporting strong anti-Iranian and even anti-Shi'ite rhetoric, efforts that have been enhanced through the bloodletting in Iraq and such events as the execution of Saddam Hussein. Nonetheless, Arab official responses toward Iran differ, with some states pursuing a much less confrontational approach than others. For example, some of the smaller and more vulnerable GCC states, such as Oman, Qatar, and the United Arab Emirates, are quite tolerant of Iran. This may be because of their vulnerability to a comparatively large and potentially menacing Iran, as well as their desires to offset Saudi Arabia, which has a tendency to try to impose its will on its smaller GCC neighbors.

Arab public opinion toward Iran also varies, largely based on regional developments (e.g., Iran gained considerable popularity in the Arab world in the wake of the 2006 Lebanon war, while it suffered in the aftermath of Saddam Hussein's execution). Iranian defiance of the United States and support for Palestinian groups fighting Israel provides Iran with considerable clout in some quarters of the Arab world and even in some official circles. Many Arabs view Iran as a fellow Islamic country and the only regional power willing or able to stand up to what they perceive as America's quest for hegemony in the region. While Arabs may dislike Iran and worry about Iranian interference in Arab affairs, many dislike the United States and Israel even more.

On the nuclear issue, for example, Arab officials who are in some ways concerned about Iran still see value in an Iranian nuclear weapons capability, which they perceive as "balancing" Israel, whose nuclear weapon capability concerns them. Arab popular sentiment largely supports Iranian nuclear ambitions. Furthermore, official and popular opinion is largely opposed to a military attack by the United States against Iran, voicing deep concern about the secondary effects such an attack would generate elsewhere in the region.[6] These divergent and

---

Against Iran," *Middle East Quarterly*, Vol. 12, No. 2, Spring 2005).

[6]   See Kaye and Wehrey, 2007, pp. 111–128.

ambivalent views toward Iran suggest caution for U.S. policymakers who envision a Cold War–style bloc of Sunni Arab states (with tacit Israeli support) to confront Iran.

Iran's conventional military capabilities are limited. Contrary to popular perception, Iranian defense spending is extremely modest, does not exceed regional norms, and is, in fact, far below that of Saudi Arabia, Israel, and Turkey. As Chapter Three describes, Iran has also made only limited progress in modernizing its force: Most of its equipment is out of date and poorly maintained, and its ground forces suffer from both personnel and equipment shortages. The IRIAF has outdated aircraft and is no match for its neighbors, and certainly not for U.S. airpower. Tehran's layered and overlapping security structures, while useful for regime survivability, inhibit battlefield performance and reduce its capability to defend against external threats. Finally, there is little reason to believe that Iranian military investments will change dramatically over the coming decade. Iranian oil production is falling due to neglect and incompetence, and Iran's economy will continue to under-perform and remain weak for the foreseeable future.

Because of its inferiority on the conventional front, Iran's defense doctrine, particularly its ability to deter aggressors, relies heavily on asymmetric warfare. Iranian strategists favor guerilla efforts (such as the example of Hezbollah in Lebanon) to counteract technologically superior conventional power likely to come from the United States and its regional allies. At the high end of the spectrum, Iran has strong motives and means to develop advanced ballistic missile and nuclear weapon capabilities.

Iran's asymmetric capabilities pose significant dangers. Iran's reliance on asymmetric capabilities can threaten Western interests in a variety of ways. Of the land, sea, and air components of Iran's armed forces, its navies appear to have made the most headway in adopting asymmetric tactics. Iran's mining, antiship cruise missile, and fast-attack capabilities could create difficult conditions for tankers passing through the critical Strait of Hormuz. Even if Iranian naval efforts could not close the passage, they would have significant effects on global energy markets, making this one of the few areas in which Iran currently has the ability to impose strategic costs on the United States (see Chapter Three).

Iranian ballistic missile capabilities are also a concern. The IRGC possesses a significant arsenal of short- and medium-range ballistic missiles that can reach the small Persian Gulf states, most of Saudi Arabia, Afghanistan, Israel, and eastern Turkey. Although these missiles are currently inaccurate and thus have limited military utility, improvements in their range, payload, and accuracy would significantly enhance Iran's ability to threaten large population centers, economic infrastructure, and military bases. Iran's development of nuclear weapons would also pose additional dangers and risks given the likely difficulty in establishing a deterrent relationship.[7] Iran also may engage in more-aggressive behavior under the umbrella of a nuclear deterrent.

Past Policies Toward Iran Have Thus Far Not Succeeded

Over the years, the United States has attempted a variety of approaches to address the Iranian challenge. To date, none have succeeded in making Iran less menacing to U.S. interests or more compliant with UN Security Council resolutions. The existing policy of creating a Cold War–like containment regime against Iran is not only unlikely to work, but it may even worsen the situation. We also believe that, although they are more appealing, policies relying on bilateral engagement and/ or hopes for some sort of grand bargain are equally unrealistic at this juncture, although laying out the contours of a normalized relationship may be useful for the future. Below we review the reasons supporting our skepticism toward such approaches, each of which has been repeatedly tried in endless versions and combinations since the Khomeini era immediately following the Islamic Revolution of 1978–1979.

Indeed, as in the past, some analysts today are calling for a combination of engagement and containment to address the Iranian chal-

---

[7] See Patrick Clawson and Michael Eisenstadt, *Deterring the Ayatollahs: Complications in Applying Cold War Strategy to Iran*, Washington, D.C.: The Washington Institute for Near East Policy, Policy Focus No. 72, July 2007.

lenge, matching in many ways the U.S. approach toward the Soviet Union during the Cold War.[8] But as the following analysis suggests, both elements of this policy are problematic, and the Cold War logic does not necessarily apply well in this context.[9] It is also unclear why Iran would respond to U.S. engagement efforts in the context of a wide-ranging U.S.-led containment regime. While pressure on Tehran is still critical, particularly concerning the nuclear question and Iran's links to terrorism, engagement approaches may bear more fruit in the context of a less antagonistic and Iran-centric U.S. strategy. Our concluding section will consider a different U.S. approach that may offer a more promising context for a future successful dialogue.

Efforts to Engage with Iran or Strike a "Grand Bargain" Have Not Yet Succeeded

Trying to find an effective vehicle to engage Iran has occupied U.S. policymakers, as well as the policy community, for well over 30 years. Although frequently co-mingled with more-coercive strategies (such as the policy of Dual Containment embraced by President Bill Clinton or the Axis of Evil perspective adopted by President George W. Bush), there have been ample, frequent, and sincere attempts by U.S. policymakers to engage Iran. These have ranged from frequent Track II meetings involving various nonofficial Americans and Iranians close to the political leadership in both countries to higher-level and more-public initiatives, such as an apology by Secretary of State Madeleine Albright for the U.S. role in the Mossadegh affair of 1953.

There have also been more-substantive engagement-type activities. The most productive of these was during the post-9/11 period, when the United States and the Islamic Republic of Iran cooperated directly and quite successfully in designing and executing a constitu-

---

[8]   See, for example, Martin Indyk's comments at a 2007 RAND conference on Iran in James Dobbins, Sarah Harting, and Dalia Dassa Kaye, *Coping with Iran: Confrontation, Containment or Engagement? A Conference Report,* Santa Monica, Calif.: RAND Corporation, CF-237-NSRD, 2007.

[9]   For an interesting discussion of the limitations of a Cold War strategy toward Iran focused on deterrence (and on the nuclear issue), see Clawson and Eisenstadt, 2007.

tion and new government for Afghanistan.[10] However, soon after this effort, President Bush referred to Iran as part of an "axis of evil" in his 2002 State of the Union address, squelching hopes for continued U.S.-Iranian cooperation in this or any other area.

But when faced with growing instability in Iraq, the United States again agreed to engage Iran in 2007 through the U.S. ambassador in Baghdad concerning Iraqi stability. These talks also failed to lead to any significant breakthroughs in U.S.-Iranian relations. And in between, there have been numerous other engagement-friendly measures proposed by Washington or those close to various presidential administrations.

We have also seen other attempts at engagement, including proposals to station U.S. government consular officials in Tehran, attempts to persuade Washington to support the appointment of Iranians to high-level posts in assorted international organizations, support for Iranian accession to the World Trade Organization, collaboration with Iran in the antinarcotics area (particularly on its eastern borders with Pakistan and Afghanistan), promotion of direct sporting ties (such as U.S.-Iranian wrestling matches), and proposals for special-interest meetings between journalists or parliamentarians. These are a few efforts among many. Although some of these measures have been successful, satisfying, and promising, none of them has led to the type of dramatic opening hoped for and often promised by their architects.

Indeed, some argue that limited engagement will not succeed because a more fundamental transformation of the U.S.-Iranian relationship is necessary in order for both sides to take engagement seriously. Proponents of such an approach advocate reaching a "grand bargain" with Iran. Although the precise components of the grand bargain are not always fully articulated, formulations usually assume that the bargain could induce Iran to abandon its nuclear program, halt all support for international terrorism, provide acceptable security assurances

---

[10] For details on these negotiations, see James Dobbins, "How to Talk to Iran," *Washington Post*, July 22, 2007; James Dobbin's contribution to James Dobbins et al., 2007. Also see Barbara Slavin, *Bitter Friends, Bosom Enemies: Iran, the U.S. and the Twisted Path to Confrontation*, New York: St. Martin's Press, 2007, pp. 193–209; Flynt L. Leverett, "Iran: The Gulf Between Us," *New York Times*, January 24, 2006.

to its Gulf Arab neighbors, and rescind its stated commitment to the destruction of the state of Israel. In exchange, the United States would offer Iran restoration of full diplomatic relations, remove all forms of international economic pressure from Tehran, and facilitate full return by Iran to its status as a "normal" member of both the Persian Gulf region and the international family of nations.

The idea of striking a deal based on mutually beneficial interests gained currency soon after the U.S. invasion of Iraq in 2003. According to a variety of reports, the Iranians offered a grand bargain deal in 2003 via the Swiss Embassy in Tehran. The comprehensive deal listed both U.S. and Iranian aims. Through a two-page unclassified fax from Swiss interlocutors (that according to Flynt Leverett, a career CIA analyst and counter-terrorism expert at the State Department at the time, had support from all of the important figures in the Iranian government), Iran sent a bulleted list of trade-offs to spark negotiations between the two countries.[11]

Iran offered to provide full transparency for its nuclear program under the policies of the International Atomic Energy Agency; provide full disclosure to the United States for tracking down al-Qaeda elements; support efforts to create a stable, democratic, nonreligious Iraqi government; halt material support to Palestinian opposition groups; and accept a two-state solution for the Israeli/Palestinian issue based on 1967 borders. In return, the United States was to forgo all economic sanctions on Iran, cease rhetoric linking Iran to terrorism, establish a fully democratic state in Iraq (ensuring a Shi'ite majority power structure), allow Iran full access to peaceful nuclear technology, and turn over Mujahedin-e Khalq Organization (an anti-Iranian terrorist organization) cadres in Iraq to Iran. Apparently, it was this last point that was the most contentious within the U.S. administration, even though it was an aim of the administration to disarm the Mujahedin-e Khalq, which is on the terrorist organizations list.[12] The offer was rebuffed by

---

[11] Leverett, 2006. Also see Glenn Kessler, "In 2003, U.S. Spurned Iran's Offer of Dialogue," *Washington Post,* June 18, 2006, p. A16.

[12] For an in-depth analysis of the U.S. administration's reaction to the 2003 offer, see Gareth Porter, "How a 2003 Secret Overture for Tehran Might Have Led to a Deal on Iran's Nuclear

the Bush administration. Whether this offer hit a dead end because of a lack of interest on the part of Washington or because of questions regarding the validity and credibility of the proposal, this episode proved yet another failed attempt to fundamentally re-order the U.S.-Iranian relationship. Either way, the United States is now in a weaker position to strike such deals with Iran than it was in 2003 and currently faces an Iranian government dominated by factions less interested in negotiation and engagement with the West.

In addition to the specific political contexts in both Washington and Tehran working against a grand bargain breakthrough, a general problem with grand bargain efforts is that they embrace the *bazaari* culture, which many in the West ascribe to Iran but which few actually understand.[13] This perspective assumes an inherent Iranian fascination with the process of negotiating and of making deals. This "let's split the difference and quickly make a deal" thinking assumes, incorrectly in our view, that Iran is as eager to reach an understanding as are those in the West who promote this approach. Thus, the West's grand bargain approach rests on an unverified belief that years of Iranian distrust toward the West can easily be swept away.

Unfortunately, the leadership of the Islamic Republic—even its more pragmatic factions—may not be as eager to make a deal as this approach assumes. The grand bargain logic tends to ignore the fact that not all rivals or adversaries are willing to make a deal at any price. History may weigh more heavily on Iran and its people than it does on those in the West. And many in the Iranian leadership, as well as among the population at large, feel deeply aggrieved by the past. There is a widespread belief and resentment throughout Iran that the United States is still unwilling to recognize the validity and legitimacy of its revolution. The West put the late Shah in power and protected him for many years from internal forces for change in Iran. Many in Iran believe that the primary goal of the United States is to subjugate the Islamic Republic, just as they believe it has tried to subjugate the government of Iraq. The

---

Capacity," *The American Prospect,* May 21, 2006.

[13] For an interesting analysis of Iranian *bazaari* mindset, see Sadjadpour, "How Relevant Is the Iranian Street?" 2007.

impact and significance of these sentiments cannot be ignored. Finally, it is worth noting that powerful elements of the regime, such as hard-line factions in the IRGC, have an institutional interest in promoting antagonism with the United States and would resist or even sabotage any efforts at rapprochement or accommodation.

The beguiling simplicity of the grand bargain to Westerners is precisely the reason it is a problematic idea from an Iranian perspective. The comparative ease with which decades-old problems can appear to be resolved trivializes the very problems which are so unsettling to so many people in Iran. Although Iran is hardly a hotbed of objectivity about the political behavior of the United States, the Iranian public is skeptical about U.S. intentions for both systemic and emotionally charged reasons. It is frequently said that Iran is the most pro-American country in the region.[14] However, some opinion polls taken in recent years arrive at opposite conclusions.[15] Whether or not these Iranian opinion polls are accurate, there exist serious reasons for skepticism about the ability of the United States and Iran to achieve a dramatic and comprehensive diplomatic breakthrough quickly given this legacy of mistrust.

Despite these shortcomings, laying out the contours of a grand bargain may prove constructive in the future given the fluidity of the Iranian political system and the factional nature of its decisionmaking process, outlined earlier in this volume. As explained in Chapter One, there are factions in the Iranian system that would be more amenable to engagement than others, and such factions could gain the upper hand in the future. Given Iran's vulnerable domestic economic situation and a desire by some Iranian leadership factions to advance Iran's normalization with the West, external stimuli can affect internal calculations, particularly if a U.S. offer is viewed as credible. Continuing limited engagement on Iraqi stability (as well as Afghanistan

---

[14] See Patrick Clawson, "The Paradox of Anti-Americanism in Iran," *Middle East Journal of International Affairs,* Vol. 8, No. 1, March 2004.

[15] For example, the 2006 WorldPublicOpinion.org poll found that 76 percent of Iranians had an unfavorable opinion of the United States. See WorldPublicOpinion.org, "Public Opinion in Iran and America on Key International Issues," January 24, 2007. However, it is important to note that the reliability of public opinion polling in Iran is questionable.

and broader antiterrorism efforts targeting al-Qaeda) may bolster the credibility of a future U.S. offer for a more expansive deal, even if such limited engagement does not produce dramatic results overnight. Our skepticism regarding a grand bargain solution stems from our desire to consider this approach realistically so that its potential in the future is not discredited by unattainable near-term expectations.

Containment Policies Have Also Fallen Short

Similarly, policies of containment—focused both on increasing Iran's economic isolation and bolstering the military capabilities of neighboring states in efforts to construct an anti-Iranian alliance—face serious limitations. They have thus far failed to curb Iran's international aspirations to support what it perceives to be beleaguered Shi'ite coreligionists around the world, as well as to pursue policies that many in the United States regard to be antithetical to the interests of Washington and its allies in the region (including the use of terrorism and nuclear enrichment activities).

As noted, epithetic U.S. policies with tough-sounding names such as "Dual Containment" or the "Axis of Evil" have accomplished very little other than hardening Iranian resolve to stand firm against them.[16] Nor has the Iran-Libya Sanctions Act succeeded in inducing compliance, even if it has had a definite impact on Iran and on its economy and oil industry. External U.S.-generated pressure on Iran and its oil sector has had an effect, as demonstrated by Iranian riots in response to the rationing of gasoline. Nonetheless, making Iran suffer economic consequences from external pressure by Washington does not mean Iran will comply with the expectations of the U.S. government and the broader international community. Many analysts argue that Iran is not even close to being weakened to the point at which it would be willing

---

[16] For analysis on how the "axis of evil" metaphor strengthened hardline discourse in Iran, see Daniel Heradstveit and G. Matthew Bonham, "What the Axis of Evil Metaphor Did to Iran," *The Middle East Journal*, Vol. 60, No. 3, Summer 2007, pp. 421–440.

to comply with U.S. expectations, despite the array of economic and political measures being deployed against it.[17]

The European Union and the United States are concurrently trying to pursue tougher sanctions on Iran than dictated by UN Security Council Resolution 1737, which freezes the assets of 10 Iranian firms and 12 people involved in the nuclear sector. The Security Council resolution also bans the transfer of materials and technology that may be used for uranium enrichment. China and Russia have predictably rebuffed harsher measures. Over 40 percent of Iran's imports come from Europe. However, starting in 2006, Iran strategically began to develop trade with the Persian Gulf region. Based on Iran's strategic maneuvering toward trade with the East, many analysts believe that these sanctions will have a minimal impact on Iran's internal political dynamics. Economist Akbar Torbat argues that, while the Iranian economy is incredibly inefficient, this is not mainly a result of sanctions, and Iran is still not faring worse than some other countries in the region. According to Torbat, financial sanctions may be more effective than unilateral trade sanctions because Iran will always find an alternative trading partner for commodities such as oil. Multilateral trade sanctions on Iran's energy sector would obviously be more effective. However, with China's growing demand, this arrangement may not be feasible.[18] China has signed several oil contracts with Iran and is ranked as Iran's second-largest trading partner.[19] Russia, likewise, will most likely not position itself against Iran. In a speech at the Munich Security Conference in February 2007, former President Vladimir Putin expressed worry over a U.S. military buildup in neighboring countries

---

[17] For an analysis of the limited effect of sanctions on Iran, see Akbar E. Torbat, "Impacts of the US Trade and Financial Sanctions on Iran," *The World Economy*, Vol. 28, No. 3, March 2005, pp. 407–434.

[18] See Lionel Beehner, "U.S. Sanctions Biting Iran," backgrounder Web page, Council on Foreign Relations, January 23, 2007.

[19] "Iran, China to Cement Cooperation," Tehran Fars News Agency, July 7, 2008.

and stated that, in opposition to U.S. unilateralism, Russia would not curtail its relationship with Iran.[20]

More recently, there has been substantial pressure on Iranian banks as a result of U.S. actions. Specifically, Iranian banks have been denied credit by major international lending agencies, while attempts have been made to discredit Iranian businesses by linking them to the IRGC and other state institutions that are believed to be involved in terrorist activities. Furthermore, there has been sporadic discussion in the United States about forcing investors holding stock in companies that do business in and with Iran to divest their holdings in these companies in an attempt at compelling such companies to cease doing business with Iran.

Other forms of pressure have also been exerted on Iran as the United States tries to broaden Iranian political and economic isolation within the global community. For example, the United States took the unprecedented step of designating the IRGC's Qods Force as a supporter of terrorism, which allows the United States to target the group's assets. The United States also has sanctioned individuals, such as Iranian generals and exiled Iraqis based in Iran, whom it accuses of fomenting violence in Iraq.[21]

Again, there is little evidence to suggest that these new mechanisms will do anything more than increase Iranian willingness to tolerate more pain. These measures may merely induce Tehran to stand firm in its refusal to comply with the expectations of what it regards to be powers hostile to the very existence of the Islamic Republic while strengthening the very conservative forces that the sanctions were meant to undermine. Although some may argue that sanctions and other financial pressures may help strengthen more-pragmatic forces (who are critical of President Ahmadinejad's economic policies), it is difficult to find concrete evidence to support such assertions. If anything, one could argue that external financial pressures may allow rad-

---

[20] See Akbar E. Torbat, "UN Financial Sanctions on Iran: Political Confrontation," Web page, Centre for Research on Globalization, March 9, 2007.

[21] Robin Wright, "Top Iranian General Hit with Sanctions," *Washington Post*, January 10, 2008, p. 15.

ical conservative elements to deflect attention from their own failed domestic policies by blaming external powers for Iran's troubled economic situation.

Another political result of these U.S. policies inside Iran has been the discrediting of the so-called Iranian moderates, or reformists, who would like further accommodation and engagement with the United States. Iranian moderates include former President Khatami, as well as less well-known intellectuals, journalists, and others who are currently enduring a crackdown on political disagreement, the extent of which is almost without precedent in the history of the Islamic Republic. While the fate of the four Iranian-Americans who were arrested by the government is well known in the West, there are countless other intellectuals who have been terrorized and otherwise threatened by those in the Iranian government who vehemently reject policies of engagement with the United States.

Finally, the most recent version of containment—the visible U.S. attempts to forge a political coalition of Arab states (the so-called GCC +2 and, more recently, GCC +3) to counter Iran—faces similar shortcomings and may even worsen the situation.[22] The idea behind this strategy is to bolster the defense and deterrence capabilities of U.S. allies to contain Iranian power and aggression in the region.[23] This evolving anti-Iranian strategy largely mirrors Cold War logic and includes proposed multibillion dollar arms packages for Persian Gulf allies,

---

[22] That is, the six states of the GCC (Saudi Arabia, Bahrain, Kuwait, UAE, Oman, and Qatar) plus Egypt and Jordan; the third state in this grouping is now viewed as Iraq according to a State Department official visiting RAND in December 2008. This explains Secretary of Defense Robert Gates's suggestion to consider including Iraq in the GCC during a speech in Manama in December 2008 (see Loveday Morris, "Gates Calls for GCC to Embrace Iraq," *The National*, December 13, 2008). For more on U.S. efforts in this area, see Anthony Shadid, "With Iran Ascendant, U.S. Is Seen at Fault," *Washington Post*, January 30, 2007, p. A1; Michael Slackman and Hassan M. Fattah, "In Public View, Saudis Counter Iran in Region," *New York Times*, February 6, 2007, p. A1; Jay Solomon, "U.S.-Arab Alliance Aims to Deter Terrorism, Iran," *Wall Street Journal*, August 9, 2007, p. 6; Robin Wright, "U.S. vs. Iran: Cold War, Too," *Washington Post*, July 29, 2007, p. B1.

[23] For further elaboration of the Cold War–like containment policy, see Vali Nasr and Ray Takeyh, "The Costs of Containing Iran: Washington's Misguided New Middle East Policy," *Foreign Affairs*, Vol. 87, No. 1, January/February 2008, pp. 85–94.

Egypt, and Israel.[24] Then–Under Secretary of State Nicholas Burns claimed Iran "wasn't the overriding factor and we certainly would have gone forward with these sales regardless."[25] However, in the statement announcing the arms sales, then–Secretary of State Condoleezza Rice said, "This effort will help bolster forces of moderation and support a broader strategy to counter the negative influences of al-Qaida, Hezbollah, Syria, and Iran."[26] A "senior administration official" involved in the negotiations further explained to the *Washington Post*, "We're paying attention to the needs of our allies and what everyone in the region believes is a flexing of muscles by a more aggressive Iran. One way to deal with that is to make our allies and friends strong."[27] Even other U.S. regional efforts, such as renewed activism in Arab-Israeli diplomacy in the aftermath of the Annapolis meeting in late 2007, are viewed by many as subordinate to and/or supportive of this broader strategy of containing Iran.[28]

While the Cold War model may be attractive and convenient, the United States cannot construct a Middle Eastern version of the Iron Curtain to cordon off Iranian expansionist designs—principally because Tehran, unlike Cold War Moscow, is not an expansionist power. Rhetoric aside, Tehran does not seek to acquire territory or export its revolution, as explained in Chapter Two. Instead, it spreads its influence by exploiting deep-seated grievances in the region—popular Arab perceptions of regime illegitimacy, Shi'ite marginalization, the festering Palestine issue, and general animosity toward U.S. policies. Military coalitions cannot easily counter this kind of power projection. That said, the nonmilitary elements of containment fostered in

---

[24] See Mark Mazzetti and Helene Cooper, "U.S. Arms Plan for Mideast Aims to Counter Iranian Power," *New York Times*, July 31, 2007, p. 6.

[25] U.S. Department of State, "Press Briefing Conference Call on U.S. Aid and Military Support to the Middle East Region," transcript of conference call, July 30, 2007.

[26] Sue Plemming, "Rice, Gates in Egypt to Persuade Arabs," Reuters, July 31, 2007.

[27] Robin Wright, "U.S. Plans New Arms Sales to Gulf Allies: $20 Billion Deal Includes Weapons for Saudi Arabia," *Washington Post*, July 28, 2007, p. A1.

[28] See, for example, Michael Abramowitz and Ellen Knickmeyer, "As Bush Heads to Mideast, Renewed Questions on Iran," *Washington Post*, January 7, 2008, p. 12.

the Cold War aimed at countering this type of ideological subversion may prove more relevant in this context, although extreme care must be taken in how such ideological "warfare" is conducted. This is particularly the case given that such attempts often put the moderate voices the United States would like to protect and strengthen at risk. [29]

The evolving U.S. containment approach also assumes a unanimity among Sunni Arab allies that does not exist. Arab states have divergent views toward Iran and the nature of the threat it poses even in the aftermath of 9/11 and the U.S. toppling of Saddam Hussein. Even those that sign up to a U.S.-sponsored "front" in the context of heightened concern over growing Iranian influence will likely pursue some form of accommodation with Iran given its dominant role in the region.[30] And such a front is likely to rely heavily on Saudi Arabia, which could dangerously bolster the Saudi inclination to inflame rather than defuse sectarian tensions as a tactic to balance Iran. Indeed, Riyadh has at times played a worrisome game, exploiting region-wide fears of sectarian spillover from Iraq and tacitly allowing its clerical establishment a platform for anti-Shi'ite vitriol. As Vali Nasr and Ray Takeyh observe, in the Cold War, containing communism "meant promoting capitalism and democracy. Containing Iran today would mean promoting Sunni extremism—a self-defeating proposition for Washington."[31]

Moreover, this type of Saudi-dominated containment approach could backfire, encouraging Tehran to accelerate its asymmetric warfare options (given its weakness on the conventional front) through terrorism, ballistic missile development, or a nuclear weapon. Finally, the containment approach may torpedo efforts to work with Iran on stabilizing Iraq and cooperating on other regional issues, such as challenging the resurgence of the Taliban in Afghanistan.

---

[29] For more information on how U.S. democracy promotion efforts are undermining Iranian reformists, see Akbar Ganji, "Why Iran's Democrats Shun Aid," *Washington Post,* October 26, 2007, p. A21; Akbar Ganji, "The View from Tehran," *Boston Review,* Vol. 32, No. 3, May/June 2007.

[30] See Marc Lynch, "Why U.S. Strategy on Iran Is Crumbling," *Christian Science Monitor,* January 4, 2008.

[31] Nasr and Takeyh, 2008, p. 91.

U.S. Policy Toward Iran in the Coming Decade Requires a New Approach

Given the themes outlined above and the difficulties confronting U.S. policy toward Iran in the past and present, we propose a different type of approach that involves a series of unilateral de-escalation measures by Washington, as well as continued muscular multilateral efforts targeted at Iranian behavior that runs counter to international norms (e.g., the nuclear issue and links to terrorism). Rather than a broad U.S.-based containment strategy, we suggest leveraging international pressure while unilaterally de-escalating U.S. rhetoric and policy toward Iran (essentially, reversing the traditional good cop/bad cop roles).[32] Keeping the pressure components of this approach multilateral (including support from Russia and China) is critical because it helps deprive the Iranian leadership of the ability to deflect domestic critique by focusing discontent solely on the United States and the United Kingdom or other European Union powers. At the same time, the United States should avoid escalating unilateral actions against Iran because they are unlikely to work and are likely to exacerbate tensions significantly. While no silver bullet, multilateral pressure—when combined with less-hostile U.S. rhetoric and policy—may prove more effective, at least in terms of the more limited aims on the nuclear issue. Having said that, the likelihood of sustained support for this approach by Russia and China remains questionable.

Policymakers Should Consider a Less Confrontational Stance Toward Iran

Over the long run (in the next ten to fifteen years), our focus is on finding a means for Iran and the United States to coexist in a region well known for its turbulence and instability. The nature of Iranian power and Iran's regional ambitions are complex. The U.S. policy response must be designed so as to take this complexity into consideration. Therefore, we suggest a fundamental unilateral shift in rhetoric and

---

[32] For this idea of role reversals (in the context of transatlantic diplomacy toward the Iranian nuclear challenge), see Robert J. Einhorn, "Transatlantic Strategy on Iran's Nuclear Program," *Washington Quarterly,* Autumn 2004.

policy toward a less confrontational stance, complemented by efforts to establish new multilateral venues for a regional security dialogue involving Iran. Specific components of such an approach could include both symbolic steps and policy actions.

Symbolic Actions Would Gradually Shift the Image of the United States

Clear statements recognizing Iran as a valid player in the region and acknowledging Iranian threat perceptions. These need to be convincing and not merely cosmetic. Actions speak louder than words; thus, issuing convincing statements could be challenging. But if such statements were accompanied by concrete proposals for confidence-building measures and exercises as suggested below, they may be viewed more seriously. Military-to-military exchanges could be particularly useful in understanding and addressing mutual threat perceptions and avoiding unintended conflict, particularly in the naval arena.

Unambiguous statements about U.S. interests and intentions in the region, particularly regarding Iraq. These must be simple and easily understood, and the United States must stick to them long enough for them to be taken seriously. The United States should reinforce the SOFA with Iraq by clearly stating that it has no long-term interest in occupying Iraq or establishing a permanent military presence there. At the same time, the United States has a right to maintain a military presence in the region, as well as ties to regional allies, to protect core U.S. interests. These statements would underscore that U.S. military postures are for defensive purposes and to ensure stability, not to develop U.S. bases in order to launch attacks on regional neighbors (i.e., Iran).

The United States should avoid bellicose pronouncements suggesting regime change in Iran. Such statements would merely isolate the United States from the very people it wishes to encourage, while emboldening Iranian hardliners and exacerbating repression of reformers and even pragmatists inside Iran. Despite this, the United States should remain true to its core principles and continue to express concern, when appropriate, about human rights abuses in Iran. Providing assurances that the United States is not seeking regime change does not mean the United States cannot continue to support human rights and civil liberties, just as it does in many countries around the world, including among its allies. Of course, given the legacy of mistrust outlined earlier, it will be difficult to convince any Iranian government that the United States is sincere.

Policy Actions

Continue strengthening international sanctions and other financial pressures targeted on the nuclear issue, but avoid unilateral punitive measures that are not likely to generate broad consensus. Secondary sanctions are particularly counterproductive in maintaining European and international support for nuclear-related sanctions in the UN.

Pursue bilateral dialogues related to areas of common interest, such as instability in Iraq and Afghanistan, narcotics trafficking, natural disaster relief, refugees, and other humanitarian crises. The United States should identify and exploit areas where genuine collaboration can be productive and profitable, without harboring expectations for broader diplomatic breakthroughs. These more limited efforts should not be trivialized by over-hyping them. News of good works will spread on its own. Even limited engagement efforts may improve the prospects for a broader dialogue and normalization process should political conditions improve.

Engage in efforts to build a multilateral regional security framework that is simultaneously inclusive of Iran and sensitive to the needs of U.S. Arab friends and allies. The Arab states remember exceedingly close U.S.-Iranian relations during the Pahlavi era and thus would be ambivalent at best about closer ties between Tehran and Washington. Therefore, the United States needs to aggressively pursue ideas to construct a broad-based multilateral regional security framework that would include Iran alongside Washington's traditional Arab allies (as well as key international players such as the European Union, Russia, and China). Such a structure would not be based on a specific threat (such as a collective security organization like NATO), but rather would provide an open-ended security forum where regional states could discuss and address a range of regional challenges (starting with more-consensual issues like narcotics trafficking, responses to natural disasters, maritime security, and economic and energy development) and engage in military confidence-building measures. The model for such a forum could be a cooperative security organization like the Organisation for Security and Co-operation in Europe, where mutual threat perceptions are aired and conflict-reduction measures are pursued. Cooperation in maritime affairs would be a useful area of focus for such a forum (such as work on a regional incidents-at-sea agreement), particularly given the potential for miscalculation and escalation in critical waterways like the Strait of Hormuz.[33]

Undoubtedly, an inclusive regional security forum would be challenging both in spirit as well as in execution. Realpolitik and balance-of-power calculations continue to dominate thinking in the region and would serve to undermine attempts to establish and sustain cooperative regional arrangements. But the effort would be worthwhile. Indeed, opportunities to pursue new regional security arrangements tend to follow major armed conflicts when regional relations are in flux. The intensity of regional interest in new regional security structures, including from Iran,[34] suggests the need to revisit ideas for multilat-

---

[33] For the applicability of a Helsinki Process model to Iran and the Middle East, see Michael McFaul, Abbas Milani, and Larry Diamond, "A Win-Win U.S. Strategy for Dealing with Iran," *Washington Quarterly*, Vol. 30, No. 1, pp. 121–138; Michael McFaul, "A Helsinki Process for the Middle East," *Journal of Democracy*, No. 8, Spring 2008.

[34] Discussion of new regional security arrangements is widespread in Iran. For Iranian views on multilateral security cooperation, see the recent ten-point proposal for a Persian Gulf Security Cooperation Council by the former Secretary of the Supreme Council for National Security, Hassan Rohani (Kaveh L. Afrasiabi, "Iran Unveils a Persian Gulf Security Plan," *Asia Times*, April 14, 2007). For other Iranian views, see Afrasiabi and Maleki, 2003, pp. 263–264; Center for Strategic Research, Foreign Policy Research Division, Expediency Council (Iran), "Negarinaye keshvarhaye Arabi nesbat be Iran dar fazaye Jadide Mantaghei [Arab Countries' Concerns About Iran in the Light of the New Environment in the Region]," Web page, 2006; Mahmoud Dehghani, "Naghsh-e Aragh-e Jadid dar tartibat-e amniyati-e mantaghe-e Khalij-e Fars [The Role of the New Iraq in the Security Orders in the Persian Gulf]," Center for Strategic Research, Foreign Policy Research Division, Expediency Council (Iran), Web page, 2003.

eral regional security cooperation.[35] Although an inclusive multilateral security structure in the Persian Gulf region would take time to build, it would contribute more to regional stability over the long run than would continuing to rely solely on competitive, balance-of-power strategies designed to isolate Iran. Such narrow strategies are more likely to encourage, even reify, Iranian hegemonic aspirations than remove them.

---

[35] The most notable previous official attempt to consider the formation of a multilateral regional security forum was the Arms Control and Regional Security working group of the multilateral peace process initiated at the Madrid Peace Conference in 1991. See Bruce W. Jentleson and Dalia Dassa Kaye, "Security Status: Explaining Regional Security Cooperation and Its Limits in the Middle East," *Security Studies*, Vol. 8, No. 1, 1998, pp. 204–238; Dalia Dassa Kaye, "Regional Security Cooperation," in *Beyond The Handshake: Multilateral Cooperation in the Arab-Israeli Peace Process, 1991–1996*, New York: Columbia University Press, 2001, pp. 76–109; Peter Jones, "Open Forum: Arms Control in the Middle East: Is It Time to Renew ACRS?" United Nations Institute for Disarmament Research, Disarmament Forum—North-East Asian Security, No. 2, 2005; U.S. Department of State, Bureau of Political-Military Affairs, "Middle East Peace Process Arms Control and Regional Security Working Group," Fact Sheet, July 21, 2001; Nabil Fahmy, "Special Comment," United Nations Institute for Disarmament Research, *Disarmament Forum*, No. 2, 2001, pp. 3–5; Shai Feldman, *Nuclear Weapons and Arms Control in the Middle East*, Cambridge, Mass.: MIT Press, 1997; Peter Jones, "Negotiating Regional Security in the Middle East: The ACRS Experience and Beyond," *Journal of Strategic Studies*, Vol. 26, No. 3, 2003; Peter Jones, "Arms Control in the Middle East: Some Reflections on ACRS," *Security Dialogue*, Vol. 28, No. 1, 1997; Emily Landau, "Egypt and Israel in ACRS: Bilateral Concerns in a Regional Arms Control Process," Tel Aviv: Jaffee Center for Strategic Studies, Memorandum No. 59, 2001; Michael Yaffe, "An Overview of the Middle East Peace Process Working Group on Arms Control and Regional Security," in Fred Tanner, ed., *Confidence-Building and Security Co-operation in the Mediterranean, North Africa and the Middle East*, Malta: University of Malta, 1994.

References

The 9/11 Commission Report: Final Report of the National Commission on Terrorist Attacks upon the United States, U.S. Government Printing Office, July 26, 2004.

Abramowitz, Michael, and Ellen Knickmeyer, "As Bush Heads to Mideast, Renewed Questions on Iran," *Washington Post*, January 7, 2008, p. 12.

Abu-Amr, Ziad, "Hamas: A Historical and Political Background," *Journal of Palestinian Studies*, Vol. 23, No. 4, Summer 1993.

Afrasiabi, Kaveh L., "Iran Unveils a Persian Gulf Security Plan," *Asia Times*, April 14, 2007.

Afrasiabi, Kaveh L., and Abbas Maleki, "Iran's Foreign Policy After 11 September," *Brown Journal of World Affairs*, Vol. 9, No. 2, Winter/Spring 2003, pp. 263–264.

Ahmed, Hisham H., *Hamas from Religious Salvation to Political Transformation: The Rise of Hamas in Palestinian Society*, Jerusalem: Palestinian Academic Society for the Study of International Affairs, 1994.

"Al-Alam TV News Director Responds to Al-Najaf Prayer Leader's Criticism," *Iranian Labor News Agency* (Tehran), Web page, in Persian, OSC IAP20040605000076, 0935 GMT June 4, 2004.

al-Aziz, Al-Khedir Abd, "America and the Sins of Coalitions," *Al Sharq al-Awsat*, in Arabic, December 18, 2006.

al-Dhiyabi, Jamil, "Fa'es America wa Ghatrasat Iran [America's Ax and Iran's Arrogance]," *Al-Hayat*, June 25, 2007.

al-Durusi, Salman, "Al-Shaykh Khalifah bin Salman: Al-Khalij La Yatahammal Harb Jadidah [Sheikh Khalifah bin Salman: The Gulf Cannot Take Another War]," *Al-Sharq al-Awsat*, July 28, 2007.

al-Fahd, Nasr, "Letter on the Legitimacy of Swearing at the Shi'a," Web page, in Arabic, date not available. As of April 12, 2006:
http://www.tawhed.ws

————, "Response to the Rejectionists (Shiites) on Their Indictment of the Companions," Web page, in Arabic, date not available. As of April 12, 2006: http://www.tawhed.ws

al-Faraj, Sami, comments on "Malaf Iran al-Nawawi wa Khayarat Majlis al-Amn [The Iranian Nuclear Portfolio and the Security Council Options]," *Akthar min Ra'i* [*More Than One Opinion*], al-Muqtada television, February 17, 2006.

al-Ghasali, Ahmad, "An Tajrubah: Makhatir Taqdim Ghusan al-Zaytoon LiIran [Out of Experience: The Dangers of Extending the Olive Branch to Iran]," *Al-Sharq al-Awsat*, No. 10341, March 22, 2007.

————, "Istifhal al-Azmah, Ma Hua al-Hal? [Exacerbating the Problem, What Is the Solution?]," *Al-Sharq al-Awsat*, July, 26, 2007.

al-Hussein, Abdullah II bin, King of Jordan, quoted in *al-Ra'y*, January 6, 2005.

al-Jabbar, Faleh Abd, "Why the Uprisings Failed," *Middle East Report*, No. 176, May–June 1992, pp. 2–14.

————, ed., *Ayatollahs, Sufis, and Ideologues: State, Religion, and Social Movements in Iraq*, London: Al-Saqi Books, 2002.

"Al-Jazirah TV Airs Documentary on Life, Rise of Hezbollah's Hasan Nasrallah," OpenSource.gov, GMP20060816637002, August 15, 2006.

al-Khazin, Jihad, "Al-Maradh al-Arabi [The Arab Disease]," *Saudi in Focus*, date not available.

al-Khudayr, 'Ali bin Khudayr, "*Fatwa* on the Shi'a," Web page, in Arabic, date not available. As of April 12, 2006: http://www.tawhed.com

al-Mun'im, Niveen Abd, *Sun' al-Qarar fi Iran wa al-Alaqat al-Arabiya al-Irania* [*Decisionmaking in Iran and the Arab-Iranian Relations*], Center for Arab Unity Studies, Beirut, Lebanon, 2002.

"Al-Nufuth al-Irani fi al-Mintaqa al-Arabiya [The Iranian Influence in the Arab Region]," *Al-Ittijah al-Mu'akis* [*Opposite Direction*], al-Muqtada television, February 4, 2007.

al-Qazwini, Jawdat, "The School of Qum" and "The School of Najaf," in Faleh Abd al-Jabar, ed., *Ayatollahs, Sufis and Ideologues: State, Religion and Social Movements in Iraq*, London: Saqi Books, 2002, pp. 245–281.

"Al-Qimma *al-Arabiya* [The Arab Summit]," Saudi Press Agency, Web page, date not available. As of late 2007: http://www.spa.gov.sa/ContentPage.php?cid=37&id=14398

"Al-Sira' al-Ta'ifi fi al-Iraq wa al-Mintaqah [The Sectarian Conflict in Iraq and the Region]," *Bila Hudud* [*Without Borders*], al-Muqtada television, January 20, 2007.

al-Umar, Nasr, "If Iran Occupies Iraq," Web page, in Arabic, date not available. As of April 12, 2006:
www.almoslim.net

———, "The Situation of the *Rafida* in the Land of Tawhed," Web page, in Arabic, date not available. As of April 12, 20067:
http://www.albainah.net

al-Zaydi, Mishari, "Uhadhir an Taqdhi Alihi al-Ama'im [Warning Against the Religious Establishment]," *Al-Sharq al-Awsat*, July 19, 2007.

"Analysis: Iran's Claim to Bahrain Sparks Media Debate," OSC Feature FEA20070723241746, July 23, 2007.

"Analysis: Survey of Iran's Arabic Satellite TV al-Alam," Iran–OSC Analysis GMF20070703684001, July 3, 2007.

"Ansar-i Hizbullah: Followers of the Party of God," Globalsecurity.org, Web page, n.d. As of February 4, 2008:
http://www.globalsecurity.org/intell/world/iran/ansar.htm

Anvari, Hamid Reza, "A Look at the Shanghai Cooperation Organization," *Central Asia and the Caucasus Review*, No. 34, Summer 2001, p. 80.

"Arming Hizbullah," *Jane's Intelligence Digest*, October 20, 2006.

"Article Views Iranian President's 'Dangerous' Proposal to Fill Vacuum in Iraq," *Al-Sharq al-Awsat* [London], Web page referencing an article by Bilal al-Hasan entitled "Ahmadinejad's Grave Mistake: The Theory of Vacuum Filling," in Arabic, OSC GMP20070902913006, September 2, 2007.

"Baalbek Seen as Staging Area for Terrorism," *Washington Post*, January 9, 1984.

"Bahrain: Mudhaharat Ihtijaj ala Maqalat Kihan [Bahrain: Demonstrations over Kihan's Article]," *Al-Sharq al-Awsat*, Web page, date not available.

Bakhash, Shaul, *The Reign of the Ayatollahs*, New York: Basic Books, 1989, pp. 279–280.

Bakhshi, Mohammad 'Ali, "Standing on the Ship of Power," found in "Iran: Report Says Iran's Navy Executed 'Ettehad-83' Maneuver in Various Waters," *Saff* (Tehran), in Persian, OSC IAP20050103000091, June 7, 2004.

Barzegar, Kayhan, "Tazad-e Naghshha: Baresiye rishehaye monazeeye Iran va Amrica bad az havadese 11 September [Conflicting Role: A Study on the Roots of Iran and U.S. Disputes After September 11]," International Relations Research Division, Center for Strategic Research, Expediency Council, 2006. As of December 26, 2006:
http://www.csr.ir/departments.aspx?abtid=07&&semid=34m

"The *Basij* Resistance Force," in *How They Fight: Armies of the World*, National Ground Intelligence Center, NGIC-1122-0204-98, 1998.

"BBC Monitoring Analysis: Arab Dilemma over Iran's Nuclear Program," OSC FEA20070627206546, June 27, 2007.

"BBC Monitoring Analysis: Arab Press Sees Iranian Gains in British Detainees Affair," BBC Monitoring, OSC EUP20070406950039, April 6, 2007.

"BBC Monitoring: Iran Media Guide," in English, Caversham BBC Monitoring, OSC IAP20070327950024, March 27, 2007.

"BBC Monitoring: Iran's Al-Alam TV Plays Role in Arab Media Scene," in English, Caversham BBC Monitoring, OSC GMP20070115950064, January 15, 2007.

Beehner, Lionel, "U.S. Sanctions Biting Iran," backgrounder Web page, Council on Foreign Relations, January 23, 2007. As of April 3, 2003: http://www.cfr.org/publication/12478/

Bergner, Brigadier General Kevin, Spokesman, Multi-National Force-Iraq, press briefing, July 2, 2007.

Berman, Ilan, *Tehran Rising: The Iranian Threat to the United States*, New York: Rowman and Littlefield, 2005.

Bilqaziz, Abed al-Ilah, "Al-Arab wa Iran: Min al-Ummah ila al-Madhhab [The Arabs and Iran: From the Umma to the Sect]," Web page, Harakat al-Adalah al-Watania [National Justice Movement], February 20, 2007. As of Novermber 20, 2008: http://www.3dala.org/print.php?id=1313&PHPSESSID=abaf5ea087b1cf63bfbe02d8776a2db0

bin Sallam, Muhammad, "Yemen Recalls Its Ambassadors to Iran and Libya," *Yemen Times*, May 13, 2008.

Black, Ian, and Benny Morris, *Israel's Secret Wars*, New York: Grove Weidenfeld, 1991.

Blackwill, Robert D., "The Three Rs: Rivalry, Russia, 'Ran," *The National Interest*, January 2008.

Bradley, John R., "Iran's Ethnic Tinderbox," *The Washington Quarterly*, Vol. 30, No. 1, Winter 2006–2007, pp. 181–190.

Brookings Institution, *The Brookings Institution Iraq Index*, July 30, 2007.

Buchta, Wilfried, *Who Rules Iran? The Structure of Power in the Islamic Republic*, Washington, D.C.: The Washington Institute for Near East Policy and the Konrad Adenauer Stiftung, 2000.

———, *Iran's Security Sector: An Overview*, Geneva: Geneva Center for the Democratic Control of Armed Forces (DCAF), Working Paper No. 146, August 2004.

"Buenos Aires: A Prime Target for Pro-Iranian Terror," *Jerusalem Post*, August 11, 1994.

Byman, Daniel L., *Deadly Connections: States That Sponsor Terrorism*, New York: Cambridge University Press, 2005.

Byman, Daniel L., Shahram Chubin, Anoushiravan Ehteshami, and Jerrold D. Green, *Iran's Security Policy in the Post-Revolutionary Era*, Santa Monica, Calif.: RAND Corporation, MR-1320-OSD, 2001. As of March 4, 2009:
http://www.rand.org/pubs/monograph_reports/MR1320/

Center for Strategic Research, Foreign Policy Research Division, Expediency Council (Iran), "Negarinaye keshvarhaye Arabi nesbat be Iran dar fazaye Jadide Mantaghei [Arab Countries' Concerns About Iran in the Light of the New Environment in the Region]," Web page, 2006. As of December 19, 2006:
http://www.csr.ir/departments.aspx?abtid=04&&semid=68

Central Intelligence Agency, "Attachment A: Unclassified Report to Congress on the Acquisition of Technology Relating to Weapons of Mass Destruction and Advanced Conventional Munitions," January 1–June 30, 2003.

Chubin, Shahram, "Iran's Strategic Environment and Nuclear Weapons," in *Iran's Nuclear Weapons Options: Issues and Analysis*, Washington, D.C.: The Nixon Center, January 2001, pp. 22–30.

———, "Whither Iran? Reform, Domestic Politics and National Security," International Institute for Strategic Studies, Adelphi Paper No. 342, 2002.

———, *Iran's Nuclear Ambitions*, Washington, D.C.: The Carnegie Endowment for International Peace, 2006.

Clawson, Patrick, "The Paradox of Anti-Americanism in Iran," *Middle East Journal of International Affairs,* Vol. 8, No. 1, March 2004.

Clawson, Patrick, and Michael Eisenstadt, *Deterring the Ayatollahs: Complications in Applying Cold War Strategy to Iran*, Washington, D.C.: The Washington Institute for Near East Policy, Policy Focus No. 72, July 2007.

Clawson, Patrick, and Michael Rubin, *Eternal Iran: Continuity and Chaos*, New York: Palgrave-MacMillan Press, 2005.

"Commentary Criticizes Iran's Fruitless Political Alliances," *Aftab-e Yazd* (Tehran), Web page, in Persian, OSC IAP20040605000057, June 5, 2004.

Cooper, Helene, "Iran Fighting Proxy War in Iraq, U.S. Envoy Says," *New York Times*, April 12, 2008.

Cordesman, Anthony H., *Iran's Developing Military Capabilities,* Washington, D.C.: The Center for Strategic and International Studies, 2005.

———, *Iran's Revolutionary Guards, the Al Quds Force, and Other Intelligence and Paramilitary Forces*, working draft, Washington, D.C.: Center for Strategic and International Studies, 2007.

————, "Iraq's Sectarian and Ethnic Violence and Its Evolving Insurgency," Center for Strategic and International Studies, April 2, 2007.

Cordesman, Anthony, and Martin Kleiber, *Iran's Military Forces and Warfighting Capabilities: The Threat in the Northern Gulf,* Washington, D.C.: Center for Strategic and International Studies, 2007.

Cragin, Kim, Peter Chalk, Sara A. Daly, and Brian A. Jackson, *Sharing the Dragon's Teeth: Terrorist Groups and the Exchange of Technologies,* Santa Monica, Calif.: RAND Corporation, MG-485-DHS, 2007. As of February 19, 2008: http://www.rand.org/pubs/monographs/MG485/

"Deconstructing Hezbollah's Surprise Military Prowess," *Jane's Intelligence Review,* November 1, 2006.

Deeb, Laura, "Hizballah: A Primer," *Middle East Report,* July 31, 2006.

Defense Threat Reduction Agency, "Special Report: Challenges of Iranian Missile Proliferation," *WMD Insights,* October 1, 2006.

Dehghani, Mahmoud, "Naghsh-e Aragh-e Jadid dar tartibat-e amniyati-e mantaghe-e Khalij-e Fars [The Role of the New Iraq in the Security Orders in the Persian Gulf]," Center for Strategic Research, Foreign Policy Research Division, Expediency Council (Iran), Web page, 2003. As of December 20, 2006: http://www.csr.ir/departments.aspx?abtid=07&&semid=306

Director of Central Intelligence, *Acquisition of Technology,* November 2004.

Dobbins, James, "How to Talk to Iran," *Washington Post,* July 22, 2007.

Dobbins, James, Sarah Harting, and Dalia Dassa Kaye, *Coping with Iran: Confrontation, Containment or Engagement? A Conference Report,* Santa Monica, Calif.: RAND Corporation, CF-237-NSRD, 2007. As of December 17, 2008: http://www.rand.org/pubs/conf_proceedings/CF237/

Dodge, Toby, *Iraq's Future: The Aftermath of Regime Change,* London: International Institute for Strategic Studies, Adelphi Paper 372, 2005.

Dreyfuss, Robert, "Is Iran Winning the Iraq War?" *The Nation,* February 21, 2008.

"Egyptian Officials, Media Escalate Anti-Iranian Rhetoric, Prompting Restrained Iranian Response," OSC Analysis GMF20070208282001, February 8, 2007.

Ehteshami, Anoushiravan, "Iran's International Posture After the Fall of Baghdad," *Middle East Journal,* Vol. 58, No. 2, Spring 2004.

Einhorn, Robert J., "Transatlantic Strategy on Iran's Nuclear Program," *Washington Quarterly,* Autumn 2004.

Eisenstadt, Michael, "Living with a Nuclear Iran," *Survival,* Vol. 41, No. 3, Autumn 1999.

————, "The Armed Forces of the Islamic Republic of Iran," *Middle East Review of International Affairs,* Vol. 5, No. 1, March 2001.

Ekvan, Samaneh, "Reserve Fund Rivalry," *Iran Daily*, December 13, 2004, p. 6.

Elan, Seth, et al., "Open-Source Research on Nuclear Doctrine and Strategy, Command and Control, and Delivery Systems in Iran and Israel," Library of Congress, Federal Research Division, Washington, D.C., December 2005.

el-Hokayem, Emile, and Matteo Legrenzi, "The Arab Gulf States in the Shadow of the Iranian Nuclear Challenge," Washington, D.C.: The Stimson Center, May 2006.

Elkhamri, Mounir, "Iran's Contribution to the Civil War in Iraq," *The Jamestown Foundation Occasional Paper*, January 2007.

England, Andrew, "Arab Street Warms to Showman Ahmadi-Nejad," *Financial Times*, April 6, 2007.

Entessar, Nader, "Iran's Security Challenges," *The Muslim World*, Vol. 94, October 2004.

Escobar, Pepe, "Twelve More Years," *Asia Times*, June 28, 2005.

"'Experts' Warn U.S. Plan Uses Arab States to Cause Sunni-Shiite Split," *Hezbollah* [Tehran], in Persian, OSC IAP20070119011004, January 14, 2007.

Fahmy, Nabil, "Special Comment," United Nations Institute for Disarmament Research, *Disarmament Forum*, No. 2, 2001, pp. 3–5.

Fahs, Hasan, "Abd al-Hadi LilHayat: Ay Sidam Irani-Amrici Sayas'ub Dhabtuhu Li'an Sahatuhu Wasi'ah wa al-Imkanat Kabira [Abd al-Hadi to Al-Hayat Newspaper: Any American-Iranian Confrontation Would Be Difficult to Contain Because the Front Is Wide and the Resources Are Huge]," *Al-Hayat*, February 9, 2007.

Farhi, Farideh, "Iran's Security Outlook," *Middle East Report Online*, July 9, 2007.

Feldman, Shai, *Nuclear Weapons and Arms Control in the Middle East*, Cambridge, Mass.: MIT Press, 1997.

Felter, Joseph, and Brian Fishman, "Iranian Strategy in Iraq: Politics and 'Other Means'," Occasional Paper Series, Combating Terrorism Center at West Point, U.S. Military Academy, West Point, N.Y., October 13, 2008.

Fisk, Robert, *Pity the Nation*, 3rd ed., Oxford: Oxford University Press, 2001.

"Focus on Hezbollah," *The Lebanon Report*, Vol. 4, No. 3, March 1993, pp. 6–7.

Fuller, Graham, "The Hezbollah-Iran Connection: Model for Sunni Resistance," *The Washington Quarterly*, Winter 2006–2007, pp. 139–150.

"FYI—Iran's *Al-Alam* TV Discusses Arab Reaction to Saddam's Execution," Al-Alam Television (Tehran), in Arabic, OSC IAP20070102950094, 1330 GMT January 2, 2007.

Ganji, Akbar, "The View from Tehran," *Boston Review*, Vol. 32, No. 3, May/June 2007.

———,"Why Iran's Democrats Shun Aid," *Washington Post*, October 26, 2007, p. A21.

Gasiorowski, Mark, "The New Aggressiveness in Iran's Foreign Policy," *Middle East Policy*, Vol. 14, No. 2, Summer 2007, pp. 125–132.

Gause, Gregory, "Saudi Arabia: Iraq, Iran, the Regional Power Balance, and the Sectarian Question," *Strategic Insights*, Vol. 6, No. 2, March 2007.

"General Rahim Safavi: America's Aim Is to Prevent Iran from Becoming the First Power in the Middle East," *Keyhan* (Tehran), in "Persian Press: Revolutionary Guard Commander on Way to Fight Unequal Enemy," in Persian, OSC IAP20061231011007, December 26, 2006, p. 14.

Ghafuri, Ali, "An Interview with General Tavakoli, Deputy Commander of the Army in Charge of Self Sufficiency Jihad," *Iran Daily Newspaper*, Vol. 9, No. 2734, February 25, 2004, p. 15.

Giles, Gregory F., "The Islamic Republic of Iran and Nuclear, Biological, and Chemical Weapons," in Peter R. Lavoy et al., eds., *Planning the Unthinkable: How New Powers Will Use Nuclear, Biological, and Chemical Weapons*, Ithaca and London: Cornell University Press, 2000, pp. 79–103.

Girard, Renaud, "The Calculated Provocations of the Islamist Iranian President," *Le Figaro* (Paris), in French, December 19, 2005.

Glanz, James, "U.S. Says Arms Link Iranians to Iraqi Shiites," *New York Times*, February 12, 2007.

Gordan, Michael, and Dexter Filkins, "Hezbollah Said to Help Shiite Army in Iraq," *New York Times*, November 28, 2006.

Grace, Robert, and Andrew Mandelbaum, "Understanding the Iran-Hezbollah Connection," United States Institute of Peace Briefing, September 2006.

Green, Jerry, "Terrorism and Politics in Iran," in Martha Crenshaw, ed., *Terrorism in Context*, University Park, Pa.: Pennsylvania State University Press, 1995, pp. 553–594.

Greenwell, Megan, "Sunnis Quit Cabinet Posts," *Washington Post*, August 2, 2007.

———, "Iran Trains Militiamen Inside Iraq, U.S. Says," *Washington Post*, August 20, 2007.

"Growing Support for Hamas Observed in Iran," BBC Monitoring, OSC Feature FEA20070622199586, June 22, 2007.

"Guards C-in-C Says Iran's 'Deterrent Capability' Extends to Entire Region," BBC Monitoring International Reports, September 11, 2004.

Guldimann, Tim, "The Iranian Nuclear Impasse," *Survival*, Vol. 49, No. 3, Autumn 2007, pp. 169–178.

Haghshenass, Fariborz, "Iran's Air Forces: Struggling to Maintain Readiness," Washington Institute for Near East Policy, PolicyWatch No. 1066, December 28, 2005.

———, "Iran's Doctrine of Asymmetric Naval Warfare," Washington, D.C.: Washington Institute for Near East Policy, PolicyWatch No. 1179, December 21, 2006.

Hajjar, Sami, "Hezbollah: Terrorism, National Liberation or Menace?" thesis, Carlisle Barracks, Pa.: U.S. Army War College, Strategic Studies Institute, August 2002.

"Hamas Minister Brings Cases of Cash into Gaza," *Independent* (London), June 15, 2006.

Hamzeh, Nizar A., "Lebanon's Hizbullah: From Islamic Revolution to Parliamentary Accommodation," *Third World Quarterly*, Vol. 13, No. 32, 1993.

Harling, Peter, and Joost Hiltermann, "Eyes Wide Shut," *Le Monde Diplomatique*, May 2007.

Harling, Peter, and Hamid Yasin, "Iraq's Diverse Shiite," *Le Monde Diplomatique*, September 2006.

Haydar, Hassan, "Inhinaa' Iran [Iran's Weakness]," *Free Syria*, Web site, February 8, 2007. As of November 20, 2008:
http://www.free-syria.com/print.php?articleid=15239

Henderson, Simon, "The Elephant in the Gulf: The Arab States and Iran's Nuclear Program," Washington Institute for Near East Policy, PolicyWatch 1065, December 21, 2005.

Heradstveit, Daniel, and G. Matthew Bonham, "What the Axis of Evil Metaphor Did to Iran," *The Middle East Journal*, Vol. 60, No. 3, Summer 2007, pp. 421–440.

Hewson, Robert, "Iran Stages Large-Scale Exercises to Underline Defence Capabilities," *Jane's Defence Weekly*, September 13, 2006.

"Hezbollah and Israeli Wage Electronic War in South Lebanon," *Jane's Intelligence Review*, February 1, 1995.

"Hezbollah's Intelligence Apparatus," *Jane's Terrorism and Security Monitor*, September 13, 2006.

"Highlights: Iranian Military Developments, 8–14 June 2007; Iran to Get SA-19 Grissom," in English, OSC Summary IAP20070615339001, June 8–14, 2007.

Hirshberg, Peter, "Getting Smart," *Jerusalem Post,* December 17, 1992.

Hodgson, Marshall, *The Venture of Islam*, Vol. 1, Chicago: The University of Chicago Press, 1977.

Hughes, Robin, "Iran Launches 'Great Prophet 2' Joint Military Exercise," *Jane's Defence Weekly*, November 8, 2006.

————, "Iran Eyes Long-Range Air Strike Capability," *Jane's Defence Weekly*, February 7, 2007.

————, "Tehran Fires Tor-M1," *Jane's Defence Weekly*, February 14, 2007.

Ignatius, David, "At the Tip of Iran's Spear," *Washington Post*, June 8, 2008.

"Inside the Mahdi Army Death Squads," *Jane's Terrorism and Security Monitor*, February 14, 2007.

International Crisis Group, "Iran: The Struggle for the Revolution's Soul," Middle East Report No. 5, Tehran and Brussels, August 2002.

————, "Bahrain's Sectarian Challenge," Middle East Report No. 40, Brussels, 2005.

————, "The Shiite Question in Saudi Arabia," Middle East Report No. 45, Brussels, 2005.

————, "Update Briefing—Iran: What Does Ahmadi-Nejad's Victory Mean?" Tehran/Brussels, August 2005.

————, "Iran: Ahmadinejad's Tumultuous Presidency," Middle East Briefing No. 21, Brussels, 2007.

————, "Where Is Iraq Heading? Lessons from Basra," Middle East Report No. 67, June 25, 2007.

————, "Shi'ite Politics in Iraq: The Role of the Supreme Council," Middle East Report No. 70, November 15, 2007.

International Institute for Strategic Studies, *The Military Balance 2007*, London: Routledge, 2006.

"Interview with Adm. Ali Shamkhani, (former) Minister of Defense of the Islamic Republic of Iran," *Military Technology*, No. 7, 2002, p. 36.

"Interview with Amir Mohebbian in *Der Spiegel*," *E'tedal va Towse'eh*, Mohammad Nasiri, trans., FBIS IAP20050715339003, February 20, 2005.

"Iran: Ahmadinezhad Government Reverses Civil Society Gains," OSC Analysis IAF20070620564001, June 20, 2007.

"Iran: Author Describes Islamic Republic's Military Doctrine," *Basis and History of Military Thought in Iran* (Tehran), in Persian, OSC IAG20021113000150, January 1, 2001.

"Iran Calls On Iraqi MPs to Scrutinize Security Pact with US," Tehran Fars News Agency, OSC IAP20081126950066, in English, November 26, 2008.

"Iran, China to Cement Cooperation," Tehran Fars News Agency, July 7, 2008. As of October 12, 2008:
http://english.farsnews.com/newstext.php?nn=8705071102

"Iran: Commander Says New Russian-Delivered Defense System Quick, Responsive," *Keyhan* (Tehran), Web page, in Persian, OSC IAP20070221397002, February 8, 2007.

"Iran: Commentator Says Shi'i Scholars Should 'Boycott' Al-Sadr," *Baztab* (Tehran), Web page, in Persian, OSC IAP20040515000085, 1122 GMT, May 15, 2004.

"Iran: Conservative Cleric Criticizes al-Sadr for Making Karbala, Najaf U.S. Targets," *Vaghaye'-ye Ettefaghiyeh* (Tehran), Web page, in Persian, OSC IAP20040520000056, May 18, 2004.

"Iran Defence Doctrine Deterrent—Defence Minister," transcript of interview on Iranian television, February 13, 2007, BBC Worldwide Monitoring, February 17, 2007.

"Iran: Guards Chief Outlines New Doctrine for Improving Combat Readiness," Tehran Fars News Agency, in Persian, Web page, OSC IAP20061217950103, December 17, 2006.

"Iran Guards' Commander Says Combat Units Can Expand Threefold in 48 Hours," Tehran Fars News Agency, Web page, from BBC Worldwide Monitoring, November 12, 2006.

"Iran: Intelligence Minister Says 'Terrorist Act' Foiled in Khuzestan Province," Tehran Fars News Agency, Web page, in English, OSC IAP20070808950147, 1025 GMT August 8, 2007.

"Iran: Magazine Looks at What Future Wars May Be Like," *Saff* (Tehran), in Persian, OSC IAP20010524000001, May 21, 2001, pp. 17–20.

"Iran: Officials Largely Remain Silent on Eve of SOFA Vote," OSC Feature—Iran FEA20081125796715, November 25, 2008.

"Iran: Political Figures Comment on Violent Groups, Elections, Other Issues," *Yas-e Now*, in Persian, FBIS IAP 2003121600005, December 8, 2005.

"Iran Press: General Discusses IRGC Role in Engineering, Economic Contracts," *Sharq* (Tehran), in Persian, OSC AP20060702011002, June 26, 2006, pp. 1, 11.

"Iran Press Military Says Sanctioned Equipment May Be Produced Internally," BBC Monitoring International Reports coverage of report by Iranian newspaper *Siyasat-e Ruz*, April 23, 2007, A2007043030-14936-GNW, April 30, 2007.

"Iran: Profile of IRGC's Shahid Mahallati Theological-Political College," in Persian, OSC IAP20061208427001, December 7, 2006.

"Iran: Provincial Cleric Urges Unity to Foil Enemy 'Threats,' 'Plots'," *Orumiyeh Vision of the Islamic Republic of Iran*, West Azarbayjan Provincial television, in Persian, OSC IAP20071026950088, October 26, 2007.

"Iran: Report Highlights 'Need' for Aerospace Security, 'Fourth Force'," *Saff* (Tehran), in Persian, OSC IAP20050210000086, October 1, 2004, p. 6.

"Iran Revolution Guards Hold 'Asymmetric Warfare' Ashura-5 Exercises," Vision of the Islamic Republic of Iran Network, in Persian, OSC IAP20040913000110, September 13, 2004.

"Iran's Domestic Political Battles Exacerbate International Crisis," *Gulf States Newsletter*, Vol. 30, No. 781, May 12, 2006.

"Iran Seeks to Allay Sunni Anxieties in Saudi Arabia," in English, Caversham BBC Monitoring, OSC GMP20070302950043, March 2, 2007.

"Iran Sees Emergence of Shiite Coalition After Elections in Iraq," Caversham BBC Monitoring, OSC IAP20090211950138, in English, February 11, 2009.

"Iran to Resort to Offensive Strategy If Attacked," Iranian Mehr News Agency via BBC Worldwide Monitoring, November 17, 2006.

"Iran Tuhadid Duwal al-Khalij al-Muta'awinah ma' America bil Sawarikh [Iran Threatens the Gulf Countries Cooperating with America with Missiles]," *Al-Sharq al-Awsat*, July 11, 2007.

"Iranian Army Personnel Undergo Irregular Warfare Training," IRNA, FBIS IAP2005041000040, April 15, 2005.

"Iranian Bassij Wishes for U.S. Defeat in Iraq," Agence France Presse, Arab News, December 1, 2003.

"Iranian Daily: Theologians Concerned by Reported Sunni Preaching in Khuzestan," *Aftab-e Yazd*, in Persian, FBIS IAP20051221011046, December 20, 2005.

"Iranian Defense Minister Urges Iraq to 'Exercise Its Authority' over Foreign 'Bases'," Tehran Fars News Agency, Web page, in Persian, FBIS IAP20050706011012, 0421 GMT July 6, 2005.

"Iranian Ground Force Tactics," *How They Fight: Armies of the World*, National Ground Intelligence Center, NGIC-1122-0097-00, August 2000.

"Iranian Media Under Pressure Tilts in Favor of Government," BBC, OSC Feature—Iran FEA20070711226066, July 11, 2007.

"Iranian Military Chief Says Evidence Shows Global Power Balance Changing," IRNA, Web page, in English, OSC IAP20060902950063, 1410 GMT September 2, 2006.

"Iranian Military Practices Asymmetrical War Tactics in Final Phase of Exercises," Iranian Student News Agency, in Persian, FBIS IAP20041208000037, December 8, 2004.

"Iranian Official Calls for Implementation of 1972 Agreement on Helmand River," IRNA, Web page, in English, FBIS IAP20050201000031, 1255 GMT February 1, 2005.

"Iranian Paper Says Airport Controversy Takes Iran's Internal Divisions 'Sky-High'," *Iran Daily* (Tehran), Web page, in English, OSC IAP20040510000022, May 10, 2004.

"Iranian Paper Says Iran's Prestige Damaged by 'Embarrassing' Airport Closure," *Iran News* (Tehran), Web page, in English, OSC IAP20040510000031, 0001 GMT May 10, 2004.

"Iranian Radio Criticizes Reported US Plans for Military Base in West Afghanistan," Mashhad Voice of the Islamic Republic of Iran External Service in Dari, FBIS IAP20041220000065, 1330 GMT December 19, 2004.

Iranian Student News Agency, FBIS IAP20050722011019, July 22, 2005.

"Iranian Transportation Ministry Denies Blaming IRGC for Closure of New Airport," IRNA, Web page, in English, OSC IAP20040831000004, 0420 GMT August 31, 2004.

"Iranian TV Describes Detained Iranian-American Esfandiari as 'Mosad Spy'," Islamic Republic of Iran Network Television (IRINN) (Tehran), in Persian, OSC IAP20070512011017, 1640 GMT May 12, 2007.

"Iraq: Al-Sadr Orders His 6 Cabinet Ministers to Withdraw from Government," *International Herald Tribune*, April 15, 2007.

"Iraq Is the Battleground—The West Against Iran," *Middle East Quarterly*, Vol. 12, No. 2, Spring 2005.

"Iraq: Transforming Iran's Shiite Proxy, Assisting the United States," Web page, Stratfor.com, May 11, 2007. As of November 20, 2008:
http://www.serve.com/Lincolnheritage2/articles/address/2004toNow/foreign/2007-05-Iraq-Transforming_Irans_Shiite_Proxy.htm

"IRGC Commander Discusses New Strategy," *Radio Free Europe/Radio Liberty Iran Report*, September 27, 2004.

"IRGC Ground Force Commander Speaks on Reorganization, Combat Plans," Vision of the Islamic Republic of Iran Network, in Persian, FBIS IAP20050309000087, March 9, 2005.

"Israeli Armor Fails to Protect MBTs [Main Battle Tanks] from ATGMs [Antitank Guided Missiles]," *Jane's Defence Weekly*, August 30, 2006.

Israeli Ministry of Foreign Affairs, "Special Survey: Bombing of the AMIA Building in Buenos Aires," July 19, 1994.

Jaber, Hala, *Hezbollah: Born with a Vengeance*, New York: Columbia University Press, 1997, pp. 11–12.

Jackson, Brian A., John C. Baker, Peter Chalk, Kim Cragin, John V. Parachini, and Horacio R. Trujillo, *Aptitude for Destruction*, Santa Monica, Calif.: RAND Corporation, MG-331-NIJ and MG-332-NIJ, 2005. As of November 20, 2008:
http://www.rand.org/pubs/monographs/MG331/
and
http://www.rand.org/pubs/monographs/MG332/

Jacoby, Lowell E., *Current and Projected National Security Threats to the United States*, DIA Statement for the Record, Senate Select Committee on Intelligence, February 16, 2005.

Jamshidi, Muhammad Husayn, "Basis and History of Military Thought in Iran," published by the IRGC College of Command, found in "Iran: Author Describes Islamic Republic's Military Doctrine," OSC IAP20021113000150, January 1, 2001, pp. 600–604.

Jane's Information Group, "Iran—Air Force," *Jane's Sentinel Security Assessment-Gulf States*, March 2005.

Jentleson, Bruce W., and Dalia Dassa Kaye, "Security Status: Explaining Regional Security Cooperation and Its Limits in the Middle East," *Security Studies*, Vol. 8, No. 1, 1998, pp. 204–238.

Jones, Peter, "Arms Control in the Middle East: Some Reflections on ACRS," *Security Dialogue*, Vol. 28, No. 1, 1997.

———, "Negotiating Regional Security in the Middle East: The ACRS Experience and Beyond," *Journal of Strategic Studies*, Vol. 26, No. 3, 2003.

———, "Open Forum: Arms Control in the Middle East: Is It Time to Renew ACRS?" United Nations Institute for Disarmament Research, Disarmament Forum—North-East Asian Security, No. 2, 2005.

Jones, Toby Craig, "Saudi Arabia's Not So New Anti-Shiism," *Middle East Report 242*, Spring 2007, pp. 29–32.

Kamrava, Mehran, "Iranian National-Security Debates: Factionalism and Lost Opportunities," *Middle East Policy*, Vol. 14, No. 2, Summer 2007.

Karimi, Nasser, "Iran Unveils Locally Made Fighter in War Games," The Associated Press, September 6, 2006.

Karouny, Mariam, "Iraq's SCIRI Party to Change Platform, Officials," Reuters, May 11, 2007.

Katzman, Kenneth, "Iran: Current Developments and U.S. Policy," Congressional Research Service, July 25, 2003.

Kaye, Dalia Dassa, "Regional Security Cooperation," in *Beyond the Handshake: Multilateral Cooperation in the Arab-Israeli Peace Process, 1991–1996*, New York: Columbia University Press, 2001, pp. 76–109.

Kaye, Dalia Dassa, and Frederic M. Wehrey, "A Nuclear Iran: The Reactions of Neighbours," *Survival,* Vol. 49, No. 2, Summer 2007, pp. 111–128.

"Kayfa Yandhuru al-Arab ila Iran? [How Do Arabs View Iran?]," *Panorama,* al-Arabiya television, February 26, 2007. As of August 24, 2007: http://www.alArabiya.net/Articles/2007/02/26/32078.htm

Kechichian, Joseph A., "Can Conservative Arab Gulf Monarchies Endure a Fourth Gulf War in the Persian Gulf?" *Middle East Journal,* Vol. 61, No. 2, Spring 2007, pp. 283–306.

Kelsay, John, *Islam and War: A Study in Comparative Ethics*, Louisville, Ky.: Westminister/John Knox Press, 1993.

Keppel, Gilles, *Jihad: The Trail of Political Islam*, Cambridge, Mass.: The Belknap Press of Harvard University Press, 2002.

Kessler, Glenn, "In 2003, U.S. Spurned Iran's Offer of Dialogue," *Washington Post,* June 18, 2006, p. A16.

Khalaji, Mehdi, "Iran's Revolutionary Guard Corps, Inc.," Washington Institute for Near East Policy, PolicyWatch No. 1273, August 17, 2007.

———, "Apocalyptic Politics: On the Rationality of Iranian Policy," Policy Focus 79, Washington, D.C.: The Washington Institute for Near East Policy, January 2008.

Khan, Abu Mohammad Ashgar, "A Look at Theories of Deterrence, Disarmament and Arms Control," *Journal of Defense Policy* (Tehran), in Persian, FBIS IAP 20021126000059, December 20, 1998, pp. 9–48.

"Khuzestan, Beating Heart of Great Iran: Ahmadinejad," Tehran Mehr News Agency, Web page, in English, OSC IAP20070102950116, 2010 GMT January 2, 2007.

Knickmeyer, Ellen, and Omar Fekeiki, "Iraqi Shiite Cleric Pledges to Defend Iran," *Washington Post*, January 24, 2006.

Knights, Michael, "Iran's Conventional Forces Remain Key to Deterring Potential Threats," *Jane's Intelligence Review*, February 1, 2006.

———, "Deadly Developments–Explosively Formed Projectiles in Iraq," *Jane's Intelligence Review*, March 2007a.

———, "Shiite Backlash—Anti-Coalition Sadrist Factions in Iraq," *Jane's Intelligence Review*, July 2007b.

———, "Rocky Road for Basra Operation," *Jane's Defence Weekly*, April 23, 2008.

Kramer, Martin, "Muslim Statecraft and Subversion," *Middle East Contemporary Survey, 1983–84,* Vol. 8, 1986, pp. 170–173.

———, "The Moral Logic of Hezbollah," in Walter Reich, ed., *Origins of Terrorism: Psychologies, Ideologies, Theologies, States of Mind,* Washington, D.C.: Woodrow Wilson Center Press, 1998.

Landau, Emily, "Egypt and Israel in ACRS: Bilateral Concerns in a Regional Arms Control Process," Tel Aviv: Jaffee Center for Strategic Studies, Memorandum No. 59, 2001.

"Larijani Describes SOFA as American Capitulation," IRNA, October 26, 2008.

"Lebanon Under the Current Circumstances," *Without Borders,* al-Jazeera television, in Arabic, January 16, 2007.

Leverett, Flynt L., "Iran: The Gulf Between Us," *New York Times,* January 24, 2006.

Levitt, Matthew, "Iranian State Sponsorship of Terror: Threatening U.S. Security, Global Stability, and Regional Peace," Testimony Before the House International Relations Committee, February 16, 2005.

Lynch, Marc, Middle East blog, February 9, 2007. As of June 10, 2007: http://abuaardvark.typepad.com/abuaardvark/2007/02/new_telhamizogb.htm

———, "Why U.S. Strategy on Iran Is Crumbling," *Christian Science Monitor,* January 4, 2008.

Mahini, Lt. Col. Rahmatollah Salmani, interview with Brig. Gen. Naser Ma'sumarast, "Electronic Warfare Past and Present," *Saff* (Tehran), in Persian, FBIS IAP2003042000149, April 28, 2003, pp. 16–18.

"Malaysia Pledges $16 Million to Palestinian Authority," *Khaleej Times,* May 21, 2006.

Malbrunot, Georges, "Golfe Alors que la tension monte entre Washington et Téhéran; Les chiites d'Arabie sous l'oeil de l'Iran," *Le Figaro* (Paris), November 17, 2007.

Maleki, Abbas, "Iran's Foreign Policy: From Idealism to Realism," *Majalleh Siasat Khareji [The Journal of Foreign Policy],* in Persian, Vol. 10, 1999.

Malley, Robert, and Peter Harling, "Containing a Shiite Symbol of Hope," *Christian Science Monitor,* October 24, 2006.

Marr, Phebe, "Who Are Iraq's New Leaders? What Do They Want?" United States Institute of Peace, Special Report 160, March 2006.

Mathee, Rudee, "The Egyptian Opposition on the Iranian Revolution," in Juan R. I. Cole and Nikki R. Keddie, *Shi'ism and Social Protest,* New Haven: Yale University Press, 1986, pp. 247–274.

Mazzetti, Mark, and Helene Cooper, "U.S. Arms Plan for Mideast Aims to Counter Iranian Power," *New York Times*, July 31, 2007, p. 6.

McFaul, Michael, "A Helsinki Process for the Middle East," *Journal of Democracy*, No. 8, Spring 2008.

McFaul, Michael, Abbas Milani, and Larry Diamond, "A Win-Win U.S. Strategy for Dealing with Iran," *Washington Quarterly*, Vol. 30, No. 1, pp. 121–138.

Middle East Media Research Institute (MEMRI), "An Eternal Curse on the Muftis of the Saudi Court and on the Pharaoh of Egypt," editorial in *Jomhouri-ye Eslami* (Tehran), July 28, 2006.

Moaveni, Azadeh, "Why Iran Isn't Cheering," *Time*, July 23, 2006.

Morris, Loveday, "Gates Calls for GCC to Embrace Iraq," *The National*, December 13, 2008.

Mubarak, Hosni, President of Egypt, statement carried on al-Arabiya television, April 9, 2006.

Murphy, Brian, "Standoff Leaves Iran Clerics on Sidelines," *Washington Post*, May 26, 2006.

Murphy, Kim, "Iran's Guard Builds a Fiscal Empire," *Los Angeles Times*, August 26, 2007.

Nakash, Yitzhak, *Reaching for Power: The Shi'a in the Modern Arab World*, Princeton, N.J.: Princeton University Press, 2006.

Nasr, Vali, "When the Shi'ites Rise," *Foreign Affairs*, Vol. 85, No. 4, July/August 2006.

———, "After Lebanon, There's Iran," *Christian Science Monitor*, August 9, 2006.

———, "Iran on Its Heels," *Washington Post*, June 19, 2008.

Nasr, Vali, and Ray Takeyh, "The Costs of Containing Iran: Washington's Misguided New Middle East Policy," *Foreign Affairs*, Vol. 87, No. 1, January/February 2008, pp. 85–94.

Nasrallah, Hasan, live televised speech given in the southern neighborhoods of Beirut, al-Manar television, January 24, 2007.

National Intelligence Council, *Iran: Nuclear Intentions and Capabilities*, National Intelligence Estimate, November 2007.

National Security Council, *The National Security Strategy of the United States of America*, Washington, D.C.: The White House, March 2006.

NAVCENT, "Iran Media Analysis, Quarterly Report, January–March 2007," April 2007.

———, "Media Analysis Report, Iran and Regional Security Quicklook," April 2007.

"No Room for WMDs in Iran's National Security Doctrine, Says Larijani,"
IRNA, distributed by United Press International, February 11, 2007.

Nu'man, Isam, *America wa al-Islam al-Silah al-Nawawi* [*America, Islam, and the Nuclear Weapon*], Beirut: Al-Matbu'at Publishing House, 2007.

Ochmanek, David, and Lowell Schwartz, *The Challenge of Nuclear-Armed Regional Adversaries*, Santa Monica, Calif.: RAND Corporation, MG-671-AF, 2008. As of December 17, 2008:
http://www.rand.org/pubs/monographs/MG671/

Parker, Ned, "Interior Ministry Mirrors Chaos of a Fractured Iraq," *Los Angeles Times*, July 30, 2007.

Plemming, Sue, "Rice, Gates in Egypt to Persuade Arabs," Reuters, July 31, 2007.

Po, Enrico, "Iran (Almost) Does It Alone," *Bergamo Rivista, Italiana Drefesa*, in Italian, translated by FBIS, FBIS EUP20030407000354, January 2, 2003.

Porter, Gareth, "How a 2003 Secret Overture for Tehran Might Have Led to a Deal on Iran's Nuclear Capacity," *The American Prospect*, May 21, 2006.

"President's Trip to Emirate Thwarted American Plans for Regional Discord," *Tehran* (Iran), Web page, in Persian, OSC IAP20070516950068, 0000 GMT May 15, 2007.

Qassam, Naim, *Hezbollah: The Story from Within*, London: Saqi Books, 2005.

Quinlivan, James T., "Coup-Proofing: Its Practice and Consequences in the Middle East," *International Security*, Vol. 24, No. 2, Autumn 1999, pp. 131–165.

Radio Free Europe/Radio Liberty, Vol. 7, No. 38, November 1, 2004.

Radio Free Europe/Radio Liberty Iran Report, December 7, 2004.

Radio Free Europe/Radio Liberty Iran Report, August 8, 2005.

Rahimi, Babak, "Muqtada al-Sadr's New Alliance with Tehran," *Terrorism Monitor*, The Jamestown Foundation, Vol. 5, No. 4, March 1, 2007a.

———, "A Shiite Storm Looms on the Horizon: Sadr and ISCI Relations," *Terrorism Monitor*, The Jamestown Foundation, Vol. 5, No. 10, May 24, 2007b.

———, "Muqtada al-Sadr Stepping Into the Power Vacuum," *Terrorism Focus*, The Jamestown Foundation, Vol. 4, No. 19, June 19, 2007c.

———, "Second Samarra Bombing Strengthens Status of Muqtada al-Sadr," *Terrorism Focus*, The Jamestown Foundation, Vol. 4, No. 20, June 26, 2007d.

———, "The Militia Politics of Basra," *Terrorism Monitor*, The Jamestown Foundation, Vol. 5, Issue 13, July 6, 2007e.

Ramati, Yohanan, "Islamic Fundamentalism Gaining," *Midstream*, Vol. 39, No. 2, 1993.

Ramazani, R. K., "Ideology and Pragmatism in Iranian Foreign Policy," *Middle East Journal*, Vol. 58, No. 4, Autumn 2004.

Ranstorp, Magnus, "Hezbollah's Command Leadership," *Terrorism and Political Violence,* Vol. 6, No. 3, August 1994.

————, *Hezbollah in Lebanon*, New York: St. Martin's Press, 1997.

————, "The Strategy and Tactics of Hezbollah's Current 'Lebanonization Process'," *Mediterranean Politics,* Vol. 3, No. 1, Summer 1998.

Raphaeli, Nimrod, "Understanding Muqtada al-Sadr," *Middle East Quarterly,* Vol. 11, No. 4, Fall 2004.

"Rationing Leads to Clashes at Gas Stations in Tehran," OSC Feature—SHANA FEA20070627205751, 0810 GMT June 27, 2007.

"Recognizing Iran as a Strategic Threat: An Intelligence Challenge for the United `tates," Staff Report of the House Permanent Select Committee on Intelligence, ιgust 23, 2006.

ˉormists Ask Sistani to Intervene in the Electoral Crisis," *Al-Sharq al-Awsat,* in ˙, February 5, 2004.

˙, Hassan, interview in *Le Figaro* (Paris), January 17, 2004.

·e' Change of Commander Consolidates Iran's IRGC," BBC Monitoring, ture FEA20070903303187, September 3, 2007.

'chael, "Dealing with Iran," interview with Kathryn Jean Lopez, *eview Online*, April 25, 2006. As of January 16, 2006: ˌnationalreview.com/interrogatory/rubin200604250606.asp

·i, "The Global Reach of Iran's Ballistic Missiles," Tel Aviv: Tel Aviv ˈnstitute for National Security Studies, Memorandum 86, November

ˑ L., "Peering over the Horizon: Arab Threat Perception and ses to a Nuclear-Ready Iran," Non-Proliferation Policy Education 5, 2005.

mal, *Hizbullah: Politics and Religion*, London: Pluto Press, 2002.

ran   ι Stokes Arab Anti-Iran, Anti-Shiite Sentiment," Middle East— ˈ20070111222001, January 10, 2007.

Path   'How Relevant Is the Iranian Street?" *The Washington* ˑ. 1, Winter 2006–2007, pp. 151–162.

ddle   Players," *Journal of International Affairs*, Vol. 60, No. 2, ˈp. 125–134.

eet   · of Propaganda in Psychological Warfare," *Saff* (Tehran), ˈ0525000001, March 1, 2001, pp. 24–26.

Sagan, Scott D., "Why Do States Build Nuclear Weapons? Three Models in Search of a Bomb," *International Security*, Vol. 21, No. 3, Winter 1996/1997, pp. 54–86.

Salame, Ghassan, "Islam and the West," *Foreign Policy*, No. 90, Spring 1993

Salim, Salaah, "Tajawoz al-Qati'a al-Misriya al-Iraniya [Overcoming the Egyptian-Iranian Estrangement]," *Elaph*, July 8, 2007.

Salimi, Mohammad, comments in *Iran Daily*, No. 2196, January 22, 2005.

Samii, Abbas William, "Factionalism in Iran's Domestic Security Forces," *Middle East Intelligence Bulletin*, Vol. 4, No. 2, February 2002.

———, "The Iranian Nuclear Issue and Informal Networks," *Naval War College Review*, Vol. 59, No. 1, Winter 2006.

———, "A Stable Structure on Shifting Sands: Assessing the Hizbullah-Iran-Syria Relationship," *The Middle East Journal*, Vol. 62, No. 1, Winter 2008, pp. 32–53.

"Saudi Website Sunni-Shiite Reaction to Lebanon Crisis," Saudi Arabia—OSC Report, in Arabic, OSC GMP20060816862001, August 16, 2006.

"Saudis to Transfer $92 Million to PA," *Jerusalem Post*, April 19, 2006.

Schake, Kori N., and Judith S. Yaphe, "The Strategic Implications of a Nuclear-Armed Iran," McNair Paper 64, Washington, D.C.: National Defense University, 2001, pp. 13–14.

Schleifer, Ron, "Psychological Operations: A New Variation of an Age Old Art: Hezbollah Versus Israel," *Studies in Conflict and Terrorism*, Vol. 29, 2006, pp. 1–19.

Shabani, Naser, "The *Basij* and National Security," *Military Knowledge*, in Persian Summer–Fall 1996, FBIS 19970711001453, July 15, 2007.

Shadid, Anthony, "With Iran Ascendant, U.S. Is Seen at Fault," *Washington Post* January 30, 2007, p. A1.

Shahidi, Farsan, "Unsuccessful U.S. Policies in the Middle East," *Sobhe Sadegh* (weekly magazine of the Islamic Revolutionary Guard Corps), in Persian, n.d.

Shanahan, Rodger, "Hezbollah's Dilemma," *Mideast Monitor*, February 2006.

Slackman, Michael, and Hassan M. Fattah, "In Public View, Saudis Counter in Region," *New York Times*, February 6, 2007, p. A1.

Slavin, Barbara, *Bitter Friends, Bosom Enemies: Iran, the U.S. and the Twisted to Confrontation*, New York: St. Martin's Press, 2007.

———, *Mullahs, Money and Militias: How Iran Exerts Its Influence in the M East*, Washington, D.C.: The United States Institute for Peace, June 2008.

Solomon, Jay, "U.S.-Arab Alliance Aims to Deter Terrorism, Iran," *Wall St Journal*, August 9, 2007, p. 6.

"Southeastern Iran Seeks Its Share from Hirmand River in Afghanistan," Tehran Mehr News Agency, Web page, in English, FBIS IAP20041110000084, 1756 GMT November 10, 2004.

Susser, Leslie, "Hezbollah Masters the TOW," *Jerusalem Report*, March 13, 2000, p. 18.

Synovitz, Ron, "Afghanistan: How Would Permanent U.S. Bases Impact Regional Interests?" *Radio Free Europe/Radio Liberty*, February 23, 2005.

"Syrian Troops Enforce South Beirut Truce; Inter-Shiite Fighting Ends," *World News Digest*, June 3, 1988.

"Tactless Mubarak Provokes Reassertion of National Loyalties by Gulf Arab Shi'as," *Gulf States Newsletter*, Vol. 30, No. 779, April 14, 2006.

Takeyh, Ray, *Hidden Iran: Paradox and Power in the Islamic Republic*, New York: Henry Holt and Company, 2006.

———, "Time for Détente with Iran," *Foreign Affairs*, March/April 2007.

Takeyh, Ray, and Nikolas K. Gvosdev, "Pragmatism in the Midst of Iranian Turmoil," *The Washington Quarterly*, Vol. 27, No. 4, Autumn 2004, pp. 33–56.

Taremi, Kamran, "Beyond the Axis of Evil: Ballistic Missiles in Iran's Military Thinking," *Security Dialogue*, Vol. 36, No. 1, March 2005a.

———, "Iranian Foreign Policy Towards Occupied Iraq, 2003–2005," *Middle East Policy*, Vol. 12, No. 4, Winter 2005b.

Tellier, Frédéric, "The Iranian Moment" Washington Institute for Near East Policy, Policy Focus No. 52, February 2006.

Tha'ir, Abbas, "Al-Hariri: Ala Hizbullah Al-Ikhtiyar bayna Lubnan wa al-Haras al-Thawri al-Irani [Hariri, Hizbullah Has to Choose Between Lebanon and the Iranian Revolutionary Guard]," *Al-Sharq al-Awsat* (London), July 16, 2007.

Timmerman, Kenneth, *Countdown to Crisis: The Coming Nuclear Showdown with Iran*, New York: Three Rivers Press, 2005.

Torbat, Akbar E., "Impacts of the US Trade and Financial Sanctions on Iran," *The World Economy*, Vol. 28, No. 3, March 2005, pp. 407–434.

———, "UN Financial Sanctions on Iran: Political Confrontation," Web page, Centre for Research on Globalization, March 9, 2007. As of April 3, 2008: http://www.globalresearch.ca/index.php?context=va&aid=5034

"Turkish PM in Iran to Ease Business Spats," Agence France Presse, July 29, 2004.

U.S. Central Intelligence Agency, *The 2007 World Factbook*, 2007.

U.S. Department of Defense, "Measuring Security and Stability in Iraq," March 2, 2007.

U.S. Department of State, "Press Briefing Conference Call on U.S. Aid and Military Support to the Middle East Region," transcipt of conference call, July 30, 2007. As of March 5, 2009:
http://www.state.gov/p/us/rm/2007/89807.htm

U.S. Department of State, Bureau of Political-Military Affairs, "Middle East Peace Process Arms Control and Regional Security Working Group," Fact Sheet, July 21, 2001.

U.S. Department of State, Office of Intelligence and Research, "Iraq Television Viewership Poll," October 16, 2003.

U.S. Department of the Treasury, "Fact Sheet: Designation of Iranian Entities and Individuals for Proliferation Activities and Support for Terrorism," press release, October 25, 2007. As of February 19, 2008:
http://www.ustreas.gov/press/releases/hp644.htm

"US, Israel Fomenting Shiite-Sunni Discord," *Iran-Daily*, November 28, 2006. As of February 20, 2009:
http://www.iran-daily.com/1385/2719/html/national.htm#s191412

"US Official Calls Hezbollah 'A-Team of Terrorists'," Reuters, September 5, 2002.

Vakil, Sanam, "Iran: Balancing East Against West," *The Washington Quarterly*, Vol. 29, No. 4, Autumn 2006, pp. 51–65.

Valbjørn, Morten, and André Bank, "Signs of a New Arab Cold War: The 2006 Lebanon War and the Sunni-Shi'i Divide," *Middle East Report*, Spring 2007, pp. 6–11.

Valinejad, A., "Is Anthrax the Most Dangerous Biological Weapon?" *Medical and Health Aspects of Bioterrorism Panel No. 005* (Tehran), translated in "Iranian Scientists Review B. Anthracis as Biological Weapon," OSC IAP20040830000037, January 1, 2001.

Visser, Reidar, "Maliki, Hakim, and Iran's Role in the Basra Fighting," www.historiae.org, April 9, 2003. As of November 20, 2008:
http://www.historiae.org/iran.asp

———, *Sistani, the United States and Iraqi Politics: From Quietism to Machiavellianism? Politics in Iraq*, Oslo: Norsk Utenrikspolitisk Institut, 2006.

Ward, Steven R., "The Continuing Evolution of Iran's Military Doctrine," *Middle East Journal*, Vol. 59, No. 4, Autumn 2005.

Wege, Anthony, "Hizbollah Organization," *Studies in Conflict and Terrorism*, Vol. 17, No. 2, 1994, pp. 151–164.

Wehrey, Fred, "Saudi Arabia: Shi'a Pessimistic About Reform, but Seek Reconciliation," *Arab Reform Bulletin*, Vol. 5, No. 5, Washington, D.C.: Carnegie Endowment for International Peace, July 2007.

"What Security for the South?" *The Lebanon Report*, Vol. 4, No. 9, September 1993, p. 5.

The White House, "President Bush Addresses the 89th Annual National Convention of the American Legion," August 28, 2007.

Wood, Graeme, "The Militant Kurds of Iran," *Jane's Intelligence Review*, August 1, 2006.

WorldPublicOpinion.org, "Public Opinion in Iran and America on Key International Issues," January 24, 2007. As of November 20, 2008: http://www.worldpublicopinion.org/pipa/pdf/jan07/Iran_Jan07_rpt.pdf

Wright, Robin, "U.S. Plans New Arms Sales to Gulf Allies: $20 Billion Deal Includes Weapons for Saudi Arabia," *Washington Post*, July 28, 2007, p. A1.

———,"U.S. vs. Iran: Cold War, Too," *Washington Post*, July 29, 2007, p. B1.

———, "Iran Is Critical as U.S. Unveils Arms Sales in the Middle East," *Washington Post*, July 31, 2007, p. 15.

———, "Top Iranian General Hit with Sanctions," *Washington Post*, January 10, 2008, p. 15.

Wright, Robin, and John Ward Anderson, "Son of Ailing Shiite Leader Steps Forward," *Washington Post*, July 1, 2007.

Yaffe, Michael, "An Overview of the Middle East Peace Process Working Group on Arms Control and Regional Security," in Fred Tanner, ed., *Confidence-Building and Security Co-operation in the Mediterranean, North Africa and the Middle East*, Malta: University of Malta, 1994.

Yaphe, Judith S., and Charles D. Lutes, "Reassessing the Implications of a Nuclear-Armed Iran," McNair Paper 69, Washington, D.C.: National Defense University, 2005.

Zimmerman, Doron, "Calibrating Disorder: Iran's Role in Iraq and the Coalition Response, 2003–2006," *Civil Wars*, Vol. 9, No. 1, March 2007, pp. 8–31.

Zogby, James, "Four Years Later: Arab Opinion Troubled by Consequences of Iraq War," Washington, D.C.: Arab American Institute, n.d.

Zogby International, "Middle East Opinion: Iran Fears Aren't Hitting the Arab Street," 2006.

Zonis, Marvin, *The Political Elite of Iran*, Princeton, N.J.: Princeton University Press, 1971.